Critical Muslim 6
Reclaiming al-Andalus

Critical Muslim is published quarterly by C. Hurst & Co (Publishers) Ltd on behalf of and in conjunction with Critical Muslim Ltd and the Muslim Institute, London.

All correspondence to Muslim Institute, CAN Mezzanine, 49–51 East Road, London N1 6AH, United Kingdom
e-mail for editorial: editorial@criticalmuslim.com

C. Hurst & Co (Publishers) Ltd.,
41 Great Russell Street, London WC1B 3PL

ISBN: 978-1-84904-316-8
ISSN: 2048-8475

To subscribe or place an order by credit/debit card or cheque (pounds sterling only) please contact Kathleen May at the Hurst address above or email kathleen@hurstpub.co.uk Tel: 020 7255 2201

A one year subscription, inclusive of postage (four issues), costs £50 (UK), £65 (Europe) and £75 (rest of the world).

A Cataloguing-in-Publication data record for this book is available from the British Library.

OUR MISSION

Critical Muslim is a quarterly magazine of ideas and issues showcasing ground-breaking thinking on Islam and what it means to be a Muslim in a rapidly changing, increasingly interconnected world.

We will be devoted to examining issues within Islam, and Muslim societies, providing a Muslim perspective on the great debates of contemporary times, and promoting dialogue, cooperation and collaboration between 'Islam' and other cultures, including 'the West'. We aim to be innovative, thought-provoking and forward-looking, a space for debate between Muslims and between Muslims and others, on religious, social, cultural and political issues concerning the Muslim world and Muslims in the world.

What does 'Critical Muslim' mean? We are proud of our strong Muslim identity, but we do not see 'Islam' as a set of pieties and taboos. We aim to challenge traditionalist, modernist, fundamentalist and apologetic versions of Islam, and will attempt to set out new readings of religion and culture with the potential for social, cultural and political transformation of the Muslim world. Our writers may define their Muslim belonging religiously, culturally or civilisationally, and some will not 'belong' to Islam at all. *Critical Muslim* will sometimes invite writers of opposing viewpoints to debate controversial issues.

We aim to appeal to both academic and non-academic readerships; to emphasise intellectual rigour, the challenge of ideas, and original thinking.

In these times of change and peaceful revolutions, we choose not to be a lake or a meandering river. But to be an ocean. We embrace the world with all its diversity and pluralism, complexity and chaos. We aim to explore everything on our interconnected, shrinking planet — from religion and politics, to science, technology and culture, art and literature, philosophy and ethics, and histories and futures — and seek to move forward despite deep uncertainty and contradictions. We stand for open and critical engagement in the best tradition of Muslim intellectual inquiry.

CM6

April–June 2013

CONTENTS

RECLAIMING AL-ANDALUS

ESSAYS

ART AND LETTERS

ET CETERA

RECLAIMING AL-ANDALUS

RETURN TO AL-ANDALUS

Ziauddin Sardar

A young surgeon seeks new techniques to relieve the suffering of his patients. He is a rationalist familiar with the latest advances in science. But his rationalism is severely tested when he meets a libertine steeped in ancient religious beliefs and haunted by the memory of his dead father. In *The Burial Chamber*, a meticulously researched dark thriller by Jeremy Cox, the entanglement between rationality and magic, dreams, talismans and ancient dogma is played out against the background of scientific advances in a nineteenth-century London of lunatic asylums, gentlemen's clubs and rowdy meetings at the Royal Society. In one particularly gripping scene set at the Royal Society, where the surgeon has been invited to present a paper, theories and cures for mental illness are heatedly discussed. It is acknowledged that the religious theories attributing insanity to the influence of Satan, as well as existing theories of medical treatment such as 'the purging of the bowels, blistering, and mortification of the extremities have not always proved effective'; although 'blood-letting and the emptying of the stomach through vomiting can still have a beneficial effect'. The discussion moves on to a new 'moral therapy' which emphasises 'kindness and patience in [the] treatment of inmates'. A stalwart of the Royal Society explains, 'I consider the mind to be an immortal, immaterial substance identical to the human soul, and therefore lunacy cannot be a disease of the mind. It has to be that of the brain. As such, it will be medical advances that bring about an understanding of insanity and new medical treatments for it in its various forms. Erasmus Darwin's rotating chair, for example. The chair spins the patient around at great speed so as to rearrange the contents of the brain into their right positions. The treatment also has the added benefit of bringing about subsequent vomiting'.

Al-Ghazzali, the Muslim theologian and jurist, considered the Muslim society of his time to be so deeply afflicted with social sickness, 'an epidemic among the multitude' as he calls it, as to be virtually insane. The only cure was a 'moral therapy', a heavy dose of religious devotion and piety. Religion, it seems, was not unlike Erasmus Darwin's rotating chair: it would spin those persistently 'straying from the clear truth', those insistent 'upon fostering evil' and 'flattering ignorance', at great speed, thus rearranging their brains into pious order, while, as an added benefit, forcing them to spew out their heresies. All of those who are lured by 'the Satan', he tells us in *The Book of Knowledge*, 'see good as evil and evil as good, so that the science of religion has disappeared and the torch of true faith has been extinguished all over the world'.

Al-Ghazzali's invective is directed at the vast majority of Muslims he saw and interacted with; although one suspects he would regard contemporary Muslim societies with equal contempt. But he was especially concerned with a particular 'class of men' who are largely missing from contemporary Muslim societies. These men have 'greater intelligence and insight', 'have abandoned all the religious duties Islam imposes on its followers', 'defy the injunction of the Sacred Law', and 'indulge in diverse speculations'. These people, al-Ghazzali squawks, hold 'irresponsible views', have 'perverted minds', and 'must be branded with diabolical perversity and stupid contumacy'. They are 'the heretics of our time'.

Just who are these men denounced so emphatically as heretics, good only for the gallows, by al-Ghazzali? They are men inspired by the 'intellectual power' of 'Socrates, Hippocrates, Plato, Aristotle'. They are philosophers. Like al-Kindi (801–873), who introduced Indian numerals to the Muslim world, and wrote on everything from astronomy to music. Like al-Farabi (872–951), the author of *The Perfect City* and *The Book of Music*, who explored the relationship between logic and grammar and was so humble that he spent his last days working as a gardener. Like ibn Sina (980–1037) whose numerous scientific works are a wonder to behold and whose *Canon of Medicine* was a standard text for eight centuries. And like ibn Rushd, the philosopher and all round polymath from Cordoba whose works fuelled the first European renaissance. The very people who laid the foundations of the Muslim civilisation, the beacons of thought and learning whose names are intrinsically linked to 'the Golden Age of Islam'.

What incensed al-Ghazzali so much? His criticism of philosophers comes in two parts. First, he accuses Muslim philosophers of taking a rather uncritical attitude to 'ancient masters'. The works of Plato and Aristotle are regarded as 'unquestionable', and their mathematics, logic and deductive methods are seen as 'the most profound' and used to repudiate 'the authority of religious law' and deny 'the positive contents of historical religions'. Second, and this is what really troubles him, their beliefs – or *aqidah* – are not correct. It is the sort of accusation that conservative Wahhabis, extremist Salafis, and militant Talibanis routinely throw at all those who disagree with them. But al-Ghazzali, a professor at the Nazamia Academy in Baghdad, was far more sophisticated: using their own rhetoric and method, he took the battle to the philosophers themselves.

The Incoherence of the Philosophers is an angry book. It is full of the sort of name-calling and livid asides not usually associated with a work of philosophy. In the preface, al-Ghazzali tries to defend the practice of offering prayer during an eclipse on the authority of a tradition of the Prophet. The philosophers explained the solar and lunar eclipse in scientific terms, as a natural phenomenon, and rejected the idea of praying during an eclipse. Al-Ghazzali acknowledges that 'these things have been established by astronomical and mathematical evidence which leaves no room for doubt'. Nevertheless, since the Prophet declared that 'when you see an eclipse you must seek refuge in the contemplation of God and in prayer', the eclipse prayer is obligatory. Then we move on to twenty 'theories' of the philosophers, such as their doctrine of the eternity of the world, their alleged denial of Divine attributes, and their belief in the impossibility of departure from the natural course of events. Al-Ghazzali sets out to demolish these theories one by one. Thirteen theories are found to be problematic. On three points (the assertion that the world is everlasting, the denial that God knows the particulars, and the denial of bodily resurrection in the Hereafter) he judges the philosophers to be totally outside Islam, *kaffirs* (infidels) to boot. The other theories and assertions are seen as heretical.

Now, I know that I am dealing with a scholar regarded by many as the most influential person in the history of Islam after the Prophet Muhammad. In certain circles, criticism of al-Ghazzali is seen almost as a blasphemy, releasing an automatic defence mechanism. And it is particularly difficult for someone like me who grew up revering 'The Proof of Islam', as al-Ghazzali is sometimes called. But, forced to take a leaf from al-Ghazzali's book, 'I am no longer obliged to remain silent'.

By any intellectual standards, *The Incoherence of the Philosophers* is not a 'major assault' on philosophy, as it is commonly depicted, but a poor polemic, and an insulting one too. Al-Ghazzali states the positions of the philosophers reasonably well, but his counter arguments are trite and often quite irrational. A couple of examples should suffice. The philosophers argued that the movement of heavenly bodies is due either to (1) the intrinsic nature of these bodies, such as the downward movement of a stone, which is an unconscious act; or (2) to an outside force that moves the body, which will be conscious of the movement. Al-Ghazzali counters with three arguments. First, 'the movement of Heaven may be supposed to be the result of the constraint exercised by another body which wills its movement, and causes it to revolve perpetually. This motive body may be neither a round body nor a circumference. So it will not be a heavenly body at all'. Second, the heavenly bodies move by the will of God. Third, the heavenly bodies are specifically designed to possess the attribute of movement. And these arguments, asserts al-Ghazzali, cannot be disproved! To the philosopher's assertion that angels are 'immaterial beings' which do not exist in space or act upon bodies, and should be understood in an allegorical or metaphorical sense, al-Ghazzali replies: 'How will you disprove one who says God enables the Prophet to know the Hidden Things?' Or deny that 'he who has a dream comes to know the hidden things, because God, or one of his angels, enables him to know them'. This is not philosophy but the notions of men, as a natural philosopher in *The Burial Chamber* tells the young surgeon who 'strenuously avoided keeping an open mind on matters of science' out of fear that their dogma and 'reputation would be undermined if they took it seriously'.

It has to be said that al-Ghazzali is big on the supernatural, an area he calls 'subsidiary sciences'. He quite likes the fact that the philosophers promote inquiry into physical sciences such as mathematics, physics, astronomy, and botany, but he is not too happy with their concept of causality, the assertion that every cause must have an effect. More than that, he is enraged at the fact that the philosophers laugh at the suggestion that the Prophet split the moon (the philosophers dismissed the tradition as a fabrication), their denial that Moses' rod literally turned into a serpent (the philosophers argued that this is an allegory of the refutation of the doubts of the unbelievers by the Divine proof manifested at the hands of Moses), and their refusal to believe in resurrection after death (the philosophers argued that the resurrection is a symbolic reference to death arising from ignorance and life emerging from knowledge).

Not everything can be explained by cause and effect, al-Ghazzali argued; and it is the job of 'subsidiary sciences' to explain things which exist beyond the domain of rationality. The reader is generously provided with a list of these 'subsidiary sciences', including astrology, dream interpretation, 'the talismanic art', 'the art of magic', alchemy, and 'physiognomy' – which 'infers moral character from physical appearance' (this science would no doubt locate me in an amoral universe). The list, including 'physiognomy', is a perfect echo of the dark supernatural world conjured up in *The Burial Chamber*. Incidentally, in *The Book of Knowledge*, al-Ghazzali describes these 'sciences' as 'blameworthy', real but not worthy of study by believers. But in the *Incoherence* he defends them aggressively – with bizarre consequences.

The al-Ghazzali that emerges from the *Incoherence* is a literalist, anti-rational scholar who is keen to cast a critical eye on philosophy yet eager to accept dogma and belief, including miracles and irrational sayings uncritically attributed to the Prophet. His main goal is to show that such metaphysical doctrines as the world having a Creator, that two gods are impossible, or that the soul is a self-subsistent entity, cannot be proved by reason. But he gets carried away and jettisons reason and 'intellectual inquiry' altogether from religion. The inductive leap to rejecting scientific inquiry per se is only natural: 'let us give up the inquiry concerning "why" and "how much" and "what". For these things are beyond the power of men'.

Given his vast oeuvre, it would be wrong to judge al-Ghazzali on a single work. In his study *Ghazali and the Poetics of Imagination*, Ebrahim Moosa gives us a different al-Ghazzali. Moosa argues that al-Ghazzali wanted to augment as well as reinterpret religion by using the Aristotelian notion of poiesis (*shiriya* in Arabic), that is, the construction of something relatively but not radically new by means of poetics. 'He constructed', writes Moosa, 'a narrative by weaving a plethora of ideas and insights into a coherent but profoundly refigured whole', and thus 'demonstrated that thoughts and ideas are not given, but made and constructed. At the same time, he elucidated a cosmology for Muslim thought that simultaneously imitated what came before it and innovated and provided something additional, some of what might be: the conditions of possibility'. Moosa presents al-Ghazzali as a modern, even postmodern thinker – and one is almost convinced by Moosa's erudite analysis. Certainly the al-Ghazzali of theological works such as *The Revival of Religious Knowledge*, *The Alchemy of Happiness* and *Jewels of the Quran*, appears to be a different category of scholar.

The al-Ghazzali of the *Incoherence*, however, is overwhelmed by his anger, and this had a genuine cause. Philosophy, or *falsifa* as it was called, as shaped by Muslims appeared positively dangerous to theology. And this danger was physical as well as metaphysical. Theologians were persecuted in Baghdad for not being rational enough, particularly during the Abbasid Caliph al-Mamun's (786–833) reign. The *Minha*, the 'testing' or 'trial', introduced by al-Mamun to force theologians to justify their positions on rational grounds, led to an inquisition and the incarceration of the noted theologian and jurist Ahmad ibn Hanbal (780–855), founder of the Hanbali school of Islamic jurisprudence. During the days of al-Ghazzali, study of the Qur'an and traditions of the Prophet was in decline; and men of learning preferred philosophy to theology. 'The people of that time went so far', writes the thirteenth-century historian Marrakhushi in his *History of the Maghreb*, 'as to condemn as an unbeliever anyone who appears to be entering upon the sciences of theology' which were seen as 'vile'. Hatred of theology and its theories was the norm. During his own lifetime, the works of al-Ghazzali were banned in the Maghreb and Andalusia. The Berber Almoravids, who controlled large parts of Spain and the Maghreb, did not take kindly to his theology. The Almoravid ruler Ali ibn Yusuf (r.1106–1142) ordered his books 'to be burnt, and issued severe threats of execution and confiscation of property against anyone found in possession of any of them; and these orders were strictly enforced'.

While al-Ghazzali's anger is understandable and his theological works demand a certain respect, we should not be carried away by his reputation. 'Conflicting forces', as Moosa argues, 'pushed and pulled him in different directions', and he found himself engaging 'with more than one intellectual and cultural tradition', as was the norm during this period. But there was no 'in-between-ness' about him, as Moosa suggests. As we learn from his autobiography, *Deliverance from Error*, al-Ghazzali moved from one extreme to another in his own life: from being a total sceptic to an enthusiastic believer who emphatically declared 'reason is false'. He supported the fanatic Almoravids even though they banned his books! And there is just too much piety and uncritical acceptance of dogma in his work for an inquiring mind to take.

For 'in-between-ness' we have to look at the object and subject of al-Ghazzali's wrath, and in particular at Ibn Rushd, who took it upon himself to reply to the *Incoherence*. Al-Ghazzali lovers often dismiss ibn Rushd as not very spiritual and too enthralled to the Greek masters. Moosa illustrates this well. Having built up al-Ghazzali as a postmodern deity, he takes a swipe at ibn Rushd. The Andalusian philosopher 'mocked al-Ghazzali as a man of all seasons, a theologian with the theologians, a mystic with the Sufis, and a philosopher with the philosophers', he says. Such 'infantine geniality' says more about Ibn Rushd than 'the target of criticism'. If, Moosa goes on to say, ibn Rushd 'had looked inwards, he might have acknowledged that a commitment to formalism and an uncritical response to Aristotelianism can be limiting'. Apparently al-Ghazzali is a 'frontier thinker' while ibn Rushd is 'intransigent'.

Given Moosa's accusations, it would be worth making a quick comparison of the two thinkers. Al-Ghazzali's position is that only correct dogma can save believers, and philosophy and rational inquiry have no place in Islamic theology. His God is so omnipotent that He leaves no room for human agency; everything can be explained by miraculous intervention. Ibn Rushd argues that the Qur'an itself urges us to pursue rational deductions, to 'look into', 'consider' and 'reflect on' (2:29; 7:14) the wonders of creation as a means to understand God as Creator. Philosophy and science are thus central to all Islamic pursuits. If it turns out that rational inquiry was not conducted by Muslims but by the ancients (that is, the Greeks), then it is incumbent upon Muslims to embrace their thought and learning. Al-Ghazzali wants to instil fear of God and Hell in his readers; ibn Rushd argues that a society is free when no one acts out of fear of God or Hell, or out of desire for reward in Paradise, but for the love of God and humanity. Al-Ghazzali freely uses hadith (authentic and weak, as well as quite irrational) and the sayings of sages and saints to make his arguments. Ibn Rushd unapologetically scrutinises the traditional sources with a critical and rational eye. Both were jurists. In his legal text, al-Ghazzali denounces most allegorical interpretations as *kufr* (disbelief). Ibn Rushd on the other hand sees such literalism as anathema. (To describe the author of *The Distinguished Jurist's Primer*, which is as full of insight and wisdom on ritual and spiritual matters as anything al-Ghazzali has to offer, as someone incapable of looking 'inwards' is a stretch of imagination too far). Moreover, al-Ghazzali was a misogynist who compared women to ten kinds of animals, all of which except one, the sheep, were nasty. Ibn Rushd, on the other hand, believed that women were prescribed the same ultimate goals as men, that there is no question of men being superior to women. It is men who consider women as animals to be domesticated, or as plants which are sought for their fruit. These are traditions made by men to serve their own ends, and they have nothing to do with Islam.

The difference between the two scholars is also illustrated in ibn Rushd's reply to al-Ghazzali in his *Incoherence of Incoherence*. There is no long preface throwing abuse and scorn at theologians in general or al-Ghazzali in particular. The book opens with a very brief and clear statement of purpose, which is to prove that *The Incoherence of the Philosophers* 'has not reached the degree of evidence and of truth'. Ibn Rushd refers to al-Ghazzali by name, and respectfully calls him Sheikh. Then it is down to business: al-Ghazzali's arguments are torn to shreds systematically and thoroughly in a series of sixteen 'discussions'. As Nazry Bahrawi writes in his contribution to this volume of *Critical Muslim*,

> first, ibn Rushd argues that God's knowledge could not be categorised as "universal" and "specific" since these are human conceptions. Given that God is not a corporeal entity like humans, His perception of knowledge differs from ours. Ibn Rushd posits that we are shackled by the limits of human understanding to comprehend, much less categorise, Godly knowledge. Second, ibn Rushd argues that human conduct could not be categorised as being either fully free or fully determined. Rather, it is a bit of both. Humanity is free to choose, but this choice is also one determined by external forces operating in tandem. Juxtaposing human will to God's will, ibn Rushd argues that humans act to fulfil their desires because these change over time. God simply acts because His eternal nature means that He is not bounded by time – past, present or future. In this sense, human desire becomes one of those extenuating "external" factors dictating an individual's choice.

But demolishing the *Incoherence* was a relatively easy task for ibn Rushd. A more challenging duty was critiquing Muslim Neoplatonist philosophers, specially al-Farabi and ibn Sina. Here, ibn Rushd restores the agency to ordinary believers that both al-Ghazzali and Neoplatonism had denied. Bahrawi again:

> ibn Rushd's middle position between al-Ghazali and ibn Sina allows for the doctrine of freewill to exist without denying God's omniscience. In other words, humanity is an active agent in Islam, and not a passive, predetermined one. It is also this recognition of human agency that leads ibn Rushd to the rejection of a key component of Islamic Neoplatonism – the emanation theory. For ibn Rushd, the idea that humanity is a 'by-product' of the First Being, as ibn Sina and al-Farabi uphold, contradicts human agency. To subscribe to the emanation theory, ibn Rushd argues, is to deprive all actual entities of any active powers, and to deny the principle of causality.

When ibn Rushd referred to al-Ghazzali as 'a man of all seasons', he was actually pointing to his shifting, changing positions – a relativistic, postmodern stance, if you like, which Moosa would argue for. As ibn Rushd points out, 'al-Ghazzali says in *The Jewels of the Qur'an* that what he wrote in *The Incoherence* was merely dialectical argument, but that the truth is to be found in his other book, entitled *What Is Concealed From the Unworthy*'. But then he changes his mind again about the nature of truth in *The Niche of Lights*. And in his autobiography, *Deliverance from Error*, he argues that certainty in 'knowledge arises by means of withdrawal (from the world) and reflection only'. He reiterates this position in *The Alchemy of Happiness*. So what is one to believe: where is knowledge finally located? Al-Ghazzali's 'confusion and muddling' and his 'doubtful and perplexing arguments', writes ibn Rushd, 'drove many people away from both philosophy and religion'.

Ibn Rushd tries to bring philosophy and religion together in *On the Harmony of Religion and Philosophy*, written in a persuasive style for the educated public. Written from the point of view of a jurist, it explores whether philosophy and logic are permitted or prohibited by the Qur'an, the traditions of the Prophet, and Islamic law. Ibn Rushd argues that philosophy is nothing more than a teleological study of the world. In as far as the Qur'an encourages a scientific, teleological study of the world, it encourages philosophy, which means reason and logic have to be amongst the tools required to study scripture and shape Islamic law. Revealed truths, he argues further, are true 'in the religious realm', and those of the world 'in the philosophic realm', but there is no contradiction between them: 'We the Muslim community know definitely that demonstrative study does not lead to conclusions conflicting with what Scripture has given us'. When apparent contradictions arise, it is the function of philosophy to reconcile the contradictions. For ibn Rushd, the method for reconciling these apparent contradictions involves an allegorical and metaphorical interpretation of the Qur'an in such a manner that the inner meanings of Quranic verses are seen to agree with observed and demonstrative truth.

Unlike al-Ghazzali, ibn Rushd was a product of a pluralistic, multi-religious society: al-Andalus. Muslims arrived in Hispania, as it was then known, during the early eighth century. They settled in a region that, as Robin Yassin-Kassab notes, 'had already been rich, and religiously and ethnically diverse'. It was not, as Gonzalez-Ferrin points out, 'the empty or uncultivated land that appears in the Arabic chronicles', written at least a century and a half after the event. Hispania had an established tradition of Hellenic scholarship, art, law, and of questioning imperial authority. 'Hispania became al-Andalus after an extended struggle of different heretical trends, substantive problems in the transition of the Visigoth kingdom, and a long and continual process of questioning Imperial Centralism as Rome shifted to Constantinople'. Moreover, Islam did not appear in Hispania as a result of a miraculous and bloody invasion; another 'worthless myth, a bare creationist concoction, devoid of historical proof', created by Muslim scholars and later expanded by European Orientalists. Rather, there was a long period of gestation that lead to the progressive formation and change of the name: 'al-Andalus, a phonetic transformation of Atlantis, located by Plato in the Lost Paradise in the western lands where the Mediterranean meets the Atlantic Ocean. Between the fourth and sixth centuries, several commentaries were produced on Plato's main writings, generating that Hellenic cultural movement called Neo-Platonism, wherein we find the origins of the transformation: Atlantis > Adalandis > Al-Andalus'. The Muslims who arrived and settled in al-Andalus did not declare followers of other religions as *kaffirs* and infidels – a tendency, by the way, al-Ghazzali demonstrates amply – but, writes Yassin-Kassab, 'intermarried with the locals and bred with their slaves, who were very often Slavs, eastern Europeans captured in eastern European wars to be traded around Europe and the Mediterranean. Soon most of the Muslim population consisted of the offspring of these mixed marriages, and of large numbers of converts'.

It was in this society of 'mixed marriages', Christians, Jews and Muslims, that Abd al-Rahman, the founder of the Umayyad caliphate in Spain (756–1031), escaping the massacre of his clan in Damascus, established the first great Western city of Islam: Cordoba. Its international fame rested on sophisticated homes in twenty-one suburbs, seventy libraries and numerous bookshops, mosques and glorious palaces. It inspired awe and admiration because it was a haven for thinkers, philosophers, musicians, and writers. In al-Andalus, ibn Rushd rubbed shoulders with revolutionary thinkers like ibn Tufayl; scientists such as Abbas ibn Firnás (810-887), the Andalusian Leonardo, who invented and manufactured many instruments, including a flying machine, which he crash landed on Cordoba's main street; feminist intellectuals such as ibn Hazm, the author of the love manual *The Ring of the Dove*, which contains surprisingly vivid anecdotes; brilliant musicians and fashion icons like Ziryab, whose achievements are described by Cherif Abderrahman Jah in his article; as well as artists, poets, architects, and mystics of the calibre of ibn 'Arabi.

But al-Andalus is not a place and time dominated solely by men. Women were more active in this period of Islamic history than in any other, enjoying freedom of movement in the public sphere and reaching high levels of accomplishment. Consider the Umayyad princess Walladah, daughter of a Cordoban Caliph, who played host to poets and artists in her Cordoba home, often engaging in poetic contests. Beautiful, gracious in speech, and never married – an 'emancipated woman' by any definition – she declared: 'By God, I am suited to great things, and proudly I walk, with head aloft'. Or al-Arudiyyah, who learned grammar and philology from her patron and soon surpassed him. Or Hafsah bint al-Hajja al-Rukuniya, whose beauty and elegance impressed the ruler of Granada, but she chose to be with a fellow poet; or the slave al-Abbadiyyah, a writer of prose and poetry who spoke several languages and eventually married the ruler of Seville. 'But women in Muslim Spain', writes Brad Bullock, 'were not just poets and artists, but also scientists and philosophers. And they were not just a handful but numerous – and during their time they were as famous as their male counterparts'. Indeed, women from diverse backgrounds were so prominent in public life that it was taken for granted that they could be leaders of men. The only question was whether they could be Prophets as well. Ibn Hazm tells us it is 'an issue on which we know of no debate except here in Cordoba and in our time'. The opinion of people, according to ibn Hazm was divided into three: those who deny that women can be Prophets and claim that it would be an innovation (*bida*) too far, those who argue that Prophethood is possible for women, and a third group who are too confused or afraid to take part in the discussion and abstain. Ibn Hazm himself had no doubt. After looking at various theological issues, and examining the arguments of the objectors, he states his conclusion emphatically: 'we find no proof for those who claim that Prophethood is impossible for women'. He points out that there are many women prophets in the Qur'an, including Mary, mother of Prophet Isa (Jesus), and Sarah, the mother of Isaac. The overall argument is that there is no limit to what women can do and achieve. For Bullock, 'the women of al-Andalus provide a vision of the way forward'. The spirit of al-Andalus, he argues, 'demands an unprecedented and urgent commitment by the *ummah* to empower women'.

The learning and thought of al-Andalus was not all 'Islamic'; al-Andalus was also home to the Jewish Sephardic community. What happened to Muslims, writes Gonzalez-Ferrin, also 'happened with another Hellenic journey from the Garden of the Hesperides to Separad > Sefarad, the Hebrew equivalent of al-Andalus'. Cordoba, Granada, Toledo and other cities had thriving communities of Arab Jews who participated in and shaped the thought and learning that emanated from al-Andalus. It was in al-Andalus that thinkers and writers of the calibre of Moses Maimonides, one of the foremost Rabbinical scholars and philosophers, who shaped the thirteen principles of Jewish faith, flourished; ibn Gabirol, the philosopher and poet who left an indelible mark on Hebrew literary heritage; and Judah Alharizi, the philosopher who composed Tahkemoni, written in Hebrew in a well-known Arabic literary genre of rhymed prose. The output of the Andalusian Jewish poets alone, writes David Shasha, would fill several libraries. But what is really unique about the Jewish thinkers and writers of Andalusia is their synthesis of the spiritual values of monotheistic religion with philosophy and science to produce a humanistic notion of religion. Jewish religious humanism, Shasha suggests, 'sought to understand the commands of God by making use of the intellectual resources of the human mind in all its workings. It combined sublime faith with rigorous scholastic analysis'. It affirmed the primacy of universal love and charity, recognised the need for tradition, but allowed 'for diversity of worship and a respect for the values of pluralism'.

It was against this background that ibn Rushd and ibn Tufayl became bosom pals. Ibn Tufayl introduced ibn Rushd, who had little sympathy with his friend's mystical leanings, to the Almohad Caliph Abu Yaqub Yusuf (r. 1163–84). The Caliph, a man of learning with a passion for philosophy, was ibn Tufayl's patron, who, in turn, was the Caliph's chief physician. The two spent a lot of time together discussing the finer points of philosophy. Abu Yaqub was also an avid collector of books and learned men. His court was brimming with thinkers, writers and poets who openly argued and critiqued each other and the Caliph. When Ibn Tufayl brought ibn Rushd into the circle, the Caliph immediately commissioned him to write a commentary on Aristotle. That commission, and the subsequent patronage by Abu Yaqub, as George Hourani notes in his truly brilliant introduction to *On the Harmony of Religion and Philosophy*, 'had far-reaching consequences in the history of thought, for it gave a new boost to philosophy in Islam at a time when it could bear fruit in Jewish and Christian circles, in Spain and the rest of Europe'. It enabled ibn Rushd not only to take on al-Ghazzali but also to reformulate Islamic philosophy.

Abu Yaqub's patronage also permitted Ibn Tufayl to write *Hayy ibn Yaqzan* ('Alive, Son of Awake'), a philosophical novel of profound significance. The protagonist Hayy is spontaneously generated on an isolated desert island. He is adopted by a gazelle, learns survival skills, and after the death of his 'mother', on whom he performs an autopsy, sets out on the road to scientific and self-discovery. Through his observations and deductions, Hayy finally reaches the ultimate truths and realises that there is a Creator. There are two significant points about Hayy. The first is widely recognised: ibn Tufayl argues that reason is a powerful tool for understanding and shaping the world, and offers us an evolutionary take both on humanity as well as on human thought and development. The second is somewhat neglected: ibn Tufayl is more than aware of the limitations of reason, despite al-Ghazzali's erroneous allegations. For a major aim of the book is to show that reason alone is not enough to experience the Divine. Indeed, ibn Tufayl insists that even the conceptualisation of the Divine is not possible through reason and mundane experience. When Hayy reaches the final stages of his philosophical journey, he realises that he cannot gain an understanding of the supernatural by studying the material world. There is also a jibe at al-Ghazzali here. The Baghdadi professor had identified the heart, in line with Sufi tradition, as the part which is receptive to the Divine unveilings, the place where God is experienced. Ibn Tufayl dismisses this notion. Rather, ibn Tufayl suggests that the experience of the Divine is spread across the human body; and to describe this experience is misguided and impossible. Our words just cannot do it justice. All attempts at such description lead straight to the authoritative version: the theology of orthodoxy, based on heresy and superficial constructions. Instead, ibn Tufayl proposes an alternative: spiritual development is a journey that individuals take for themselves. Having brought the reader to a level of understanding of the world and purpose of life in which words no longer suffice, ibn Tufayl declares: now you are on your own, the teacher can't help you, the Sheikh can only give you false directions. From here you have to take the next steps yourself to experience what I have experienced in my immersion in the Divine. Once again, al-Ghazzali ends up looking rather lame.

The legacy of ibn Tufayl and ibn Rushd had a profound impact on Europe. As Gonzalez-Ferrin argues, it shaped the original Renaissance. Ibn Rushd produced a whole school of philosophy, Averroism; his works became widely available at universities throughout Europe, and were responsible for the development of scholasticism, which examined Christian doctrines through the lens of reason and intellectual analysis. Indeed, he 'reached such a level of prominence in Europe that his translations were forbidden in thirteenth-century Paris, where he was accused of promoting free-thinking'. The 1671 Latin translation of *Hayy* under the title *The Self-Taught Philosopher* caused a sensation. As Bahrawi notes, it became the foundational text for British empiricism. John Locke's *An Essay Concerning Human Understanding* was greatly influenced by *Hayy*; Locke's first draft of the *Essay* was completed in the same year his friend Edward Pococke finished and published the English translation of *Hayy*. It went on to influence a string of influential philosophers and writers, including Baruch Spinoza, Jean-Jacques Rousseau and Daniel Defoe.

While Europe embraced Andalusian philosophers and writers, the story in the Muslim world was somewhat different. The reasons for the evaporation of learning, philosophy and critical thought, and hence the decline of Muslim civilisations, are many and diverse. It probably has something to do with the so-called closure of 'the gates of ijtihad', which basically outlawed reason. While no one actually closed the gates, it came to be treated, as Sadakat Kadri suggests in his *Heaven on Earth: A Journey Through Sharia Law*, 'as a historical fact rather than a poetically pleasing way of saying that jurists were no longer as good as they used to be'. A lack of patrons like Caliph Abu Yaqub also meant that the support that philosophers and free thinkers needed was just not there. In the later stages, the colonisation of the Muslim world no doubt contributed a great deal to the malaise. But there is little doubt that al-Ghazzali made a major contribution to the downward spiral of Muslim civilisation. It was not the *Incoherence* itself, which as I have argued, is simply not a work of enough power to dethrone philosophy, and was probably read only by a select few. Rather, it was the aura built up around the book, within a context of an anti-philosophy hysteria whipped up by theologians, that did the most damage. Even before al-Ghazzali there were efforts to outlaw philosophy, most notably by the Abbasid Caliph Abdul Qadir (d.1031), who issued a famous decree in 1017-18 requiring the philosophers 'to repent' and ordering his subjects to dissociate themselves from 'the counter to Islam' ideas of philosophers. Al-Ghazzali became the epicentre of an anti-rationalist storm. He succeeded in resurrecting 'the science of religion' but in the process his arrogant dismissal of philosophy confined the Muslim civilisation to *The Burial Chamber*, the earthly representation of the Hereafter, a place full of talismanic artefacts, where the walls are illustrated with magical texts, and where the living start foaming at the mouth and become completely irrational.

The true extent of al-Ghazzali's influence is well illustrated by C. Snouck Hurgronje, who spent a considerable time in Mecca in the latter part of the nineteenth century. Hurgronje found that only the works of al-Ghazzali were taught in Mecca to students who came from all over the world. *The Revival of the Religious Sciences* was the main text; it was memorised by students parrot fashion. Other texts 'were more or less excerpts or compilations from the works of Ghazzali'. Not 'one new word' was to be heard anywhere. Philosophy was totally forbidden. 'The industrious students', Hurgronje writes, only understood that the philosophers 'were stupid pigheads who held human reason to be the measure of truth – a terrible superstition'. The professors openly mocked and ridiculed philosophers like ibn Rushd, ibn Tufayl and ibn Sina: 'I have seen a smile of mocking astonishment pass over the faces of all students present when the professor told them how the ignorant heathens who opposed Muhammad, had, like the philosophers, believed in human reason, and the professor smiled too with a shrug of his shoulder'.

After its initial love affair with ibn Rushd and ibn Tufayl, Europe became just as unjust to the legacy of al-Andalus. 'The fall of Granada in 1492', Merryl Wyn Davies says in her 'Last Word', 'is a clear and precise historic moment': 'the time the life-blood of plurality was drained from European consciousness'. As the Spanish monarchs Ferdinand and Isabella sealed the final end of Muslim rule, Europe 'discovered' the Americas and used their wealth to dominate the eastern sea routes and kick start its imperial adventure. But it was not just the Muslims who were expelled from al-Andalus; Jews too were driven out.

Those who were left behind were forced to convert to Christianity. The converts, known as Moriscos ('little Moors'), writes Matthew Carr, 'were often depicted as inherently backward, inferior and uncivilised.' And there was always the suspicion that Moriscos were not 'good and faithful Christians'. On 7 November 1567, King Philip II of Spain issued a royal decree ordering the Moriscos of Granada 'to cease speaking or writing in Arabic and learn Castilian and destroy all Arabic books and texts'. Public baths were to be demolished, Morisco songs, dances and musical instruments were banned, and Morisco householders had to leave their doors open on Fridays and Christian festivals so that their religious observance could be monitored. Morisco men and women who persisted in wearing Moorish clothing were to be fined, flogged or deported. 'In a stroke, Philip II issued what amounted to a charter for the complete eradication of Morisco culture from Granada, which demanded that the Moriscos disappear as a distinct and recognisable group'.

The Moriscos entrusted an elder of the community, Fernando Nuñez Muley, to plead with the authorities and defend their cause. According to Carr, Nuñez Muley's *Memorandum for the President of the Royal Audiencia and Chancery Court of the City and Kingdom of Granada* is one of the key historical documents of sixteenth century Spain. Not everything, Nuñez Muley argued in the *Memorandum*, that goes under the rubric of Islam is actually Islamic. There is a distinction between cultural traditions and religious practices. He insisted that 'Morisco dances were a folkloric rather than a religious custom that was anathema to pious Muslims; that the clothes worn by

Granadan Moriscos were merely a form of regional costume without religious significance; that Arabic had "no direct relationship whatsoever to the Muslim faith"'. Moreover, Morisco women did not cover their heads for illicit romantic liaisons, but out of modesty; neither were bathhouses of religious significance or had anything to do with ritual ablution, but were only there for the purpose of health and hygiene. Despite the *Memorandum* the decree was enforced, leading to a Morisco rebellion. It provided yet another excuse for religious cleansing: the Moriscos too were banished from Spain. 'In the space of five years, nearly 350,000 men, women and children were expelled from Spain in what was then the largest forced population transfer in European history'.

Indeed, Europe in general, and Spain in particular, has constantly been expelling al-Andalus from the continent as well as from history. As Gema Martín-Muñoz notes, 'ideological positioning has marked the interpretation of Andalusian history'. The Enlightenment historians saw al-Andalus either as a part of the history of progress, 'an uninterrupted progression until the triumph of reason', or as an exotic ingredient of the Romantic vision. Romanticism and Orientalism fashioned their own version of a stereotypical al-Andalus that happened to be in Europe but was firmly outside European history. The Spanish nationalists, on the other hand, sought to link 'real Spain' with 'Western Christianity to avoid sharing her destiny with Muslims' and to 'establish a continuity of national essence, defined by rules of religion, language and race (Christianity, Latinate, Hispanic)'. An example of the nationalist tendency is provided by the Orientalist Francisco Javier Simonet (1829–1897): his 1903 *The History of the Mozarabs* demonstrates 'a great hostility toward the presence on the Iberian Peninsula of Islam, to which he attributes persecution, violence and evil'. Martín-Muñoz discusses the output of a number of Spanish Arabists, who negated the Muslim contribution, presented al-Andalus as an outsider, and emphasised the ideas of the 'Europeanness' of Spain. In more recent times, when eight centuries of Islamic presence and experience in the Iberian peninsula could not be ignored and written off, a new answer was found: a 'Muslim Spain' and a 'Spanish Islam' was created that isolated al-Andalus 'completely from its global Arabic and Islamic context'. The works of old and new Orientalists and nationalists have inspired, writes Martín-Muñoz, 'a good part of the historical interpretation of Spanish education in the twentieth century'.

As a consequence, al-Andalus is 'hardly mentioned' in the secondary school curriculum in Spain, Jordi Serra del Pino tells us. 'Instead, we were regaled with the exploits of the Reconquista, which, we were taught, forged modern Spain'. As in Mecca, where nothing mattered except religious doctrine, Reconquista is taught 'as dogma and its main actors, the Catholic Monarchs' projected 'as legendary characters'. Indeed, the Reconquista is presented as 'a spiritual endeavour'. Everything good in Spain, the students are told, comes from the Reconquista; the previous history, the time of al-Andalus, is dark and evil; 'hence, the need to wipe out any traits, features, remains, history and heritage of al-Andalus'. So, it is hardly surprising, writes Serra del Pino, that 'I grew up knowing little about al-Andalus; even worse, what I thought I knew was largely propaganda'.

Serra del Pino suggests that Spain is now engaged in a Reconquista 2.0. The old Reconquista imagery is being resurrected: the fierce El Cid is now being projected on billboards as a hero of Spain and Queen Isabella is depicted in a new television series as a modern woman, a feminist, spiritual mother of Spain. There is a drive to force Castile and its language on everyone, to homogenise the state, and purge Spain of its linguistic and ethnic diversity. Reconquista 2.0, argues Serra del Pino, is aimed at subduing Catalan and other autonomous regions of Spain. Andalusia, one of the least advanced and poorest regions, suffers from 'an archaic property distribution that concentrates great portions of territories into the hands of a few landlords', and has already 'become one of the most subsidised European regions'. Furthermore, 'the rich Andalusian cultural heritage has been reduced to banal folklore for the consumption of tourists: the bullfighter, the flamenco guitarist and dancer have become global references for Spain, perverting the deep meaning and relevance these cultural forms had for Andalusia. Andalusians are told they are good at looking after the tourists and entertaining them with flamenco, great at parties, but not very good at working hard'.

These sentiments are shared by Carr, who refers to the 2006 statement of former Spanish Prime Minister José Maria Aznar comparing al-Qaeda to the eighth-century Muslim 'occupation' of Spain, and Gonzalez-Ferrin, who describes expulsion as Spain's 'endemic sport that has continued to the twentieth century'. But al-Andalus stubbornly persists, to use the words of

Yassin-Kassab, 'as the jasmin in the air'. It is the future that Serra del Pino envisages for his beloved Catalan as well as for Spain.

The spring shoots of a re-emerging al-Andalus are most evident amongst the young of Andalusia, fighting to recover their heritage, culture, and historic identity; and the Spanish converts that Marvine Howe meets in her travels across Iberia. A few positive steps towards 'normalisation' have been taken in recent times, she writes, and one can now find a host of well-established Muslim communities throughout the region. There is a small community of 'old Muslims', people of Moroccan descent, who inhabit the two Spanish enclaves of Ceuta and Melilla in northern Morocco. But the first Muslims to venture back to Iberia, centuries after it had been ethnically and spiritually cleansed, were university students who arrived from the late 1950s to the early 1970s. Seen as 'pioneers', they have worked hard to build their communities. Howe introduces us to a host of Spanish Muslims: converts, the well-settled, and new arrivals. Individuals like the late Mansur Escudero, who ran the Islamic Junta; Abdel Rahman Essaadi, a Moroccan professor of Arabic; and Braima Djalo, a thirty-five-year-old shopkeeper who fled his native Guinea-Bissau, sailed through perilous seas in a fragile fishing boat, only to be detained on arrival. Howe relates some heart-warming stories of Muslims who overcame tremendous odds to make a home for themselves in Spain. She sees 'a new solidarity' emerging 'among Muslims in Spain, more cooperation between the main communities, the Moroccans and Pakistanis and the Spanish converts'. There is more confidence, more political involvement, and more eagerness 'to show a public face, heedless of emerging anti-Muslim attitudes'.

The anti-Muslim sentiments of Spain and Europe are a product, Gonzalez-Ferrin tells us, of amnesia: 'the forgetfulness of having been something more, something else'. Both Europe and Islam were something more, something greater than the European constructions of al-Andalus 'as an operetta set on an Orientalist stage', something more profound than the anti-rational 'cosmology' of post-al-Ghazzali Islam. They can come together and become whole if they reclaim their mutual histories – and return to al-Andalus.

In their re-imaging of the celebrated Cordoba Mosque, Zara Amjad and Gulzar Haider show us how the past can be remade to heal our present and to build a more viable and pluralistic future. Built in 785 by Prince Abd ar-Rahman I, the founder of the Umayyad Caliphate of Spain, the Mosque is located on the southern edge of the city on the banks of river Guadalquivir. Its most iconic feature is a forest of colonnades which make the space inside appear weightless and create a sense of infinity. The Mosque was consecrated as a Cathedral in 1236, and a Renaissance Cathedral was built within the Mosque in 1523. The Cathedral destroyed the harmony of the Mosque, 63 pillars had to be moved to locate it exactly in the centre, and the Mosque which was originally flooded with light became exceptionally dark. The Cordoba Mosque now functions largely as a tourist site, although there is a Sunday service. Muslims are forbidden from praying inside.

Amjad and Haider begin by 're-locating the Renaissance Cathedral to its metaphorically equal place across the river. The Cathedral is moved stone by stone so that it can continue to function but now has a more clear identity, with an opportunity to reflect on itself and focus on the previously occupied Mosque across the river'. The re-located Cathedral leaves a huge void in the centre of the structure. The natural conservative Muslim tendency would be to rebuild it as a Mosque. But Amjad and Haider redesign the interior as a pluralistic sacred space for all religions. The void is turned into 'a new altar that employs spiritual signs and religious symbols of all religions and is an ode to light, sound, and water', a pool '*mandala*' replaces the dome of the Cathedral and collects rain water which is recirculated back to the river, a series of pilasters in place of the columns of the Cathedral serve as the memory of the Cathedral, and an arcade of glass columns serves as reminders of the Mosque columns. There is also a carved courtyard, steel columns that are left open to the sky, ramps that take you down in the carved spaces around the courtyard, a library under the floor of the mosque, and an underground tunnel that opens onto the river to let in the breeze and the music of the wind. The minaret is turned into four residences named after Ibn Rushd, Maimonides, the thirteenth-century Roman Catholic philosopher and theologian Thomas Aquinas (who, by the way, was inspired by and sided with al-Ghazzali against ibn Rushd), and the Subcontinental philosopher and poet Muhammad Iqbal, whose poem 'Mosque of Cordoba' still reverberates throughout India and Pakistan. Pavillions dedicated to different world religions are built on the small islands on the river Guadalquivir: 'each pavilion will show the essence of the religion it is representing in context with nature; together they will provide a space for the common goal of our different spiritual traditions – a symbolic journey from a place of one individual differentiated religion to a place, the Inhabited Void, the Courtyard, that is for all'.

Like the Cordoba Mosque, al-Andalus too can be reimagined and relocated, liberated 'from the wounds of history', and infused, as Amjad and Haider assert, with 'the essence of life' so that pluralism and humane futures flourish. 'Al-Andalus is not merely a past time', says Gonzalez-Ferrin. 'It is also a time present, a component, and an essential ingredient of all our histories'.

The legacy of al-Andalus belongs to us all.

THE JASMINE BREEZE

Robin Yassin-Kassab

Every Muslim has heard of al-Andalus, where Europe meets Africa, where the Mediterranean almost closes its lips. It's a land of sonority and luminosity, a storied land, an imagined land. Millions know the story of Boabdil (or Abu Abdullah Muhammad XII), the last Andalusi sultan, shedding a tear as he turned to view Granada one last time, bidding farewell to eight and a half centuries of civilisation, and his mother reproving him: 'You weep like a woman for what you failed to defend like a man'. The phrase comes from Washington Irving, American Romantic author of *Tales of the Alhambra* and other fairy stories, but no matter. There's a place in the Alpujarras mountains called the Pass of the Last Sigh, and Salman Rushdie wrote a novel called *The Moor's Last Sigh*. For Muslims, al-Andalus represents lamented past glories, a standard against which to measure the decadence of the present, and hope for the future. For Spaniards and other Europeans it provokes reactions including embarrassment, denial, and delirious enthusiasm. Its image is burningly relevant to our contemporary global arguments over multiculturalism and migration.

So Muslims ruled a chunk of Western Europe for the best part of a millennium, until Europe's Renaissance, which was in important ways provoked or fed by Europe's Muslim civilisation. The final end of Muslim rule in 1492 provides one of those temptingly portentous dates by which to simplify history, for Christian Europe discovered the Americas in the same year, and in following years, funded by New World silver, dominated the eastern sea routes too, establishing the long ascendance which is only ending now.

The Muslims and Jews were driven out of al-Andalus, but still something of Islamic Spain persists as piercingly as the jasmin in the air. As 'The Mosque of Cordoba', a poem by philosopher Muhammad Iqbal, exclaims:

> Its breeze even today is laden with the fragrance of Yemen
> Its music even today carries strains of melodies from the Hijaz

It's confusing being there. You glance over your shoulder and see Tangier or Meknes, then look closer and see a church or a pork delicatessen. There are Arabic survivors in the language, words like aceite from the Arabic az-zeit, meaning olive oil. The rice in the paella was brought by the Moors and became a staple in Moorish times. Certainly the tapas custom of offering a small plate of food with a drink mirrors Levantine drinking culture. Andalucians, like Arabs, take an afternoon siesta. Like Arabs they place a high value on family life, employ a wealth of gestures when they speak, and enjoy a healthy attitude to time. There's even a Spanish version of Arab *wasta*, *enchufe* – using connections to get things done. The Andalucians are Mediterranean people, southern Europeans, Christians and post-Christians, Latins, and almost Moroccans. 'To be a cubist one has to have been born in Malaga', said Picasso, who was born in Malaga. Surely he was making a joke, but if not, it isn't the southern light he was referring to but the multiplicity of perspective inherent in the human landscape.

Malaga airport, servicing Marbella, Torremolinos and other resorts, is where you tend to arrive in southern Spain. I'd been expecting the city to be a transplanted northern European holiday nightmare, a Boschian canvas of pink boys and girls in extreme states of intoxication and undress. Perhaps that's what I was hoping for. Instead I found, as well as the Moorish courtyard and carved wooden ceilings of the Picasso museum, palms from Arabia and trees from the Americas, and Latin Americans and Moroccans running restaurants. The Moorish *alcazaba* (or *kasba*, an Arabic word, related to my surname, meaning 'strong place') dominates the city from its hill top. A surviving horse-shoe arch from the Nasrid-era shipyard is now the entrance to a contemporary neo-Moorish market.

The Moors arrived in 711. It seems significant that the word 'Moor' should have two possible derivations, two potential cultural-geographic perspectives behind it. In Greek, *mauroi* means black; in Phoenician, *mauharin* means western, maghrebi. The land the Moors arrived in had already been rich, and religiously and ethnically diverse. The Tartessos civilisation in the south-west, trading tin, copper and bronze, was influenced by Phoenicians and Greeks. The most popular religions during the Roman period were mystery cults like Mithraism, which originated in Persia, the Egyptian Isis cult, and the worship of the Anatolian god Cybele. Then Christianity arrived from Africa. When Muslim armies swept over the Iberian peninsula, into France and even to the Alps (where the bodies of an Arab and his camel were preserved under the snow), the Andalusian natives were Romano-Iberians, speaking dialects of proto-Spanish. Then there were the Germanic Visigoths, the old ruling class. The Vandals had also passed through, and perhaps gave al-Andalus its name.

The Muslims were divided between Berbers, the greater number, and Arabs. The conquering general Tariq bin Ziyad, from whom Gibraltar (Jebel Tariq) derives its name, was a Berber, and his fellow commander Musa bin Nusair was an Arab from the east. The Muslims intermarried with the locals and bred with their slaves, who were very often Slavs, eastern Europeans captured in eastern European wars to be traded around Europe and the Mediterranean. Soon most of the Muslim population consisted of the offspring of these mixed marriages, and of large numbers of converts. The Muslims would not have been able to take and keep al-Andalus had large sections of the native population not found benefits in their presence.

Christians and Jews were considered People of the Book. So long as they paid the *jizya* tax (which worked as something like an income tax, on a sliding scale), their priests, places of worship and communal legal systems were protected. For the Jews in particular, this was a definite improvement. Furthermore, the Muslims divided the latifundia slave plantations between local tenants. Slaves could now buy their freedom or win it by conversion to Islam.

Cordoba

In 756 the Umayyad prince Abd ar-Rahman, who fled from Syria and the Abbasid conquerors of his dynasty, made Cordoba his capital. His successors in the city would claim the title of caliph.

And what a city. Cordoba enjoyed universal schooling, public hospitals, street lighting, bookshops, libraries and hundreds of mosques. The greatest library housed 400,000 books. No other library in Europe was on anything like the scale. The city's population reached half a million, making it the second biggest city in the world after Baghdad. It was also a global centre of philosophy, mysticism and science, first importing then exporting scholars to the Middle East. One such was ibn Hazm, a typical Muslim Renaissance man, who wrote 400 works on law, ethics, history, theology and love, and who upheld the view of the earth as round rather than flat.

Even if they weren't usually persecuted, Christians and Jews remained second class citizens. In many areas, for instance, the ringing of church bells was forbidden. According to the standards of peaceful countries today, al-Andalus at its diverse peak comes across as an unacceptably discriminatory state. But it was better than what came later in Islamic Spain, and far better than what came centuries later with the Christian conquest. It was better than Franco's Spain, which lasted from 1936 until 1975. Indeed, for its time and its surroundings, al-Andalus was something remarkable, and it remains something for Muslims, Christians, Jews, Europeans, and pluralists to take pride in and to be inspired by.

Monasteries kept alive the Catholic faith, and synagogues the Jewish, but more than that, the '*convivencia*' or coexistence meant not only the development of cultural, artistic and religious ideas within each community, but a rich cross-fertilisation. As it had done in the east, the Arabic language slipped its immediate identification with tribal Arabs and became the medium in which the sciences and concepts of the new Islamic world, from India to Africa, bobbed and swam. It was public property. Non-Muslim Andalusans became known as Mozarabes or *must'arabeen*, the Arabised.

Through the language, Christians and Jews were put in touch with their coreligionists in the old heartlands of their faiths, and with the revived writings of ancient Greece. Spurred by Arabic grammatology, Hebrew grammar was developed and analysed, and a diverse, sometimes 'heretical' Christianity was able to flourish away from the enforced orthodoxy of a Christian ruler. Through Arabic books and scholarship, the raw materials of modernity dribbled into Europe and percolated over centuries.

This vast, cosmopolitan city possessed plenty of *savoir vivre* too. In his *Moorish Culture in Spain*, a work of enthusiasm as much as history, Titus Burckhardt quotes the eleventh-century traveller Ahmad al-Yamani, who on his visit to Malaga, found that 'in the neighbourhood, the strains of lutes, drums and harps intermingled with singing would sound all around me.' Al-Andalus was also, controversially, famous for its wine. Its poetry provided the roots of the European courtly love lyric and the cult of chivalry.

And at Cordoba's centre stood the mosque.

The Mezquita

The mosque consists of a forest of columns linked by white and terracotta double arches. The Cordoban arches are unique, but the column forest also sprouts in the congregational mosque in Fes, and as far back in time as in the hypostyle hall at Egypt's Temple of Karnak. Guidebooks suggest the design evokes a desert landscape, or palm trees, which is possible. What is certain is that it produces the illusion of endlessly rising and spreading space. It's a metaphor for infinity. As such, there is no centre point. Or rather, any point could become a centre of private meditation or public instruction. Sit down, support your back against a column, and you've constructed a centre; stand up again and walk, and the centre dissolves.

Of course, it's not a mosque any more. You have to pay to enter, a distressing eight Euros, which changes the nature of the visit. You have to treat it like a museum and see all you can in one go. You can't wander in and out for prayer or reflection or a simple rest between the business of your day. Most of the arched entrances to the mosque are now blocked, separating it from the secular life outside and necessitating artificial light. Nobody is sitting or prostrating or snoozing on the floor. Parts of the space are cluttered by pews. Sentimental, sometimes garish paintings (one of a Christian conqueror receiving obeisance from kneeling Muslims) hang on walls and in alcoves. There's an overemphasis on gold and heraldry. The divine here is an image of earthly power and glory, and of monarchy.

Still, you can imagine how it used to be, a huge shaded space, the (uncentred) focal point for a huge city.

In his poem, Iqbal lamented:

Stars look upon your precincts as a piece of heaven
But for centuries, alas
your porticoes have not resonated with the call of the muezzin

I met a young group of bearded British-Pakistani brothers deciphering the calligraphy on one of the mosque doors. When I asked what the place meant to them, their spokesman answered, 'It means a lot. It's our history, our heritage. It shows what we could do if we were real Muslims. We could rule.'

Loss is what very many Muslims must feel when they come to this place, loss mingled with pride and a touch of resentment. But I'm not going to whine about the Christianising of the mosque in Cordoba or lament the larger defeat of Islam in Andalusia. Powers and civilisations, and religions too in their organised manifestations, rise and fall. They are transient human efforts and to mourn them greatly would be a great vanity. Cordoba's mosque was a cathedral before Abd ar-Rahman purchased first half the space, then the whole thing as the Muslim community grew. Istanbul's Aya Sofia was transformed from Christendom's greatest cathedral into a mosque, and then under Ataturk's forced secularisation into a museum. The great Umayyad mosque in Damascus was first a temple to Haddad, the Aramaic thunder god, and then Jupiter's sacred precinct, and then a cathedral of such import that John the Baptist's head is interred there. I've heard Syrian Christians complaining because it's a mosque now and not a church, and I was annoyed. Get over it, I thought. So I won't whine.

But still, there's something wrong here, purely from an aesthetic and cultural point of view. If you walk half way over the Puente Romano and look back at the Mezquita you see what it is. The building's basic elongated structure is that of a mosque which has been violated by a cathedral, as if the cathedral has landed from the air, like a bomb. The cathedral is too heavy. It crushes and ruins the mosque. This isn't fusion but vandalism. It looks like an insult.

From inside too. In the cathedral area you feel boxed in, and the mosque's democracy dissolves. The Gothic architecture crushes the soul into awareness of its lowly insignificance. There's a power organisation coded entirely differently to that of a mosque. Naves and altars commandeer the gaze and control the walker's direction. Partitions and priest-only areas are like doors slamming on the notion of infinity. Burckhardt describes the mess as a 'dark church structure that was built between the Renaissance and Baroque periods, and arbitrarily placed at the centre of the light forest of pillars like a giant black spider.' The whole point of the mosque structure was that it had no centre, that it was therefore an image of infinity. As I stood on the bridge I thought the mosque structure is both more secular – an extension of the city beyond – and, because it's open, abstract, eternal, a more effective pointer to the spiritual.

Back to Iqbal's poem:

Annihilation is the end of all beginnings, annihilation is the end of all ends
Extinction is the fate of everything, hidden or manifest, old or new

and then:

O, the ever-flowing waters of Guadalquivir
Someone on your banks is seeing a vision of another period of time

What the reader expects here is that Iqbal, like most Muslims of the modern and contemporary periods, is looking backwards into the reassuring past. Yet as the reader continues reading he finds that Iqbal is not peddling nostalgia. Quite the opposite. He is looking to the future. After referencing the Protestant Reformation and the French Revolution, he writes:

Were I to lift the veil from the profile of my reflections
The West would be dazzled by its brilliance
Life without change is death
The tumult and turmoil of revolution keep the soul of a nation alive

To be a 'real Muslim' doesn't simply mean to strictly observe rules and rituals, to grow facial hair and pray on time. This is what I suspect it meant to the British Muslims I met outside the mosque. But for Iqbal, the kind of faithfulness to Islam which would result in universal dazzlement requires revolutionary progress, reform, reinterpretation, renewal.

The fate of the city's surviving synagogue is perhaps sadder than that of the mosque. Now it's no more than an empty room for tourists to traipse through. But contemporary Cordoba is bright and beautiful, friendly and tolerant, if significantly smaller than a millennium ago. Jasmin climbs on whitewashed walls. Luxuriant patios are glimpsed through doors. The old city walls stand as strong as the walls encircling Rabat in Morocco. Further out, rose gardens sprout between the main roads. Even the bus station, balancing nature with perforated concrete, possesses a mild beauty. In some ways it looks like what the Arab world should be, what it would be were it not in such a mess.

Madinat az-Zahra

I took a tourist bus to a terraced, partially 'rebuilt' archaeological site a few kilometres out of town, at the foot of the Sierra Morena mountains. If you ignore the recent building, there's nothing more here than foundation stones. It is difficult to envisage that these were once a far greater set of constructions than those at the Alhambra in Granada, vaster and richer, marbled and bronzed, silvered and gilded, built during a flowering rather than a shrivelling. The Byzantine Emperor Constantine Porphyrogenitus sent 140 marble columns as a sign of goodwill. The builders extended the old Roman aqueduct and fed water into a network of channels, basins and fountains, with stone animals often serving as water bearers. The complex was a marvel to equal the Abbasid palaces in Samarra, also long lost to time.

The guidebook tells a nice story about the site being named for Zahra, the caliph's wife, but the prime purpose of this place was to exercise and display caliphal power. The Umayyad successor Abdul Rahman III had himself proclaimed caliph in 929 in response to the claim of the Shia Fatimid dynasty in North Africa. The Caliphate in al-Andalus often allied with the Byzantines against the common Fatimid enemy. Founding this administrative city, like minting gold coinage, was therefore a political act, a demonstration of supreme authority, and a nod to the caliphal tradition established when the Abbasids founded Baghdad in 762. The Fatimid rivals had founded Cairo.

As much as it is foolish to dream of a golden age when Muslims worked together in brotherhood against their common foes, it is a mistake to romantically believe that the Islamic states of the past were ruled according to our contemporary notions of Islamic justice and equality. In Madinat az-Zahra the palace very deliberately occupied a position higher than the mosque, leaving no doubt as to who was in charge. The palace contained the *dar al-mulk*, or House of Power, where the caliph lived, with the residences of the crown prince and the *hajib* or chief minister, and a grand reception hall. Beneath the mosque stretched the town, housing court officials, servants, artisans, traders and scholars. A basin looted from az-Zahra and taken to Granada shows lions (symbolising the caliph) preying gloriously on deer (lesser mortals). Before the mass media, the display of authority was essential to rulers, and a theatre of power was enacted here. The twelve grand portico arches which welcomed visitors were designed as an illusion, and in functional terms were far too large for the buildings they led into.

There was substance behind the theatre, but not for long. Only seventy years separate the city's foundation in 940 and its first ransacking in 1010. During a civil war in 1012 one claimant to the Caliphate lodged a Berber army here, which did even more damage. But still earlier, in 976, the usurping minister al-Mansur had transferred the state administration to his nearby, similarly named Madinat az-Zahira.

The impression I gathered was one of pointlessness. Each state builder or warlord is a Sisyphus, rolling the rock up the mountainside only for inevitability to work, for the thing to roll down again, as sure as gravity.

This was the poet al-Sumaysir's response when he visited the ruins later in the eleventh century:

I stopped in az-Zahra, tearful and meditative
and cried out among the destroyed ruins
'O Zahra, return to existence!'
She replied – 'Can the dead return?'

A popular uprising ended the caliphate in 1031. In the following decades and centuries, Muslim control of northern and central Iberian territories slipped, and in 1236 Cordoba itself fell to strengthening Christian forces.

My final visit in Cordoba was to the Alcazar de los Reyes Cristianos, or the Castle of the Christian Monarchs. The conquest of Muslim Granada was planned from here, as was the conquest of the Americas. For a long time it served as a base for the Inquisition. The castle is built on Roman and Moorish foundations, and today displays impressive Roman mosaics excavated in the surrounding area. It also encompasses beautiful fifteenth-century gardens: fish-filled pools, hedges and pomegranate trees.

After the fall of the caliphate, Islamic Spain split into small, often warring principalities known as *taifas* (the word is used in modern Arabic to signify 'sects'). These states came under the control of two north African-based Berber dynasties. The first, in the eleventh and twelfth centuries, was the Almoravids, or *murabitoon*, named after the *rabat* or fortified seminary on the Niger river from which they originated. Their leader, Yusuf bin Tashufin, founded the Moroccan city Marrakesh. In the twelfth and thirteenth centuries they were replaced by the Almohads, or *muwahhidoon*, unitarians. Both dynasties, but especially the Almohads, failed to maintain al-Andalus's previously high standards of tolerance. These periods saw the destruction of synagogues and churches. Persecutions and forced conversions caused many Jews and Christians to flee to Toledo, recently conquered by Christian forces, and other northern cities. Cordoba lost its place as the leading city to Seville.

Yet two of al-Andalus's greatest philosophers were born in Cordoba in the Almoravid period. Ibn Rushd, or Averroes, developed a Hellenistic-Islamic rationalism which ultimately had more influence on European than Islamic thought. Ibn Rushd held several court positions in al-Andalus and Morocco, but abruptly fell out of favour, and his books and other works of philosophy were burnt. The great Jewish thinker Musa ibn Maymun, or Maimonides, whose seminal *Guide for the Perplexed* incorporates Greek philosophy into Jewish theology, was also a victim of intolerance. He fled forced conversion, first to Morocco then to Cairo, where he served as physician to Salahuddin al-Ayubbi (or Saladin).

So I too left Cordoba, through a landscape of dry and rocky high peaks bursting from hills cloaked in gorse and citrus. Bridges leap over deep narrow gorges. Between the mountains, plains bear interminable row-planted olive orchards, their leaves shimmering hyper real. The earth is red, yellow or white, according to its richness. Further to the east, green scrub gives way to semi-desert, and almonds and carobs are the dominant trees. Parts of it are very like the Rif mountains of northern Morocco; parts reminded me of the hills of coastal Syria.

I was heading for Granada, three hours by bus. Between the thirteenth and fifteenth centuries this was the frontier zone beween Islam and Christendom, so the tiled and whitewashed villages huddle high around hilltop forts, either ruined or restored. From high points on the road, the millions upon millions of olive trees made a pointillist landscape. Piling grey clouds brought out the metallic tone of the leaves.

Granada

I arrived in Granada in heavy rain.

It's a much bigger city than Cordoba, and at first sight gritty rather than quaint. The suburbs are shabbier, the central maze of alleyways more exciting; there are more students and more immigrants – Moroccans, Iraqis, Syrians, Turks, Chinese. The area where I found my hotel is painted in earth colours – red and ochre – and its streets lead into Renaissance squares. On the Gran Via de Colon, my nearest main street, a church's high doors were directly open on the pavement and a wedding in progress was spilling out. I found a Moroccan restaurant, ate the best couscous royale in years, stopped for a while at the nearby Afrodisia club (black American music, Africans and Spaniards dancing), and then slept.

Next day I walked up through the winding alleys of Albayzin, so-called since Muslim refugees fled here from Baeza, captured by Christians in 1227. Long before that, this was Granada's first Muslim settlement and power centre, before the Alhambra palace-city was developed. It continued briefly as the surviving Muslim quarter after the fall of 1492, and was once home to twenty-seven mosques.

In the streets lowest on the slopes, workshops sell patterned inlay boxes and tables, very similar to the inlay sold in the Damascus souq but in its own subtly distinctive Andalucian style. I came across a lute (or *oud*) workshop. Higher up there are *carmens* or walled gardens, from the Arabic *kurm*, which means both 'vineyard' and 'hospitality'.

I visited the Palacio Dar el-Hurra, supposedly the palace of Aisha, Boabdil's unforgiving mother. This was darker, quieter, more intimate than the Alhambra palaces I'd see the next day. The birds in the courtyard were making deep sea noises, twirls and trills from another planet. I sat between ochre plaster, climbing plants, wooden eaves. The drip drip of time sounded in a sunken pool.

Everywhere there were mosques pretending to be churches (or churches pretending to be mosques), the bell towers indistinguishable from rectangular Moroccan-style minarets. There were arches linking the alleyways (I was remembering Nablus when one arch opened onto a graffittied wall – *Fuera de Palestine!* it screamed, Get Out of Palestine!), and stately buildings, and tapas bars packed at late lunchtime. Darker flashes of gate and wall under dispersing cloud made me think of Aleppo or even Istanbul, but those images bounced off as soon as the Mediterranean whitewash reasserted itself. I stopped to buy some calligraphed poetry from a man from Casablanca. Being here was like being in Paris and Fes at the same time, and no clash between the elements. Italian coffee and Moroccan mint tea seemed equally suitable options. I ran into another group of wispy-bearded British-Pakistani brothers, these ones bright-eyed and grinning, enchanted by the living heritage. Granada is full of Muslim visitors from Europe, the Middle East and Pakistan, working class and middle class, wearing expressions of bemusement and delight.

I walked higher up the dry slope past cave housing in the Sacromonte neighbourhood where Gypsies, Africans and others live. Several were tending their gardens as I passed – prickly pears, tomato vines, the occasional citrus. There are 650,000 Gypsies in Spain. Their life expectancy is a decade lower than the national average, and only one per cent go to university. Some wear tattoos of the Star of David and the Islamic crescent as a reminder of the common fate of the persecuted. Famously, Gypsies are the masters of Flamenco, the distinctive Andalucian music of *pena y alegria*, pain and joy, and I'd heard some – two guitars and three voices – on a terrace in Albayzin. Flamenco, of course, is very different to the Gypsy music of eastern Europe, and sounds similar to some Arab music. It is safe to say, therefore, that Flamenco is what happened when the originally Indian ideas of Gypsy music met the Muslim-Jewish-Christian music of Moorish Iberia. It sounds good, anyway, and so did the saxophones, trumpets and tin drums I met round every other corner. Granada is the first city I've visited where all the buskers without exception are excellent.

I climbed until the buildings gave way. Up here the city meets the countryside very abruptly. I sat under a conifer outside a section of old city wall, where the besieging Crusaders must have sat as they slowly starved the city beneath, with bird song and strings floating up from below, and gazed across the Darro valley at the Alhambra, or al-Hamra, the red. Red it is, and dazzling to the eye, too complex to arrange in the mind. It's an elegant confusion of battlements, towers and pleasure walkways. Trees sprout thickly between the architecture. After a few enraptured minutes I decided the place represented an ideal compromise between defence and decoration.

The broad high snows of the Sierra Nevada rise behind, falling in cliffs and serries, tree-dark beneath the white tops.

The Alhambra

I spent a half hour in the ticket queue. Apparently it takes much longer in the peak season. My slow and staged approach seemed somehow apt. Like an ancient petitioner, yesterday I'd seen the fort from afar, today I begged entrance at the gates. On the inside the ergonomic herding continued – the one-way system, the closed-off areas, the checkpoints – and it truncated the interconnection and interplay of palaces and gardens. You're only allowed to view things from certain perspectives, you can't repeat your steps, you can't walk backwards. This is how the authorities process their six thousand daily visitors.

In the palace city's heyday, perhaps 40,000 people lived here. The complex contained a mosque, markets, artisanal workshops, a barracks and a zoo as well as luxurious halls and gardens for the Nasrid dynasty's enjoyment. In his myth-busting and slightly cantankerous book on the Alhambra, historian and novelist Robert Irwin reminds us that the place was also 'a monument to murder, slavery, poverty and fear'. Christian slaves were set to work on the palaces, which, unlike the Madinat az-Zahra, were constructed in a decadent and declining age. The decorators had to make do with stucco, wood and tiling rather than marble, silver and gold.

More generally, Nasrid court culture in this last Muslim hold-out was fixed on past glories. Its poetry, for example, was deliberately archaic and tinged with nostalgia – always a bad sign. Relying for its survival on military aid from the Merenid dynasty in North Africa, and paying tribute (or protection money) to the Kingdom of Castille, the Nasrids knew their past was more attractive than their future. External pressures only mirrored the internal rot. Irwin also describes the internecine conflict, brother against brother, which frequently led to *al-mowt al-ahmar*, blood red death, for the royals and their ministers.

Yet the beauty and proportion of the buildings communicate nothing of this turbulence. What they represent is a contradicting and perhaps psychologically necessary vision of order projected out of the chaos. The Alhambra architects were greatly influenced by the theories of the *ikhwan as-safa'*, the Brethren of Purity, a secret philosophical society based in Iraq which had married Pythagorean numerology to Islamic science and mysticism. The Brotherhood was obsessed by the divine one, the universal four, the perfection of seven. That is – the unity of the one from which all multiplicity arises; the structure of the four, the basic shape with which to build all objects; and the seven heavens. Secretive certainly, the Brotherhood was nevertheless something like a tenth- and eleventh-century Bauhaus. Its scholars wanted their theorising to be applied in the world, and architects, calligraphers, town planners and craftsmen took note.

The Alhambra was influenced too by the Merenid architecture of Morocco, especially by the madrasa in Salé where ibn al-Khatib, poet, minister and architect, spent an exile. Merenid style continued to develop in Morocco after the fall of Granada, and in a different way in Spain's Mudéjar art (a word from the Arabic mudajjan, meaning 'domesticated', referring to the Muslim artisans who remained after the fall of the Muslim kingdoms). And in the nineteenth century, there was a neo-Mudéjar revival throughout Spain.

Irwin tells us that there is surprisingly little information on Muslim Granada. The primary texts were burnt, the people were driven out or enslaved, the poets were panegyrists who preferred high-flown metaphor to detail. He warns us therefore not to take the claims of guidebooks too seriously, and not to think of the palaces as authentic originals. It is better to see them as we would see towns on tells, used again and again, or coral reefs constantly encrusting with new life. And we certainly shouldn't set store by the arbitrary titles of the rooms. What is labelled a harem, for instance, could equally have been a reception hall. Rooms in Islamic palaces usually didn't have fixed functions but served according to the occasion, like shifting theatre sets. Usefully, Irwin suggests sitting on the floor to view the rooms, as the first inhabitants did.

The Alhambra museum gives a sense of the old furnishings. Gathered here are fountain bowls shaped like shells or shields, rugs and fabrics, sundials, fine Qur'ans, a chess board, silver dirhams and gold dinars (the currency was used across Muslim and Christian Iberia), glazed jars, an enormous and enormously beautiful carved wooden door, capitals in various styles, and mosaic columns and slabs excavated from the palaces showing a quite different, darker decoration than what is currently in place.

As with the Medinat az-Zahra, the first function of these buildings was to signal power. The representation of the seven heavens in the building known as the Court of the Ambassadors is more earthly than it seems, for the planets were thought of as a celestial court, a mirror of a human court, with the sun replacing the sultan, the moon the chief minister, Jupiter the *qadi*, and so on.

The power long-dissolved, the Alhambra retains a rare and overwhelming beauty of the tear-provoking sort. (It worked on me, and I was not at all in sentimental mood during my visit). The roses, figs and peach trees have something to do with it, the many-coloured flowers and their aromas, the birdsong again – it's a multi-sensory assault. The buildings are uplifting in a literal as well as metaphorical sense: the gaze is lifted up to greet the light. Indeed, the Alhambra illustrates why the two senses of 'light' are conjoined in one English word. Here light is filtered by honeycomb stucco and reflected in pools. The rock is thinned and purified to wax or lace by light, is symmetrically separated by light.

Jorges Luis Borges, although or because he was blind, wrote the greatest poetic response to the Alhambra, and in it he talked of a 'fine labyrinth of water'. The sound – running, splashing, gurgling – and sight of water is an essential element in the whole. Like the use of light, it enacts and emphasises constant change.

As well as politics and reflection, the complex was built for music. Ribbed ceilings to the palaces reduced echo and focused the sound's clarity. The long-disappeared cemetery was also used for musical entertainments, a location which added the melancholic celebration of transience to musical pleasure. Reading this information in Irwin's book, I remembered sitting by the graves at Shah Jamal in Lahore six months earlier and listening to drums. Music, again, is an art which exists in shifting time, and which heightens the awareness of change. It is also closely related to mathematics, its sounds to the ears of Nasrid scholars hinting at the Pythagoran music of the heavenly spheres.

Pattern everywhere – a metaphor for both higher consciousness, pure thought, and for the abstract laws underlying the creation. In the *rasa'il* of the Brotherhood of Purity we find mystical justification for patterned abstraction: 'The divine works are the forms abstracted from matter and created from nothing by the Creator of everything.' It wouldn't be surprising to find such a line in a text by Andalusia-born ibn 'Arabi, the greatest mystic of them all.

The Alhambra is, as Robert Irwin points out, an 'inhabitable book', both for the calligraphy – ibn al-Khatib and ibn Zamrak's verses low in the walls, the Qur'an higher up – and for the mathematical proposals it embodies. The text most obsessively repeated is *wa la ghalib illa ullah* – there is no victor but God. This was the Nasrid dynasty's motto, and in a strange meeting of European heraldry and Islamic calligraphy, it's written inside stone shields as well as on wall panels. I'm glad the phrase is everywhere. Perhaps only by coincidence, it suggests a degree of self-awareness coded into the buildings, for of course the Nasrids were conquered by Christian monarchs, who were eventually conquered by Republicans, who were then conquered by Franco. Today the Alhambra is in the hands of the tourism industry. The *wa la ghalib illa ullah* phrase reminded me of the inscription *umbra summus* – we are shadows – on the sundial on the fronting of east London's Brick Lane mosque, which was first a Huguenot chapel, then a Wesleyan chapel aiming to convert the Jews, and then a synagogue, before the Bengalis arrived. Each comes, each passes.

Like the cemetery, the Alhambra's congregational mosque, once its most impressive building, was destroyed long ago to make way for King Carlos V's renaissance palace. Irwin sums up this construction perfectly: 'a fine, imposing building, but on the wrong site.'

From the seventeenth century the palaces served as debtor's asylum, gunpowder store (a huge explosion did a lot of damage), slave housing and barracks. In the nineteenth century the Alhambra was rediscovered, provoking two Orientalist responses: Romantic infatuation and neo-classicist disgust. These positions are echoed by contemporary responses to the political meaning of al-Andalus. In any case, writings and drawings of the Alhambra were widely circulated, and these influenced buildings and decorative styles all over Europe and Latin America.

But the conservationist attitude was yet to fully develop. Early tourists frequently chipped stucco or tiles from the ruins and pocketed them for their private collections. In 1843 the Nasrid-era mental hospital across the valley in Albayzin was demolished. In 1959 an original garden layout and irrigation system were discovered on the Alhambra site, and were promptly destroyed.

Civil War

We must thank the 'Catholic monarchs', Ferdinand and Isabella, for not destroying the Alhambra as soon as they took it. They may have hated Islam, but they greatly appreciated Islamic art and architecture, and for a time they resided in the conquered palaces. Their marriage in 1479 had unified the kingdoms of Aragon and Castile and established the Spanish nation state. This makes Spain a very old power, unlike Italy and Germany (unified in 1861 and 1871 respectively), but one which by the twentieth century had lost its reach and therefore felt something of the humiliation felt by the other European states which were ruled by fascists.

By 1489 Muslim power on the Iberian peninsula had been reduced to the city of Granada. The final fall of the city in January 1492 was witnessed, fittingly, by Christopher Columbus. He considered his voyage to the Americas later that year as an extension of the anti-Muslim crusade. Believing that he was sailing to the East Indies, he took the Arabic-speaking Jew Luis de Torres to act as interpreter to the supposedly Arabic-speaking tradesmen he would find there. The strategic aim was to establish direct trade and military links with the Far East and thereby undercut Muslim wealth and political alliances. So the European discovery of the New World was a by-product of the Spanish crusades. That it radically changed the global balance of power need not be repeated. A mass migration of Spaniards across the Atlantic ensued. Christian Seville soon became the richest city in the world, and for a century Spain became the pre-eminent Atlantic power and the possessor of an empire stretching to the Philippines.

Ferdinand and Isabella are buried in Granada's Gothic-style Real Capilla, in front of an elaborately befigured golden screen (on which is depicted, beneath the crucifixion and the beheading of the baptist, the Muslims surrendering the Alhambra), and beneath their sculpted images. Graven words celebrate them as *Mahometice secte protatores et heretice pervicacie extinctores* – 'subjugators of the Mahometan sect and extinguishers of obstinate heresy'.

The Jews were expelled immediately. Refugee communities of Ladino-speaking Sephardim spread through Morocco and Algeria to Egypt and Istanbul, later through Europe and eventually to America. Along with Tsarist pogroms and Nazi genocide, the expulsion from Spain, such an important locus for the development of Jewish culture, represents the greatest tragedy of European Jewish history.

At first Muslims were promised freedom of religion under Christian rule, but the promise very quickly turned out to be hollow. The fanatical Cardinal Jimenes de Cisneros ordered enormous book burnings (the Nasrid library was one of many lost to the flames), mosque closures, and forced conversions. Converted Muslims (often only nominally converted) were known as Moriscos. In the 1560s the Moriscos of the Alpujarras mountains rebelled against Philip II's attempt to ban the Arabic language and customs, Muslim dress, even Muslim bathing habits. The rebels were defeated and savagely repressed. In 1609 the decision was taken to expel the Moriscos, and in the following years 275,000 were driven out, permitted only to take what possessions they could carry. By now there was no racial difference between Muslims and Christians; the majority of those expelled were by blood as Iberian as the Christian cousins who were kicking them out of the peninsula. Many of these Muslim Iberians were killed as invaders as soon as they arrived in North Africa. And Christian Spain suffered too from its barbarism. It took decades for the economies of Valencia and Aragon to recover. (Matthew Carr covers these events much more extensively in his essay in this issue 'The Memorandum of Fernando Nuñez Muley').

I got talking, in my terrible Spanish and her terrible English, with a woman in Cordoba's Jazz Café. 'A lot of Spaniards,' she told me, 'don't like Arabs. But we are Arabs, our culture and our blood is Arab. We have forgotten that.'

Well, some Spaniards have forgotten, but not all. She obviously hadn't forgotten. A plaque in Cordoba's archaeological museum describes 'our contemporary reality as men and women whose identity is the product of centuries of hybridisation'. Such a realisation is more common in Cordoba, Granada, Toledo and Seville, cities whose tourism industry necessarily foregrounds the Moorish past, than in other parts of Spain. The truth is that when it comes to al-Andalus, Spain, as on so many topics, is deeply split.

Back in the sixteenth century, the Mozarabe Christians of Cordoba did not want the new cathedral structure to damage the mosque that they already used as a cathedral, but the official pamphlet given to visitors at the mosque/cathedral today talks of 'the inconvenience of celebrating the liturgy amid a sea of columns'. In triumphal tones it also describes the conquered precinct as 'a sacred space that had suffered the imposition of a faith that was foreign'. Muslims lived in Cordoba for over four and a half centuries, and Andalusian blood ran in their veins. Was that not enough to erase their foreignness?

Basques and Galicians are proud they were not conquered by Muslims. For Basques especially, this differentiates them from other Spaniards and feeds into their nationalist-separatist claims. In other words, the other Spaniards are foreign because of their Muslim roots.

For fiercely anti-separatist former prime minister Jose Maria Aznar, Spain's unified national identity exists in direct opposition to the Muslim past. In a lecture at Georgetown University a few days after the March 2004 Madrid train bombs, he said this: 'Spain's problem with al-Qa'ida starts in the eighth century ... when a Spain recently invaded by the Moors refused to become just another piece in the Islamic world.' Seldom has a contemporary European politician made a more simplistic and ahistorical statement.

The train bombs had killed 191, most of them working class, fifty-four of them immigrants. In the immediate aftermath Aznar, despite his Islamophobia and despite a lack of evidence, was determined to blame the Basque separatist group ETA, probably because he didn't want the attacks to be seen as blowback for his unpopular decision to join in the occupation of Iraq. Over 80 per cent of Spaniards opposed the Iraq war, but Aznar still sent a large military contingent. His soldiers wore the cross of Santiago 'the Moor slayer' on their uniforms.

I talked about Spanish attitudes to the Muslim past with Amira Kedier and Xavier Rosom of the Casa Arabe in Cordoba. The Casa Arabe (or Arab House) is a state organisation which seeks to improve relations between Spain and Arab countries. Its base in a restored house in Cordoba, on the Calle de Samuel de los Santos Gener near the Mezquita, hosts lectures and art exhibitions and is well worth a visit.

'Our education system,' Xavier pointed out, 'somehow avoided the Andalus period.' Amira added that the very notion of 'reconquista' is deeply problematic, as if there was a unified Christian Spain before the Muslims arrived, as if eight hundred and fifty years was a mere parenthesis. The historian Angel Gonzalez Palencia argues that the reconquista should instead be understood as a civil war between two Spains. The poet and playwright Federico Garcia Lorca, executed by fascists in 1936, saw the contrast between the Nasrid palaces and Carlos V's palace as symbolic of the divide in Andalucian society in his own times.

I was thinking about civil war as I travelled through Andalusia because of the revolution and repression in Syria, which is what tea and couscous serving Moroccans often wanted to talk about when they heard my Arabic. And also because I was thinking of the wars of swords and rhetoric which have divided Spain between *taifas*, between Moors and Christians, between visions of the past, and between left and right. I was reading Giles Tremlett's book *Ghosts of Spain* and realising that many of the towns and villages I passed through contained mass graves from the thirties and forties, my grandfather's era. Half a million were killed in the war between republicans and nationalists, almost half by execution.

There were clear parallels between the wars in Spain and Syria. Both class wars, both catalysts and symptoms of larger ideological conflicts (fascist/democrat and Sunni/Shia), both attractors of foreign fighters. For Franco's German and Italian troops, Assad's Iranians and Lebanese; for the Republicans' International Brigades, the Free Army's small complement of Salafists and democrats from Libya, Tunisia and Iraq. There were parallels too between Spain's twentieth century and fifteenth century wars, parallels of which Franco was keenly conscious. The General described the programme of his Falange party as 'National Catholicism' (his variety of fascism soon inspired a Falangist movement amongst Lebanese Maronites), and he saw in the '*cruzada*' against the Reds a new reconquista, a new and necessary purging. 'We must eliminate without scruples,' said General Mola, 'all those who do not think like ourselves.' Priests played an important role in identifying subversives for execution, and many priests were murdered by leftists.

Obviously, the bad feeling has not yet dispersed. The name of Jose Antonio Primo de Rivera is stencilled into the wall of an official building in Granada – de Rivera, founder of the Falange Party. Someone has spattered the wall with red paint, to suggest blood.

But official Spain celebrates its historic diversity much more than it celebrates the fascist past. In Cordoba I came across a roundabout called Glorieta de las Tres Culturas. Amira Kedier calls this kind of municipal idealism the 'three cultures myth'. She says, 'Part of the population is proud of this supposed peaceful coexistence, especially in the last twenty or thirty years. It's a nice idea, but a little bit far from reality.' Maybe it is, but it has its uses, including perhaps a more welcoming attitude to immigrants than in most of Europe.

There is a thriving community of Spanish converts in Andalusia. Historically and culturally, these people have more reason than most converts to identify themselves as 'reverts', and according to Amira, they are often very keen indeed to stress that the faith they are embracing is in no way exotic or foreign but one which runs in the Spanish blood.

Converts are responsible for setting up numerous national organisations and institutions, including Spain's Cordoba-based Halal Institute. They are also behind Granada's new mosque, constructed with Emirati money in 2003, the first in the Albayzin quarter for five centuries. The mosque is simple and beautiful in a classical Islamic Moroccan/Andalusi style, white-washed, with a rectangular minaret. As such, it fits perfectly with its surroundings. Viewed from across the valley it is culturally indistinguishable from the neighbouring church. The atmosphere is peaceful, friendly and welcoming. The mosque's beautiful garden, and its remarkable view of the Alhambra, are open to all.

THE ANDALUSI SECULAR

Nazry Bahrawi

Somewhere in the Gobi desert lurks a wormlike creature so elusive that no one can fully describe its attributes properly. Some say it spews acid when threatened. Others allege that it dispenses electric charges, or even explodes at will. While it has not yet been proven to exist, the Mongolian death worm is nevertheless 'real' to many who live in that part of the world. Despite the multifarious, often fabulous accounts of this mythical animal, one thing that those who believe in it can agree on is its uncompromising lethalness. A similar paradox afflicts traditional Islamic discourse on the secular. It is a great many things to a great many thinkers: colonialism, Godlessness, and moral degradation, to name a few. Like the Mongolian death worm, those who believe in it can only imagine it as deadly.

The Malaysian scholar Syed Muhammad Naquib al-Attas aptly summarised the normative perspective of Muslim traditionalists on secularism. In his *Islam and Secularism*, he suggests that expressions of the secular were not only westernised beliefs 'opposed to the worldview projected by Islam' but in fact 'pose an immediate threat to us' – Muslims. The secular can spew acid, discharge electricity, explode, or perhaps even do all three. But in vocalising this threat to the Muslim world, al-Attas is not alone. The popular Sunni cleric Yusuf Qardawi also regards the secular as toxic. As political scientist Nader Hashemi points out in his book *Islam, Secularism and Liberal Democracy*, the al-Azhar-trained cleric had written in his 1977 book tellingly titled *al-Hulul al Mustawradah wa Kayfa Jaat 'alaa Ummatina* (or, How the Imported Solutions Disastrously Affected the Muslim Community) that 'secularism may be accepted in a Christian society but it can never enjoy a general acceptance in a Muslim society' because 'secularism among Muslims is atheism and a rejection of Islam'. Such vitriol only serves to entrench what Hashemi calls the 'Islamic exceptionalism' thesis, or the postulation that Islam is uniquely incompatible with notions of secularism and liberal democracy because of the faith's 'inner antimodern, religiocultural dynamic' (ibid. xi). Islamic exceptionalism is a twentieth-century phenomenon that carries the baggage of European colonialism. It is an all-inclusive hypothesis: Sunnis like al-Attas and Qaradawi subscribe to it, but so too the Shi'ites. Hashemi points to Iran's Ayatollah Seyyed Ali Khamenei who reminded his colleagues at the Assembly of Experts in 2002 that 'colonialist powers have always advocated a separation of religion from politics'.

To relieve their 'death worm' fear of the secular, Muslims need to return to al-Andalus, where philosophy, or *falsafa*, thrived and philosophers and polymaths such as ibn Tufayl, ibn Rushd and ibn 'Arabi had already tamed the beast.

But what exactly is the secular? Talal Asad, son of the famous translator of the Qur'an Muhammad Asad, makes an important distinction in his *Formations of the Secular*: the secular must be differentiated from secularism. The former is an 'epistemic category', the latter a 'political doctrine'. Thus, Khamenei's chastisement gestures to the second sense of the term – one that signals an anti-colonial stance against the oppressive expeditions of Europe to conquer vulnerable societies under the disingenuous pretext of civilising barbarians. However, intimations of the secular in Andalusian philosophy appeal to the first sense of the word – the secular as ontology. As a way of framing the world, the secular ontology is built on several themes and dichotomies, most particularly reason and human agency that are fuelled by the binary oppositions of faith/reason and freewill/determinism respectively.

The Andalusian philosophy is associated with a certain type of philosophical disposition in Islamic thought, typified by a commitment to conclude Islamic thought's engagement with Neoplatonism – either by incorporating it, denying it, or proposing it altogether as new way of viewing metaphysics. All three positions are represented in the personages of ibn Tufayl, ibn Rushd and ibn 'Arabi respectively.

Secularism as a contemporary condition, as the philosopher Charles Taylor has pointed out, is mistakenly premised on the simplistic view that 'science refutes and hence crowds our religious belief'. This faith-reason dichotomy has become the yardstick for judging Muslim societies. Consider the October 2012 tweet by the British comedian Ricky Gervais: 'Dear Religion, this week I safely dropped a man from space while you shot a child in the head for wanting to go to school. Yours, Science.' Gervais was contrasting the Austrian skydiver Felix Baumgartner's record-breaking stratosphere jump with the Taliban shooting of fourteen-year-old Malala Yousefzai in Pakistan. Doubtlessly, the first represents a step forward for humanity, and the latter a condemnable act. Yet has there truly been a neglect of reason in Muslim societies?

To answer this question we have to consider the genealogy of a central assumption fuelling the idea of secular 'reason' – empiricism. Simply put, this is the view that the human mind is a blank slate, or *tabula rasa*, and can only make sense of the world by way of experience. It follows that knowledge must therefore be supported by evidence, or be provable – a key feature of scientific enquiry. It is precisely this notion of secular reason that ibn Tufayl, or Abubacer as he is known in the West, alluded to in his philosophical novel *Hayy ibn Yaqzan* ('Alive, Son of Awake'), which was published in the mid twelfth century.

Ibn Tufayl fictionalises the intellectual development of a feral child named Hayy, raised by a gazelle on an undisclosed island in the Indian Ocean. The first thing the child does following the death of his surrogate mother is to perform surgery on the gazelle in an attempt to bring the animal back to life. This does not happen, but the child learns about anatomy. Hayy also begins to ponder about his environment and reasons for life. The boy finds himself alone in the world, yet manages to fend for himself, picks up survival skills by observing events in his environment and rationalising his observations. As he enters adulthood, Hayy's intellectual developments lead him into the spheres of theology and philosophy.

In narrating the novel, ibn Tufayl latches on to the great eleventh-century Persian polymath ibn Sina's treatise on *tabula rasa*. Ibn Sina argues that a person's intellect begins as an empty slate that develops through two consequent phases of intellectualising. Firstly, the mind engages with the immediate world to develop what he calls *al-'aql al-hayulani*, or material intellect. Then, it begins to wrestle with abstract concepts like God as the mind develops as *al-'aql al-fa'il*, or the active intellect. The latter, a more developed state of mind, can only be reached through a process of deductive reasoning.

Hayy ibn Yaqzan was a foundational text for British empiricism, an intellectual movement that had come to define secular reason as that which necessitates proof and can be validated by sense experience. In 1671, the novel was translated into Latin as *Philosophus Autodidactus* by Edward Pococke, the son of the famous Orientalist professor by the same name at Oxford

University. Pococke's translation, sub-titled *The Self-Taught Philosopher*, hinted at the limitless potential of the human mind to develop itself in amazing ways just by observing its immediate surroundings. In short, nurture matters more than nature. One of the older Pococke's most attentive students was the seventeenth-century English philosopher, John Locke. Fascinated by the human potential implied in ibn Tufayl's novel, Locke immediately called for a meeting with his intellectual peers to discuss 'this novelty' in London. Locke incorporated *tabula rasa* into his philosophy and seminal work *An Essay Concerning Human Understanding*. Locke believes that humanity is malleable, ultimately shaped by what it learns. No one is born good or evil as he outlines in another work *Some Thoughts Concerning Education*: 'all the men we meet with, nine parts of ten are what they are, good or evil, useful or not, by their education.'

Several translations of *Hayy ibn Yaqzan* appeared in Dutch and English in subsequent years. Among the first Dutch translation was one by I. Bouwmeester, a friend and associate of another western philosopher who had an influential role in defining secular philosophy, Baruch Spinoza. So influential was ibn Tufayl's novel that it inspired a series of like-minded fictional tales of feral children, abandonment and isolated islands in European literature, such as Daniel Defoe's *Robinson Crusoe* (1719), Jean-Jacques Rousseau's *Émile, or On Education* (1762) and Rudyard Kipling's *The Jungle Book* (1894). Yet one important point has to be made about the European appropriation of *Hayy*. While the protagonist in ibn Tufayl's story eventually becomes a firm believer in Islam, European thinkers ignored the religious aspects of the novel and used it to forward the aims of the Enlightenment. Specifically, *Hayy* has allowed the likes of Locke and Rousseau to make a clear distinction between faith and reason, and to hold reason in greater esteem in this juxtaposition.

Underlying the notion of secularity is the idea of human agency. That is to say, humanity can uninhibitedly exercise freewill to effect change and engage in emancipatory action. Secularity in this sense also means the irrelevance of divine determinism inferred in the following oft-cited verse of the Qur'an: 'Verily never will Allah change the condition of a people until they change it themselves' (13:11). In the thick of the Enlightenment, Rousseau appeals to this preference for freewill over determinism when he opens *The Social Contract* with one of the most unforgettable displays of irony: 'Man was born free, and everywhere he is in chains.' Free from what? Rousseau would say the authoritarian rule of the monarchy. But writ large, this freedom holds true to dogma of all shades. Yet to claim that freewill originated in the European Enlightenment would be disingenuous.

Centuries before, Muslim philosophers had debated the idea of freewill rather fervently – with two Persian thinkers, al-Ghazali, the eleventh-century theologian, and ibn Sina, taking diametrically opposite positions on the matter. The middle ground was reached in al-Andalus through the figure of ibn Rushd, or Averroes as he is called in the West – thus entrenching the importance of Andalusian philosophy in shaping secularity.

To appreciate the discussion on freewill in classical Islamic philosophy, we need to first understand the emanation theory of the tenth-century philosopher al-Farabi, known in the West as Alpharabius and in the Muslim world as 'the Second Teacher', that is, the successor to 'the First Teacher', Aristotle. Simply put, this is the theory that the universe – and the things within it – were created as emanations of the First Cause, or First Being: that which is God. While the theory is far more complex, it would suffice to highlight that it upholds humanity as a 'by-product' of God. Accepting al-Farabi's thesis, ibn Sina, a century later, asks: how can one justify the theological narrative of reward and punishment in the hereafter given that the nature of humanity as a 'by-product' of an omnipresent God must mean that they are somewhat 'determined' by this First Being?

The question is further complicated by another oppositional pairing – good and evil. If God as the First Being causes humanity to commit evil acts and then punishes them, this makes Him unjust. Hence, God cannot be omniscient or omnipresent, making the idea of God itself ludicrous. Thus, how can evil exist? To get past this dilemma, ibn Sina argues that the presence of evil in the material world is incidental; and that good is in fact its essence. Fire demonstrates this best, he says. Fire is generally utilised for good purposes such as cooking and light, yet it can also be incidentally evil when it comes in contact with the skin. Similarly, the inequality of skills in a human society is to ensure interdependency but in certain circumstances can also be crippling for that society if certain skills are under-represented. But this still does not answer the question of why rewards and punishments are necessary. So ibn Sina argues further that these act as stimulants and deterrents. The onus for performing good and evil deeds in the course of one's corporeal existence thus falls squarely on one's own shoulders. To this end,

God is a guide. As such, rewards and punishments are not so much acts dished out by an unjust God as they are effects of the soul's conduct on earth. This is congruent with the cause and effect premise that underpins the emanation theory. Ibn Sina is able to retain the Godly ties of al-Farabi's emanation theory while discarding the idea of determinism.

For al-Ghazali though, ibn Sina's theory of freewill suggests that God has knowledge only of universals and not specifics. This is nothing short of heresy, al-Ghazali proclaims in *Tahafut al-Falasifa* (The Incoherence of the Philosophers), because it transgresses the Islamic notion that God is omniscient as alluded to, say, in the Qur'anic verse 6:59: 'He has the keys to the Unseen: no one knows them but Him. He knows all that is in the land and sea. No leaf falls without his knowledge, nor is there a single grain in the darkness of the earth, or anything fresh or withered, that is not written in a clear Record.' Al-Ghazali thus posits that God knows both universals and specifics, even if it were the activities of an ant.

Enter ibn Rushd. His crucial intervention in this theological impasse rescued ibn Sina's idea of freewill from certain obscurity following al-Ghazali's formidable onslaught. He does this in two ways in his sarcastically titled book *Tahafut al-Tahafut* (Incoherence of the Incoherence), which is in fact a response to al-Ghazali's attack on philosophy. First, ibn Rushd argues that God's knowledge could not be categorised as 'universal' and 'specific' since these are human conceptions. Given that God is not a corporeal entity like humans, His perception of knowledge differs from ours. Ibn Rushd posits that we are shackled by the limits of human understanding to comprehend, much less categorise, Godly knowledge. Second, ibn Rushd argues that human conduct could not be categorised as being either fully free or fully determined. Rather, it is a bit of both. Humanity is free to choose, but this choice is also one determined by external forces operating in tandem. Juxtaposing human will to God's will, ibn Rushd argues that humans act to fulfil their desires because these change over time. God simply acts because His eternal nature means that He is not bounded by time – past, present or future. In this sense, human desire becomes one of those extenuating 'external' factors dictating an individual's choice.

Ibn Rushd's middle position between al-Ghazali and ibn Sina allows for the doctrine of free will to exist without denying God's omniscience. In other words, humanity is an active agent in Islam, and not a passive, predetermined one. It is also this recognition of human agency that leads ibn Rushd to the rejection of a key component of Islamic Neoplatonism – the emanation theory. For ibn Rushd, the idea that humanity is a 'by-product' of the First Being, as upheld by ibn Sina and al-Farabi, contradicts human agency. To subscribe to the emanation theory, ibn Rushd argues, is to deprive all actual entities of any active powers, and to deny the principle of causality.

Ibn Rushd's position and arguments were embraced by the Enlightenment thinkers. For example, the Muslim victory at the battle of Badr is seen by Voltaire in terms of human agency. The battle, a crucial event in Islamic history, witnessed a highly outnumbered Muslim force defeating a larger army belonging to the hostile tribe of the Quraish. The Qur'an describes the day of the battle as the 'day of the furqān' (8:41) – furqān denoting 'the moment of truth' – and speaks of God's intervention in the way He reinforces the Muslim force with an army of thousands of angels. Voltaire downplays the 'miraculous' nature of the outcome by highlighting the episode's preference for human agency. As Ziad Elmarsafy notes in *The Enlightenment Qur'an*, for Voltaire 'the lesson is simple: God helps those who help themselves. The operative distinction, the Enlightenment furqān, that makes this lesson cohere is the binary opposition between those who change the world through their own initiative and those who wait for a higher power to do it for them.'

In the post-Voltaire era, the turn towards freewill becomes more pronounced in Immanuel Kant's discourse. According to Kant, humanity can speculate about moral law, a system of codes governing what is ethical, without any recourse to religion. As rational creatures, humanity will only agree to the tenets of moral law through free consent because accepting these blindly will only position them as slaves. Thus, the onus for acting responsibly falls on the shoulders of humanity and not a divine being.

Yet Kant also argues that God is a necessary postulate in the human quest for morality. This is grounded in the belief that God is the dispenser of rewards and punishments, an idea, Kant argues, that must be solely based on faith. In *The Critique of Practical Reason*, Kant suggests that it is only through the belief that God exists and plays this gatekeeper role that humanity will ensure that the 'transgression of the [moral] law would indeed be avoided; what is commanded would be done'. So while Kant argues for the primacy of human agency in determining our moral action, he is also disdainful of totally subtracting God from the equation.

That radical task was performed by Friedrich Nietzsche, the early twentieth century German philosopher. His (in)famous maxim 'God is dead' in *The Gay Science* represents him as God's grim reaper. For Nietzsche, humanity is driven to act by a natural, active force within us that Nietzsche calls our 'will to power'. This force pushes humanity to become better selves by appealing to traits such as action, spontaneity, domination, pride, and even cruelty. It is will to power that has ensured human flourishing over the ages, upholding the Darwinian precept of the survival of the fittest. However, Nietzsche argues that organised religions have suppressed humanity's will to power by relegating its values as undesirable, even sinful, traits. He prophesises that the time is nigh for humanity's will to power to make a re-appearance, a revolution that will be heralded by the promulgation of atheism. In true 'secular' style, Nietzsche writes that atheism will bring about 'a victory of the European conscience, won at last and with difficulty, the most momentous act of a two-thousand-year-long discipline in truth which ultimately forbids itself the lie of faith in God'. Nietzsche's statement is not just an endorsement of human agency over determinism; it is also a powerful protest against Godliness. His absolutist stance can be seen as the apogee of centuries of debates dichotomising free will and determinism that began with a subtle differentiation between the two categories as we see in ibn Rushd's defence of philosophy, and his predecessor ibn Sina, against al-Ghazali's assault.

While ibn Tufayl and ibn Rushd resided in al-Andalus for the most part of their lives, ibn 'Arabi left his homeland at the age of thirty-six. He wrote two of his most renowned works, *al-Fusus al-Hikam* (The Bezels of Wisdom) and *al-Futuhat al-Makiyyah* (The Meccan Openings) in Mecca. Yet al-Andalus never left him. His treatises suggest a keen engagement with ideas of Islamic Neoplatonism, though in surprising new ways.

If the ideas of ibn Tufayl and ibn Rushd entrench the secular, those of ibn Arabi take us to a whole new level of understanding its ontology. For ibn Arabi, there is no such thing as reason or free will. Indeed, there is no secularity. His was a philosophical position premised on the cryptic adage he champions: *huwa la huwa*, or He/not He. In these three seemingly harmless words lies ibn 'Arabi's most powerful protest against the principles of dualism that characterises the secular such as the dichotomies of faith/reason and free will/determinism.

With *huwa la huwa*, ibn ʻArabi denies the idea that God is anthropomorphic or incomparable, as postcolonial scholar Ian Almond argues convincingly in his book *Sufism and Deconstruction*. Anthropomorphism was denoted through the creed of *tashbih* (immanence), while God's incomparability was implied by the doctrine of *tanzih* (transcendence). These notions were championed by two seminal movements of classical Islam: the Ash'arites, the tenth-century school of speculative theology; and the Mu'tazilites, the school of rational philosophy that saw its heyday between the eighth and tenth centuries. The Ash'arites professed immanence; their primary ideologue al-Asha'ri upholds God's likeness to humanity in the way He sits on the throne, has two eyes, two hands and a face. The Mu'tazilites, meanwhile, were so bent on endorsing the uniqueness and perfectibility of God that their members concluded that He can never be like anything of this world, protesting against any efforts to make God appear pseudo-human. Their radical form of negative theology led to several controversial conclusions, one of which was the idea that humans will not encounter God even in the afterlife.

Though both groups employ Aristotelian logic to prove the validity of their stances, ibn ʻArabi believes that 'reason' could not possibly explain God's essence, which he calls the Real or *al-Haqq* in Arabic. This is what is entailed in his doctrine of *huwa la huwa*. Godliness for ibn ʻArabi is predicated on the doctrine of 'divine vastness' (*al-tawassu' al-ilahi*). Thus, any rational attempts at defining Him would only serve to limit God rather than facilitate human understanding. This was certainly what the Ash'arites did, but so too the Mu'tazilites, whose form of negative theology was – ironically – an attempt at depicting God's vastness.

The two groups' concept of Godliness was also limited by another aspect of 'reason': the Socratic dialectical method in which a hypothesis gets advanced by way of pointing out contradictions inherent within it so one can arrive at a better argument. In the nineteenth century, the dialectical method was surmised by the German philosopher Hegel by the triad phrase: 'thesis, anti-thesis, synthesis'. Yet for ibn ʻArabi, the polemics of the *tashbih-tanzih* debate did not lead to a better understanding of God. On the contrary, it was deceptive. The doctrine of divine vastness meant that God is not one or the other, but all and sundry. It is this recognition of God's 'inter-textuality' that led ibn 'Arabi to embrace the virtues of perplexity. According to Almond, confusion for ibn 'Arabi is not so much helplessness, as it is the ability to recognise the boundless, and boundary-less, essence (*dhat*) of God. In this sense, confusion is the antidote to scientism if one takes the latter to be a philosophy that sieves, focuses, and divides. Confusion leads us to see the bigger picture, and not be lost in minute details – fascinating as they may be. It helps us understand not just God's divine vastness, but also His Oneness, denoted in Islamic terminology as *tawheed*. In intimating the latter, Ibn 'Arabi also references the emanation theory of ibn Sina and al-Farabi, which posits some divinity in all of us. After all, we are all 'by-products' of the First Being, God.

The radicalism of his thought makes Ibn 'Arabi possibly our best hope at breaking the contemporary impasse that has come to define secularity: that is, its inherent binarism, the duality of faith and reason as well as free will and determinism. Erudite as they are, ibn Tufayl and ibn Rushd still hover around the idea of the secular in their thoughts, upholding its inherent binarisms. Ibn 'Arabi, on the other hand, ushers us into the sphere of the post-secular. By this, I do not mean the idea that 'religion' has returned as some have come to understand the term. No, religion has never been away. Rather, I am inferring that the human condition is a cacophonous one in the same way that Godliness is 'divine vastness'. Human existence, metaphysically speaking, is both terrestrial and otherworldly. There are no Mongolian death worms, nor secularity. There is no need to fear monsters. They have already been tamed and domesticated in al-Andalus.

A THOUSAND AND ONE HISTORIES

Gema Martín-Muñoz

The Arabs conquered the Iberian Peninsula in 711, integrating it into the Islamic Empire, and in 1492 the Catholics put an end to the peninsula's last Muslim entity, the Kingdom of Granada. These eight centuries represent the longest civilisational period in the history of what we now call Spain, and the Arabs called al-Andalus. The Andalusi cultural component did not disappear with the last Islamic political domain, but survived first through the Mudejars, the Muslims who remained for some time in the Christian kingdoms, and above all later through the Moriscos, Muslims forced to convert to Christianity, until their expulsion in the early seventeenth century. Al-Andalus thus represents a historical experience almost a millennium long.

Few historical periods have been more controversial. Few demonstrate more clearly how the past can be made to serve current ideologies. Al-Andalus and its significance have been the objects of multiple polemics and contradictory historiographical visions, and a fount of myths that have frequently obstructed balanced and contextualised study. Most approaches to al-Andalus have suffered from an excess of grand emotions and *a priori* assumptions.

Ideological positioning has marked the interpretation of Andalusi history. The 'Catholic Kings' paradigm was based on the unity of Spain and the negation (and persecution) of religious diversity. Christianity was the major constructor of an ideology which stubbornly excluded the eight Islamic centuries from the Spanish historical memory. 'Hispania' (from which 'Spain' is derived) was imposed on al-Andalus in both name and meaning. The Romans named the Iberian Peninsula Hispania when it was integrated into their empire. Of course, this conquest never provoked the historiographical controversy of the subsequent Islamic conquest. The Greco-Roman heritage was presented as the essential source of European being and thought, definitively excluding any oriental contribution.

The Romans, succeeded by the Visigoths of the Kingdom of Toledo and then the Christian kingdoms of the north after the formation of al-Andalus, were presented as part of the line that culminated in the Catholic Kings, guaranteeing continuity with Hispania and, as a consequence, with the essence of Spain ('Spain as a historical unity' was Spanish historian Claudio Sánchez Albornoz's central idea). Al-Andalus, due to its Arab and Islamic identity, was excluded, interpreted as a historical anomaly, a foreign experience lying beyond the true Spanish personality of Christian and Latin roots. This historical construction nourished official interpretations until the eighteenth century when, for a brief period, Enlightenment thought brought a new approach.

During the eighteenth century, Enlightenment thought caused a rupture with the negationist interpretation of al-Andalus, approaching the reality instead from an assimilationist perspective. According to Maria Antonia Martínez Núñez, 'Enlightenment thinkers conceived of history around the rationalist paradigm of modernity, viewing the past as an uninterrupted progression until the triumph of reason (in fact, of the bourgeoisie and its values). Renowned Enlightenment thinkers wanted to reclaim al-Andalus as part of that history of progress seen as a worthy alternative to feudalism.' The new interest in al-Andalus brought such advances as the founding of the first Chair in Arabic at El Escorial at the behest of Charles III in 1786 (suggesting a surprising degree of interest in learning the Arabic language), the publication of *Arab Antiquities* by San Fernando's Royal Academy of Fine Arts in 1770, the beginning of Andalusi numismatics studies and, more generally, research into al-Andalus and its archaeological remains which had until that point been rejected and abandoned, where they had not been destroyed.

Nevertheless, this Enlightenment effort had little reach, and the nineteenth century saw the birth of other visions of al-Andalus which, for all they were new, were no more objective. Medievalism and exoticism would be the two major ingredients of the Romantic vision; and Romantic travellers of the eighteenth century, such as Francis Carter, Washington Irving and Cavanah Mourphy, encountered in Spain an inexhaustible source of attraction in the material traces of al-Andalus, divulging in their writing an Orientalist fascination for all things Andalusi. This in turn developed an Orientalism to accompany the European colonial venture: a world view in the minds of imperial officials and academics who developed a purportedly scientific knowledge that would dominate narratives concerning the east and which would justify colonialism. Orientalism is one of the ways by which Europe sought to define itself in opposition to an Orient recreated to fit European fantasies and interests and Europe's need to feel superior.

The Orientalism most directly linked to the colonial venture represented 'natives' of the African and Asian lands as inferior and intrinsically foreign to European modernity – and susceptible therefore to a civilising process. In this way a moral justification was found for colonial domination, converted to the historical mission of superior beings obligated to bring civilisation to backward or savage peoples. The progressive contact of travellers and artists with oriental lands also generated a Romantic and aesthetic Orientalism which sought to highlight that which was most different and picturesque. The orient was a world of palaces, of beautiful and sensual women, of desert landscapes and cities composed of domes and labyrinthine buildings arranged in medinas and kasbas. Romanticism was an ideal that transported European society to attractive worlds that were supposedly distant, although in reality they were very close geographically. This aesthetic Orientalism was as unreal and distant as the political one, but it had a great power of social attraction.

Spain counted on a rich production in which its particular local orient, al-Andalus, was added to the Far East. Icons of the Andalusi legacy, such as the Mosque of Cordoba, the Alhambra, and the Alabaicin of Granada, provided a rich fount of oriental inspiration that was reflected in art and literature as well as in other popular arts such as advertising posters. Al-Andalus was a rich advertising pitch for unusual products such as beverages, biscuits, and tobacco. By reinterpreting al-Andalus through the Orientalism of the *Thousand and One Nights*, these billboards sold their products as if they were something particularly exotic and different.

The 'Hispanic' Nationalist Reaction

Romanticism and Orientalism fashioned their own version of a stereotypical al-Andalus to present an orientalised Spain as a relevant marker for the West. Spanish nationalism reacted to this by demonstrating its univocal Christian and Latin character. Historiographical schools of the nationalist type would develop during the course of the nineteenth and twentieth centuries, and would define the prevailing interpretations and significations of al-Andalus until our time.

According to this vision, 711 is identified as the date of the 'loss of Hispania/Spain', and the Battle of Covadonga in 722 as the beginning of the 'Reconquista'. Covadonga, situated in Asturias in the north of Spain, was where the local political and military leader, D. Pelayo, defeated the troops of al-Andalus and prevented further conquests in the northern part of the Iberian Peninsula. The term and concept of 'Re-conquista' dominated the teaching of medieval Spanish history; it has allowed the guiding ideology of the 'real Spain' which, invaded and occupied by the Arab-Muslims, finally managed to recover its territories and expel the invaders, to establish itself. The Reconquista concept's transcendental intention is to link Spain with Western Christianity and to avoid sharing her destiny with Muslims. In this interpretation there is a desire to establish a continuity of national essence, defined by rules of religion, language and race (Christianity, Latinate, Hispanic), positing a direct link between the Visigothic heritage and the Catholic Kings. Al-Andalus is thereby converted into a mere hiatus of almost a millennium, and the fact that the inhabitants of al-Andalus were the natural population of that territory, with longer residence – eight centuries – than the time that has passed from 1492 until the present day, is completely ignored.

With this same ideological bias, nationalist historians held up figures such as D. Pelayo, Omar ben Hafsun and El Cid as grand representatives of Hispanic nationalism, when in reality both D. Pelayo and Omar ben Hafsun (first as a neo-Muslim or *muladi*, then as a convert to Christianity, depending upon his interests) were two local political and military chiefs (*caudillos*), neither of whom, in their different contexts, represented anything but the battle for power over certain territories, and who were not in the least motivated by nationalist ideology. With respect to El Cid, he was a mercenary who fought on behalf of the Muslim *taifa* kingdoms as well as for the Christian kingdoms. For him, it was a question of remuneration rather than of nationalism. In fact, 'El Cid' was the nickname bestowed on him by the Arabs, deriving from the term 'sidi', meaning 'my lord'. It is an anachronism and an exercise in historical voluntarism to attribute nationalist concepts to these historical figures, concepts that are entirely alien to their epoch.

Historia de los mozárabes (The History of the Mozarabs), published in 1903 by the Orientalist Francisco Javier Simonet (1829–1897), is a significant contribution to reactionary Spanish thought. His interpretation of history was determined by a great hostility toward the presence on the Iberian Peninsula of Islam, to which he attributes persecution, violence and evil. Simonet consequently rehearses a discourse of religious confrontation with Islam, and focuses on the Mozarabs as the only element of al-Andalus to represent Christian continuity and therefore the persistence of Spanish identity. The Christians of al-Andalus were called Mozarabs and, due to their status as *dhimmis* (protected non-Muslim citizens), they had the same rights as the Jews to practise their faith. The term Mozarab signified 'Arabised', which indicated their integration into the Andalusi cultural and linguistic milieu, provoking complaints from the Mozarab archbishops when they observed how the community was rapidly losing its Latin in favour of Arabic. This ecclesiastical hierarchy would maintain a profound anti-Islamic spirit, but not monolithic control over the community. Simonet and his followers distorted history by constructing 'Mozarabism' as a bastion of Hispanic nationalism in al-Andalus. They attributed to Mozarabic art a specific character that essentially does not exist: imbued with Arab and Islamic culture, Mozarab churches reproduced those artistic elements.

Among the modern historians who countered the liberal school and the more open spirit illustrated by the *Historia General de España* (General History of Spain) of Modesto Lafuente (1806–1866), was the ultraconservative historiographical school represented by Marcelino Menéndez Pelayo (1856–1912), which took up the Spanish nationalist spirit and added to it a sectarian Catholic sentiment. This school was to inspire a good part of the historical interpretation of Spanish education in the twentieth century. Ramón Menéndez Pidal (1869-1968), director of the Centre for Historical Studies, though unquestionably much more restrained and balanced, also stressed this idea. Disregarding the liberal school, Menéndez Pelayo not only extolled the ancestral values of an inherited European civilisation of Greco-Latin and Christian tradition, but also negated any Arab contribution whatsoever:

> What is designated under the name of Arab civilisation is far from being a spontaneous emanation or the work of Semitic genius; it is from any perspective foreign and contradictory. This is proven by the fact that there has never flourished any genre of philosophy or science among either Arabs or Africans, but only among Islamic peoples in which the Indo-European element predominates, such as in Persia or in Spain where the vast majority of renegades (those converted to Islam) far superceded the pure Arab, Syrian and Berber element.

That is to say, Arabs were a people foreign to creative genius, and their scientific culture was limited to that which was taken from other civilised people of predominately Indo-European type. Menéndez Pelayo later adds that the transmission of 'Arab-Spanish' science to Europe was accomplished by Christian Spaniards. These ideas, contrary to expectations, far from being outmoded, have been revitalised by Sylvain Gouguenheim in his highly publicised book *Aristote au Mont-Saint-Michel* (Aristotle in Mont Saint-Michel), published by the French house Seuil in 2008. The book is a veritable exercise in academic imposture that nonetheless inexplicably received the prize of l'Academie des sciences morales et politiques (Academy of Moral and Political Sciences) in France. All this speaks of the important link between these negative historical interpretations and the growing wave of Islamophobia in Europe.

During the course of the twentieth century, Sánchez Albornoz came to stress the idea of the 'Europeaness' of Spain based on the Gothic and Germanic heritage, pitting a foreign Islam against the Western Christian civilisation. Sánchez Albornoz uses D. Pelayo and the Asturian kingdom as the founding moment of the Spanish nation: 'Because on an imprecise day of the 8th century (D. Pelayo), in whom the ancestral virtues of the race were incarnated, rose in rebellion against the Muslims who lorded it over Hispania ... This started the multi-secular battle between Islam and Christianity that was decisive in the forging of Spain and all that is Spanish.' The legendary and moving polemics between Albornoz and Américo Castro, for whom Spanish civilisation was the fruit of mixing between Muslims, Jews and Christians, did not prevent Albornoz's version of history from becoming the most widely accepted, although that of Castro, assimilationist of Islam and the Arabic language as it was, was still accommodated within Spanish nationalist parameters.

Spanish school books from the curriculum of 1938 until the General Education Law of 1970 used the theses of Sánchez Albornoz and Menéndez Pelayo. They have improved significantly since 1970 with regard to the teaching of al-Andalus, even if they follow the vision of the traditional school of Arabists which still tries to contort history in order to 'nationalise' al-Andalus, as we will see below. Since the new education law of 1990 the Eurocentric and Occidentalist vision of history predominates in such a manner that the problem lies not in transmitting the most objective interpretation but rather in the manifest lack of interest in anything that does not have a clear link to Europe and the West.

The 'Nationalisation' of Al-Andalus

The school of Spanish Arabists at the beginning of the twentieth century (Francisco Codera, Julián Ribera, Miguel Asín Palacios, and later Emilio García Gómez), besides wishing to legitimise its object of study, had to resolve something as basic as making sense of the Islamic experience in the Iberian Peninsula, because the simple ideological negation of the other could not ignore such a considerable part – over eight centuries – of the national past. They found the answer in a new interpretation of al-Andalus that would meet the requirements of 'Hispanisation' to allow it to be accepted as part of 'our' history. Accepting al-Andalus required the establishment of a fundamental divide between 'ours' – the 'Spanish' – and the 'exogenous' – belonging to the Arabic and Islamic Maghreb and Mashreq.

These scholars created a 'Muslim Spain' and a 'Spanish Islam', isolating it as much as possible from its global Arabic and Islamic context. Their historical reimagining was based on an explanatory context whereby the cultural and demographic superiority of the (Hispanic) natives rapidly absorbed the supposedly small Arab and Berber military contingent that arrived on the Peninsula in 711. In other words, native Hispanics, with a superior majority culture, Hispanised the dominant minority. The result was the development of a specifically Spanish Islam that was alien to the rest of the Islamic Empire. To accommodate this ideological change, terminology was also changed: the Andalusi was converted to a 'Hispano-Arab' or 'Hispano-Muslim'. So if al-Andalus could be integrated into a few chapters of the national history, even if they were secondary chapters, it was included for its 'Hispanic' aspect, according to the interpretation of Spanish Arabism that dominated the major part of the twentieth century.

This school of Spanish orientalists, together with other European specialists such as R. Dozy (*History of the Muslims of Spain*) and Henri Terrasse (*Arabo-Hispanic Art: From its Origins to the 13th Century*), were concerned with highlighting the specificity of al-Andalus. To this end they established a set of special qualities of 'Hispano-Arab' exquisiteness – artistic splendour, refinement, tolerance, *convivencia* (coexistence) – and converted them into myths serving to demonstrate the superiority of 'Spanish Islam' over the other Islamic lands. Al-Andalus was torn from its orient and made out to be a uniquely specific splendour, in spite of the various proofs to the contrary: the links and exchanges between al-Andalus, the Maghreb, and the Islamic Orient never ceased, and such grand civilisational development also occurred in the same manner in Baghdad, Cairo, Fes and Marrakech, each of course with its own particularities according to local context and circumstance.

As the historian Eduardo Manzano noted with deserved severity, 'the intention to make of "Muslim Spain" a historical period whose Hispanic character is clearly differentiated from contemporary North African or Oriental societies lacks all foundation. The Andalusi Muslims were no more or less tolerant than their coreligionists in other latitudes. The Arab and Islamic traces on Andalusi society cannot be denied simply for the sake of arguing that the conquest had a negligible impact.' The number of Muslim conquerors, although larger than traditionally supposed, is not as important as is claimed. But in any case, as Manzano continues, even

> a relatively small number of conquerors are able to produce great social and cultural transformations, as is well attested by the Roman conquests or those of the Spanish in America. Neither Romanisation nor Spanish colonisation were the result of a massive immigration of Romans or Spaniards, but of the imposition and acceptance by the conquered of the newcomers' social and cultural norms. This is what happened in al-Andalus, where the politically dominant position of the conquerors made their assimilation by the natives unthinkable from the start, even if the indigenous population was greater in number. As soldiers and administrators of an Empire, it was they who imposed the rules, not the populations that ended submitting to them.

It is interesting to note that these scholars of Spanish Arabism – children of the colonial thought of which they are contemporaries – continue the idea that the civilising impulse has but one direction – from north to south – and apply the idea to al-Andalus. This meant that Spain radiated its cultural excellence towards 'primitive' North Africa. Such historical voluntarism is encountered with particular insistence on the Almoravid and Almohad periods. Far from allowing al-Andalus to stand out as an independent emirate or caliphate to establish its particular and superior Spanish specificity, the Almoravid and then Almohad periods unambiguously link al-Andalus to the Maghreb. Moreover, al-Andalus became a dependent province of these north African empires;

hence the insistence on establishing the idea that the best Maghrebi art during those periods of undoubted splendour was produced by 'Hispano-Arab' artisans and artists in Marrakech, Fes, and Meknes. In any case, these Almoravid and Almohad periods which trace such an indelible link between al-Andalus and the Maghreb, moving from south to north, are regarded with indifference, and are consequently rarely studied unless cloaked by the unjust popular myth which reduces the periods to a fanatical government that destroyed the refined and tolerant 'Hispano-Arab' society. Their undisguised lack of interest in anything other than their vision of an Andalusi ivory tower left these scholars on the margins of research in the north of Morocco during the protectorate established there by Spain between 1912 and 1956. In contrast to French and British Orientalists in their respective protectorates and mandates, the specialists of Spanish Arab studies were not concerned with the contemporary Arab world. This Orientalist knowledge of anthropological and sociological studies was developed instead by the well-known school of Africanists, staffed primarily by military personnel and professionals who lived in northern Morocco during the protectorate.

While new studies and rigorous scientific works have revised and delegitimised the diverse interpretations that we have discussed (those of Eduardo Manzano, Pierre Guichard, Manuela Marín, Maria Antonia Martínez Núñez, Alejandro García Sanjuán, and various other distinguished academics), and have established that it is most correct and objective to speak of 'al-Andalus' rather than of 'Muslim Spain', they have not extended their reach beyond the academy. The old ideas therefore continue to flourish in popular books, in schools, in media discourse, and in political visions related to Islamophobia and the concept of the 'clash of civilisations'.

Three Religions and One Culture, More or Less

The clichés of the refined splendour, tolerance and superiority of Spanish Islam have ended up producing the very popular myth of the 'three cultures': that is, the exaltation of *convivencia* and tolerance between Jews, Christians and Muslims that supposedly occurred primarily during the tenth and eleventh centuries. The myth posits this time as something unique and exceptional. Objectively, the presumptions on which this definition is based are very debatable indeed. The concepts of religion and culture are confused, and this introduces a serious distortion, and the modern concepts of tolerance and *convivencia* are attributed to a medieval epoch in which these ideas did not exist. Reality was much more mundane. In al-Andalus as in the rest of the Islamic Empire, Christians and Jews were permitted to maintain their faiths because they belonged to the same monotheistic tradition as the Muslims (Ahl al-Kitab), but this did not signify an idyllic equality. They paid a special tax and limitations were imposed on their social integration. The Christian kingdoms initially treated the Muslims in their territories (*Mudejares*) in the same way, until they succumbed to a progressive persecution that finally resulted in the Inquisition.

But attempting to turn the three creeds into distinct and self-contained cultural realities is the weakest and most ideological part of this project. The Jews and Christians of al-Andalus were Arabised and partook of the Andalusi cultural construction which was, more or less, the common culture. This is what permitted cohesion and a reasonably satisfactory interchange between the three religions. So a more precise approximation would be the existence of three religions within one culture, or at least within a shared cultural dynamic that was Andalusi, and speaking the same language: Arabic. To move from here to discussing cross-breeding, as Américo Castro wanted, is much more questionable. Each religious community was basically very protective of its confessional identity. When the intolerance of the Catholic kings led to expulsion, Andalusi Jews as well as Muslims logically chose the Islamic Empire as the principal place to settle, not only because they were afforded the acceptance there that Christian Europe denied them, but also because they shared Arab-Islamic cultural elements and language. As such, the *convivencia* in al-Andalus was neither exceptional nor miraculous.

The widespread reach of the idea of al-Andalus and its 'three cultures' in recent times can be explained (besides it is an appealing advertisement for political agendas concerning multiculturalism and the Arab World) by the fact that it fits ideologically with a conceptual structure spread by the theory of the 'clash of civilisations'. The presentation of the cultures, with a special focus on the Islamic one, as closed, and antagonistic separate entities mirrors Huntington's peculiar theory; the 'miracle' of *convivencia* seems to presuppose, as Huntington suggests, that *convivencia* is almost impossible. The proclaimed success of the *convivencia* is at first sight a positive thing, but it hides this pernicious concept, implicitly stressing the incompatibility and antinomy between

Islam, Christianity and Judaism – except for one surprising and never repeated moment.

It is quite probable that no other period in history has been as interpreted, manipulated and struggled against as al-Andalus, this period which still has not achieved the 'historical normalcy' it has demanded for more than six centuries; that is, to assume its legitimate existence and to be recognised as an important part of both Islamic and European history without amputating its undoubtedly Arab and Islamic characteristics or adorning it with extemporaneous qualities to portray it as something exceptional. Far from achieving that normality, it remains subject to ideological manipulation. The irrelevant but noxious theory of the clash of civilisations, the 9/11 attacks and the growing Islamophobia that has been unleashed since, have ensured that al-Andalus remains an object for barter at the service of ultra-Catholic, nationalist and Islamophobic ideologies. While enlightened intellectuals continue their endeavours to inscribe al-Andalus in historical normality, their work does not enjoy the wide dissemination in media and society of the dominant theories which connect better with voguish anti-Islamic perceptions.

The nationalist visions based on the idea of 'Spain, unity of destiny', a Spain of exclusively Christian, Latin and Germanic roots, have once again found followers and publicists through whom they express their negation of everything Arab and Muslim. And from an opposite position, they have also managed to resurrect 'super Spanish' interpretations of al-Andalus; hence the unusual interest awakened in various circles (Muslim converts, academics and publishers) by Ignacio Olagüe's implausible theory published in Paris in 1969 and titled *Les Arabes n'ont jamais invahi l'Espagne* (The Arabs never invaded Spain). According to Olagüe, the Arabs were incapable of conquering the Iberian Peninsula, and what happened in 711 was simply an internal dispute between Visigoth factions. Islam and the Arabic language may have entered the peninsula through a process of acculturation by native, peninsular Hispano-Romans attracted by the development and cultural superiority of the Islamic world in that epoch. The cultural and intellectual contributions of al-Andalus were therefore an exclusive work of Spanish genius. Everything stays at home.

THE ORIGINAL ENLIGHTENMENT

Emilio Gonzalez-Ferrin

1

History, wrote the Roman Catholic saint Gregory of Nyssa (335–395), is a non-stop sequence of new beginnings. Some sixteen centuries later, we are still tied up with the idea that history is all about decline, thanks largely to the influence of Edward Gibbon's *History of the Decline and Fall of the Roman Empire*. Indeed, we tend to think of history as a non-stop sequence of declines, and constantly search for causes of degeneration. It is like looking at a weather map to spot a coming storm. One of these overwhelming storms seems to be the 'Middle Ages', or the 'Dark Ages', as the historians describe the period between the fifth and fifteenth centuries in Europe, following the collapse of the Roman Empire

The history of dates and proper names, History with capital letters, tends to live on this perception of passing time. It consists largely of the biographies of heroes, great men who conquered territories for their motherland, and shaped the world and their times – a perception best illustrated by Thomas Carlyle's *On Heroes and Hero-Worship* and the *Heroic in History*; and Carlyle's numerous crypto-followers.

But this perception of history is guilty of incoherence and self-contradiction. Life is not a downhill road to a perceived end. Life always expands and spreads in all directions, although not necessarily in the way we expect. In fact, in life and in history everything interacts with everything else, morphs, changes, synthesises, is always on the verge of becoming something different, something new. We cannot understand the past if we select and isolate a portion, take it out of context. So here is a truism: everything was born from something previous.

2

New beginnings and continuity. That's the essence of history, which is always subjected to perceptions and verdicts. Most historians are ever ready to judge, to pass verdicts, but are not so keen on evaluations. Perhaps it is not surprising in a discipline that is so old, with methodologies so fixed. Historians thus behave as though they are scroll curators and file keepers, committed to the established mores of blind philology: if it's old and hard to translate, it is the truth. Once this truth is established, there is reluctance to revisit certain inconvenient periods of time where truth is murky, not easy to decode and discern.

One of these inconvenient periods is al-Andalus, a long and strange time of Arabic and Islamic culture in European lands, set against a dark medieval stage. It is inconvenient because it refers to a past time in which we were different; but ideology does not permit us to acknowledge that we were different from what we are today. But who were we? And who are we today?

There are two prerequisites for tackling this subject of al-Andalus. First, we have to move from creationism to evolution in the way we understand passing time. It is futile to maintain in history what has been disregarded in science: the old fashioned tenet about things emerging from nothing, from nowhere, at once. This history, based as it is on romantic ideals that fall from above and create anew by means of invasions and amazing cavalries, is no longer comprehensible. So here is another truism: everything flourishes in a context from which it emanates.

Second, we have to be aware of our current, mediated vision of the world. There is an old pseudoscience called phrenology that imagined the brain as the organ of the mind, divided into neat localised boxes with specific functions that could be inferred by examining and measuring the skull. A phrenology bust described and depicted a grotesque distribution of brain lobes through which you could acquire a magical ability to read the human mind. That disregarded procedure is the basis of our current description of the world. In this assumed phrenology globe there are places out of time, others out of culture, a section out of religion, another vast northern paradise of reason, another repulsive land with an endemic proclivity to violence – complete phrenologic description of the world of archaic cultures and enduring topics that points out every single tendency of a region and its historical background.

3

In this phrenologic vision of the world, al-Andalus appears as an operetta set on an Orientalist stage. It provides mythological nourishment in essentialist times, serving all needs. After a casual reading of al-Andalus, one may say 'this is not me', although belonging to the same land. Another may say 'this is me' in spite of belonging to a tradition and culture two or three continents away. Faulty perceptions are fitted for a faulty sense of identity.

So nothing is allowed to appear as it once really was, everything has to be fitted to our current concerns. Religions as flags, as vertical motherlands, as teams with a collection of medals and awards gained in the past, are never allowed to be forgotten. Let us suppose I am a Muslim, say an Indonesian Muslim. Do I inherit al-Andalus simply because of the coincidence that I follow the same religion as al-Andalus? Does a man from Panama, for example, inherit the cultural legacy of Byzantium just because he follows the same religion? Let us suppose I am a Christian, say a Swedish Christian. Should I bypass the medieval roads and ignore my own western tradition, simply because they were written in Arabic?

4

Revisiting al-Andalus without ulterior motives, with no stage machinery, means something quite different. It is about admitting the role of connections and movement in history and, thus, discovering a path that led to the first Enlightenment. In the common vision, al-Andalus displays itself as a Punch and Judy Show of history – currently labelled 'The Clash of Civilisations'. Its initial strangeness, and hence shock, comes from the fact that it is a civilisation located in Europe but developed in Arabic in the Gothic 'with me or against me' world of the Middle Ages. And the Middle Ages are seen as dark because the creationists of the Renaissance needed darkness to highlight their core. If 'the Middle Ages were less dark and less static', as the American historian of the Middle Ages, Charles Homer Haskins, once wrote, then 'the Renaissance [would be] less bright and less sudden'. The Middle Ages are not dark but hardly understood because they are written in Arabic.

But al-Andalus is not merely a past time. It is also a time present, a component and an essential ingredient of all our histories. And it is an unavoidable seed of Europe: the Europe that we take as matrix of the West. For without al-Andalus and its first renaissance in Arabic, there would be no Europe as we know it. Given the over-arching re-interpretations of the origins of the European Renaissance now in vogue, we should admit that the starting point of that flourishing new age includes a wide-spread stream of previous histories.

The European Renaissance was not an absolute beginning; it did not emerge out of nothing. Its myth of Greek roots is itself a product of cross-fertilisation of histories. When the Turks conquered Constantinople in 1453, the men of learning of Byzantium took refuge in Italy; and took their books, in their own language (Greek), with them – and the 'Greek seed' of the 'Renaissance' was planted. The European Renaissance is in fact a product of wide-spread and different acculturations. Where did they come from? From the east, such as the trading contacts of Venice with China, and the acculturation of Sicily, where a Norman king, Frederick II (1194-1250), had a realm of Arab lands and decided to translate the Qur'an, commentaries on Aristotle, and other Arab scholarly works into Latin. And, last but not least, the long and dense crossroad of al-Andalus.

5

The crossroad of al-Andalus, a quite atypical portion of Europe in Arabic, was created like sediment, after prolonged and constant gestation. It is the final step after a long series of eastern grafts, just like anywhere else all over the Mediterranean. To talk about Arabic-Islamic conquest in 711 is to talk about a worthless myth, a bare creationist concoction, devoid of historical proof. In 711 there was no Arabic culture or 'Islamic civilisation' able to spread out from a very limited portion of the Middle East. In later propaganda, Islam expands by force, Christianity by conviction, and Judaism by genetics. These three well-grounded myths evaporate with a serious, cold look at history: there were always conversions to the three religions, as well as traffic of populations, and social and religious unrest, and troubles all over.

Regarding the insistent myth of a miraculous and bloody Islamic invasion, we ought to note the complete lack of Arab sources – at least, till 858. But several Latin, Syriac and Greek contemporary sources describe numerous causes for the destruction of two central empires, the Roman and the Persian. We just need a comparative reading of two authors living during the first universal steps of Islam: Saint John of Damascus in the East, around year 750; and Eulogy of Cordoba, in the West, almost one hundred years later. Both of them shed enough light on the gradual spread of Islam to al-Andalus, and highlight a key element in the origins of a wider cultural world: Islam, at least during its first century and a half, was a Hellenic culture. This would change after the foundation of Baghdad, which itself was planned as a Greco-Roman polis, in 762. However, this was the starting point of a new lingua franca: the Arabic language.

6

These Hellenic origins can be traced not only through the progressive replacement of Byzantine coinage, art and law but also in two significant details that lead to the progressive formation of al-Andalus. One is the name: al-Andalus, a phonetic transformation of Atlantis, located by Plato in the Lost Paradise in the western lands where the Mediterranean meets the Atlantic Ocean. Between the fourth and sixth centuries, several commentaries were produced on Plato's main writings, generating that Hellenic cultural movement called Neo-Platonism, where we find the origins of the transformation: Atlantis > Adalandis > al-Andalus. Something quite similar happened with another Hellenic journey from the Garden of the Hesperides to Separad > Sefarad, the Hebrew equivalent of al-Andalus.

The second Hellenic trace is paradoxically included in the first valuable Arabic source that provides us information about al-Andalus. It is called *Akhbar majmua*, or Collected Chronicles, dated 858, and is responsible in part for the official version of the origins of al-Andalus, insistently repeated till today. This chronicle narrates the European uprising of the old Syrian Umayyad dynasty and involves the adventure of ten thousand soldiers commanded by a general called Balj. They faced a defeat in North Africa, followed by a tactical retreat that led them to al-Andalus where they became the principal party that supported the first emir of Cordoba. It is interesting to note that this is exactly the narrative plot of the *Anabasis*, written by the Greek professional soldier and writer, Xenophon, who with an army of ten thousand tried to seize the throne of Persia. But *Akhbar majmua* provides two other Greek literary tropes. One is that first Ummayad Emir was precisely the last of the eastern kings, just like in the plot of the Aeneid, Virgil's epic Latin poem and the foundation of Rome. The other element is that the alleged conquest of Spain was due to the kidnapping of a maid by Spanish Visigoths, which led to an organised invasion in revenge. Exactly the detonating flame of the Iliad.

7

Hispania was not the empty or uncultivated land that appears in the Arabic chronicles; written, let us remind ourselves, at least a century and a half after the presumed conquest. Hispania became al-Andalus after an extended struggle of different heretical trends, substantive problems in the transition of the Visigoth kingdom, and a long and continual process of questioning Imperial Centralism as Rome shifted to Constantinople. The encyclopaedic writings of Isidoro de Sevilla (556-636) provide us with the cultural heights of Hispania that in the next Iberian phase – al-Andalus – were not only known but wisely exploited and turned into an advantage. Isidoro, along with the Latin-Visigothic legacy of Hispania, fertilised the science produced in Arabic in the same lands, which were permanently influenced by the cultural tides originating in the East. Once again: new beginnings and continuity.

This new beginning grew in natural and constant interaction with a similar evolution in the rest of the south and east Mediterranean. It was the continuation of the Roman culture, not its decline and fall. Rome and Persia did not disappear but fell into the subsequent and emerging Mediterranean cultural model: Dar al-Islam. The gap between these two different worlds, East and West, Constantinople and Rome, provoked a definitive European disconnection. Hispania, on the verge of becoming al-Andalus, aligned itself with the rest of the Mediterranean south and east. Thus, it cut itself off from the rest of Europe, which aligned in turn with a future configuration: the Carolingian project.

8

The Carolingian Empire (800–888), which begins with Charlemagne, established France and Germany. It played a leading role in the canonical definition of Europe, and produced a key concept in European history: the idea of restoration. Disregarding the existence of a living Roman Empire in the East, a new emperor set out to restore the Empire at the beginning of the ninth century. And so it seems that Rome resumed in the West, overlooking the way of being Roman in the rest of the Mediterranean basin.

The point is that Europe loves re-ism: every restoration rejects the past from which it emanates. It was so in the Carolingian restoration, as well as the reconquest to come in the Iberian Peninsula, or even in the Renaissance itself. In the future, every single great project in Europe will have to be anchored in an assumed distant and golden past, bypassing the immediate twists and turns of history, in a myth of eternal return.

9

Al-Andalus is not a product of some mythical invasion but of Arabisation, which enabled it to become a substantial part of what we may call 'the spirit of the time'. The American scholar of Arab culture Dimitri Gutas has shown the connection between the development of Greek lower-case letters and the spread of Hellenic cultural heritage. When Baghdad became established as an economic and cultural fortress, the Greeks in Byzantium developed practical small letters to save time in copying manuscripts they were selling to Baghdadi translators eager to render them into Arabic. And it is quite interesting that in the commercial interchange between Bagdad and Constantinople, the Baghdadis would always refer to themselves as 'sons of the igriqis', the Greeks, while the others were simply 'sons of Rome', or rumis.

The Arabised populations of the Middle East (and not only Muslims) were eagerly translating the canons of science and philosophy not because they had suddenly discovered a love for letters and learning, but because they needed the knowledge of the elders to understand and shape the world. It is always the practical and pragmatic that moves the engine of civilisation. But Dar al-Islam was not simply a company of carriers, a conveyor belt, translating and preserving Greek heritage to pass on to its rightful owner, the European Renaissance. No: for more than eight centuries, Mediterranean knowledge ranging from philosophy to astronomy, from theology to medicine, was developed, shaped and composed in Arabic, not merely translated into it. And this knowledge was delivered all over a world already steeped in Arabic through commercial routes – silk, slaves, gold, paper, spices – with a compulsory stop in al-Andalus. The Dar al-Islam, the territories with a common civilised structure, was never a single state, but a certain and critical commonwealth, a network of cities and routes. We must emphasise: it was never a unique empire, and always urban, maintaining certain Bedouin roots in dress and as an implant of collective memory. Belonging to the Dar al-Islam, was just like belonging today to the West, embracing certain ideas as well as tools and instruments of modernity.

10

The Dar al-Islam, as civilised network, had a pluralist system of laws derived from the Roman and Persian laws. In general, this dichotomy always persisted: the so-called Sunni Islam comes from Byzantium, while the Shia Islam comes from a Persian and Zoroastrian background, in spite of the fairy-tale tradition of familiar disputes.

Al-Andalus was a very active part of this network, without being politically dependent on the East. But there was some dependency on North Africa after the mid-eleventh century, where the Almoravid dynasty of the fanatical Murabits was pre-eminent. This was not very different from the north Iberian dependency on the equally fanatic Cluny, a French abbey in charge of re-Christianising Europe. Torn between these two similar and opposite pressures, al-Andalus developed a culture that would deliver a heritage to all of Europe.

11

A specific Arabic culture called 'Andalusian' emerged around 850. From then on, a young and formative vision of the world began to spread, one we may recognise as pre-Renaissance, provoked, in part, by occasional political uncertainty. In fact, a driving force of al-Andalus was the political turmoil, the stability/instability, in Cordoba, the most modern capital of its time. Then, one morning the system collapsed. It was 1031, the beginning of an age always disregarded or looked down on with scorn in the manuals. Again, new beginning and continuity.

It was a new age based on the core of Andalusian identity: the city-states of the Taifas. Cordoba, the ancient capital of sciences, poetry and bureaucracy, did not disappear. On the contrary, it was absorbed into one thousand and one small Cordobas whose rivalry and competition contributed to raising the level of all al-Andalus. It was the beginning of a golden Arab and Hebrew age in the Iberian Peninsula.

12

The city-states of the Taifas, like the Italian city-states that preceded the Renaissance, generated enough political tension to stimulate thought and creativity. Several books appeared which kindled our thinking on anthropocentrism, the assessment of reality through human perspective, and other typically European themes. For example, ibn Tufayl's *Hayy ibn Yaqzan*, or The Self-Taught Philosopher as it came to be known in Europe, produced the genre of utopian inquiry and the beau savage. The courtly writings of ibn al-Khatib, whose poetry decorates the walls of Alhambra in Granada, became a model for the European genre of political education, inspiring Machiavelli's *The Prince* and Baldassare Castiglione's works such as *The Book of the Courtier* and *The Fortunes of the Courtier*. Ibn Hazm's treatise on love and lovers, *The Necklace of the Dove*, influenced generation after generation.

Empiricism and experimentation also spread during the Taifas due to the competition between the mini-courts, leading to the golden age of European astronomy and medicine, as well as numerous other disciplines. For instance, the post-*taifa* period could be considered the road that led to Averroes (ibn Rushd), the European commentator on Aristotle. That philosopher from Cordoba reached such a level of prominence in Europe that his translations were forbidden in thirteenth-century Paris, where he was accused of promoting free-thinking. All these writings and works are, and should be considered, as part of the European Renaissance. Indeed, that would be the case if they had been written in languages other than Arabic.

13

It is now time to recognise the diversity of European cultural roots. Europe was the final destination of Andalusian cultural thought, devices, artefacts and items. If Averroes was prohibited in Paris, it was because his writings were avidly read. And if Columbus reached America it was in part because an Andalusian astronomer called Azarquiel (ibn al-Zarqali) invented mobile instruments and devices that permitted ships to sail across continents. Science often arises from the needs of a society; and al-Andalus had set a course, a long time ago, for the Renaissance, in that universal game of taking over.

Geopolitical interests shaped the whole peninsula as northern Christian kingdoms sniffed the wealth of southern Taifa states. To maintain peace, contain the whims of Christian kings and preserve the status quo, the Taifa paid a special tax called *parias* to northern states – Leon, Castilla and Aragon. The money from al-Andalus financed the building of northern cathedrals, and in their crypts were buried the Christian kings and courtesans dressed-up in the silk produced and bought in al-Andalus. This circulation of money and goods created an atypical mutual prosperity that lasted till the final eclipse of the Arab world and a new beginning: the European Renaissance itself, as well as an invented religious rivalry.

14

The arrival of the year 1000 brought a sense of foreboding millenarianism: 'the end of the world is nigh'. Soon after that, and largely due to previous propaganda, the Christian fundamentalists of Cluny started to enter Spain. At the same time, the Almoravid Muslim fundamentalists came from Morocco. Torn between these two exclusive identities, al-Andalus began to filter and seep through in three different but important ways. First, there was the expulsion of Arabised Andalusian Jews who fled to France, where they worked as translators. But what did they translate? The Andalusian scientific and philosophical works from the original Arabic into Latin and Hebrew. This is one of the main streams that fertilised Europe, preparing the future Renaissance. Second, the Arab city controlled by Castilians, Toledo, began an extensive programme of translations – the second branch of Latinisation of Arab scholarship. But this would become a means of converting the whole of Spain to Catholic ideology. Third, al-Andalus spread throughout Spain via converted Jews and Muslims, who enriched the cultural life of a sad and closed Spain. This became a general trend in the centuries to come, a time of flexible frontiers and an elastic sense of nation.

The tragic, national sport of the Iberian peninsula began at the same time: deportation. Wave after wave of Andalusians were forced into exile: after the Andalusian Jews, the Muslim Moriscos, then a new wave of Hispanised Jews. It was an endemic sport that continued to the twentieth century. In the end, all that was left was a fearful Third Spain: trapped between the Inquisition and Expulsions, it maintained a proud silence on being anything else, anything more.

But al-Andalus still made its presence felt. It had surreptitious influences on the Golden Age of Spanish literature, on movements like Erasmism, a form of Christian humanism, and many heterodox cultural and religious trends. If we were able to 'inhabit our history in Spain', just as one of our most prominent historians Americo Castro (1885–1972) suggests in *The Structure of Spanish History*, we would perceive and understand the precious Andalusian remainders left in masterpieces of our literature, such as Don Quixote, that unrivalled protest against oblivion. In the pages of Cervantes' novel, we find the missing Moriscos as well as an enlightened fool who shouts 'I know who I am' in a forgetful land. The forgetfulness of having been something more, something else.

THE MEMORANDUM OF FERNANDO NUNEZ MULEY

Matthew Carr

More than any other period in Islamic history, the Moorish kingdom of al-Andalus has always shown a remarkable capacity to insinuate itself into the present. The early twenty-first century is no exception. Osama bin Laden frequently referred to the 'tragedy' or 'loss' of al-Andalus as a template for contemporary 'Zionist-Crusader' occupations of Muslim lands. In 2006, the former Spanish president José Maria Aznar attempted to establish an equally tenuous historical connection between al-Qaeda itself and the eighth century Muslim 'occupation' of Spain.

Both bin Laden and Aznar were attempting to use very specific and selective interpretations of al-Andalus to mobilise their respective constituencies, and both of them shared a common belief that Moorish Spain 'ended' in 1492, the year in which Ferdinand and Isabella conquered the last Muslim kingdom of Granada. It is doubtful whether either of them was aware of the existence of a sixteenth-century Spanish Muslim named Fernando Nuñez Muley, or whether they would have found much use for him if they had been. For Nuñez Muley belongs to a chapter in the history of al-Andalus that is often overlooked or ignored in the shifting debates on the legacies of Moorish Spain; the fate of the tens of thousands of Muslims who remained in Spain after 1492, trapped in a tragic religious and cultural struggle that was to culminate in their expulsion

Nuñez Muley's brief contribution to that tragedy was a direct consequence of one of the most disastrous policy decisions in sixteenth-century Spanish history. On 7 November 1567, King Philip II of Spain promulgated a radical *prágmatica* (royal decree) regarding the Muslim converts to Christianity in the Kingdom of Granada. Within three years, all Granadan Moriscos, as these converts were known, were ordered to cease speaking or writing in Arabic, to learn Castilian and destroy all Arabic books and texts. Morisco dances, songs and musical instruments were also prohibited, and municipalities across the kingdom were ordered to demolish or close the public baths that the Moorish Iberian kingdom of al-Andalus had introduced into Spain.

In addition Morisco men and women were to cease wearing Moorish clothing or face the prospect of fines, flogging and deportation from the kingdom. Morisco householders were ordered to leave their doors open on Fridays and other Christian festival days, so that their religious observance could be monitored.

As an example of cultural repression, the severity and scope of these draconian proscriptions had few parallels in European history. The 1367 'Kilkenny Statutes', passed by the English government in Ireland, had once banned a similarly wide range of indigenous cultural practices, from hairstyles to the speaking of Gaelic, but these laws were intended to prevent English/Norman settlers from 'going native'.

Ostensibly at least, the 1567 pragmatic had a very different purpose: to complete the transformation of Granada's 'native' Morisco population into 'good and faithful Christians'. This drastic decision was the culmination of a process of enforced assimilation that had begun in the last decade of the fifteenth century, when the surrender of the Muslim emirate of Granada to the Christian armies of Ferdinand and Isabella brought the last remnant of al-Andalus under Christian control.

With the reconstitution of Granada as a new Christian kingdom, its inhabitants joined their co-religionists elsewhere in Spain, and became another Muslim minority within a unified Catholic state that regarded Iberian Islam as an un-Christian and un-Spanish aberration, and was committed to the long-term eradication of the medieval multi-religious and multi-ethnic society inherited from al-Andalus.

Throughout much of the fifteenth century, these aspirations were largely pursued through an aggressive campaign of enforced assimilation directed at Jews rather than Muslims. At the beginning of the century, tens of thousands of Spanish Jews were forcibly converted to Christianity and the new converts were subsequently policed by the Inquisition. In the aftermath of their triumph at Granada, Ferdinand and Isabella signed an Edict of Expulsion ordering all Spain's unconverted Jews to adopt Christianity or leave the country. Between 100,000 and 150,000 Jews chose the latter option, in a tragic exodus that had grave implications for all Spain's Muslims. The expulsion of the Jews was intended to speed up the assimilation of converted Jews or *conversos*, but the more supremacist and chauvinistic officials within the church and state exhorted Ferdinand and Isabella to impose a similar 'choice' on Spanish Muslims, beginning with those of Granada.

Economic self-interest and the complicated regional relationships between Christians and Muslims tended to neutralise Catholic triumphalism and religious ardour. Many Christian employers and municipalities regarded their Muslim communities as an important source of labour and income – as did the Crown itself. Though the interactions between Muslims and Christians varied widely across the country, they continued to be regulated by old medieval arrangements, which allowed the former carefully circumscribed religious and legal autonomy. This often grudging tolerance did not indicate a commitment to religious pluralism per se, but it nevertheless provided the basis for a *modus vivendi* that in some parts of Spain had endured for centuries.

Anxious to bring a speedy end to the war in Granada and ensure the post-war stability of the kingdom, the Catholic monarchs chose to extend these traditions. The conquest of Granada was made possible through extremely generous surrender agreements signed beforehand with the emirate's last king Boabdil, which allowed Granadan Muslims full religious and cultural autonomy. This conciliatory stance was confirmed by the appointment of the moderate Hernando de Talavera as the first archbishop of the new Church of Granada. Talavera, unlike many of his fellow clerics, favoured the gradualist assimilation of Granada's Muslims, and attempted to win them over to Catholicism through various methods of persuasion rather than force. These included translating parts of the Scriptures into Arabic, the use of Arabic words during mass, and the incorporation of some Muslim dances into the annual Corpus Christi procession.

The commitment of the Catholic monarchs to this policy remains a subject of debate amongst historians. What is certain, however, is that this magnanimity came to an end in the last years of the century, with the arrival of the fanatically anti-Muslim archbishop of Toledo, Cardinal Francisco Jiménez de Cisneros, in the city of Granada. Appalled and disgusted by the open presence of Islam in the city, Cisneros began forcibly converting Muslim nobles to Catholicism.

These efforts provoked a Muslim rebellion in the kingdom, which was quickly suppressed. Ferdinand and Isabella cynically used the revolt as a pretext to renege on the Granada surrender agreements, and ordered the general conversion of Muslims in the kingdom through various forms of pressure and inducements. By the beginning of the sixteenth century, Granada's Muslims were all nominally Christian, and these developments had a knock-on effect in the rest of Spain. By the mid-1520s, Iberian Islam had ostensibly ceased to exist and all Spain's Muslims had become Catholic converts who were known under the pejorative name Moriscos ('little Moors').

Having 'converted' the Moriscos to Christianity through varying degrees of force, Spain was now obliged to absorb a minority that many Christians feared and despised and preferred to keep at arm's length, and ensure that they remained steadfast in their new faith. From the beginning this objective was pursued in a contradictory and often haphazard fashion. On the one hand its rulers demanded that Moriscos become 'good and faithful Christians', while at the same time they remained constantly suspicious of the sincerity of these conversions. Such suspicions were not without reason. Reports from church and Inquisition officials around the country frequently found – and sometimes simply alleged – that Moriscos were not fulfilling their Christian duties or were continuing to worship as Muslims in private.

Such backsliding was to some extent a natural consequence of conversions that had taken place under duress, but it was not universal. If some Moriscos accepted Catholicism reluctantly and paid lip service to it, others eventually came to embrace their new faith. But this transformation was not rapid enough to please the more bigoted hardliners in the church and state, many of whom did not believe that former 'infidels' were worthy of Catholicism or capable of it.

The sincerity of the Moriscos was further called into question, in the eyes of many ecclesiastical and state officials, by the continued prevalence of 'Moorish' cultural traditions in various parts of the country. To Spanish officialdom, Morisco cultural and religious practices were equally 'Moorish' and Islamic, and even dances and songs without any religious component were often interpreted as evidence of crypto-Islamic worship. Religious hostility to Islam was only one component of Christian antipathy.

Moriscos were often depicted as inherently backward, inferior and uncivilised, and viewed through a prism of prejudices and false assumptions. Then, as now, female dress codes were often cited as a particularly unacceptable expression of Muslim difference. Christian clerics tended to obsess about the white veil or *almalafa*, with which many Morisca women, particularly in Granada, covered their face and hair in public. In the eyes of the church, Moriscas who covered their faces in public were likely to be engaged in sexual transgressions, and a string of laws and punishments were introduced in an attempt to 'unveil' Morisca women in Granada, most of which were disregarded. These early attempts at repression were nevertheless an indication of the priorities of Spain's rulers towards their 'new Christians'. Not only were the Moriscos expected to transform themselves internally into devout Catholics; they also had to look, talk and behave like Christians and Spaniards.

The assimilationist pressures were particularly strong in Granada, whose inhabitants were the most visibly 'Moorish' of Spain's Morisco minorities, in terms of their language and customs. In 1526 a congregation of church officials in Granada drew up a comprehensive list of Morisco customs to be banned from the kingdom, many of which were subsequently incorporated into the 1567 pragmatic. But a delegation of Granadan Moriscos negotiated an agreement with King Charles I, in which they agreed to pay the Crown not to implement these proposals.

For the next thirty years these arrangements remained more or less in place in Granada. In the same period, Christian settlers, fortune-hunters and officials seeking positions in the new Hapsburg bureaucracy poured into the kingdom, many of whom regarded the Moriscos as defeated infidels, and treated them as illegitimate occupants of land and property that they wanted for themselves. The more politically influential Christian settlers often used their positions to dispossess the Moriscos of their lands, and the priests and clerics entrusted with guiding the Granadan Moriscos in their new faith also routinely fleeced and exploited their new parishioners, in ways that did little to promote assimilation.

The Spanish government did little to prevent such abuses, and more often than not ignored them altogether. By the mid sixteenth century, the upper echelons of the church and state were becoming increasingly frustrated at the slow pace of assimilation and the continued evidence of crypto-Islamic worship in various parts of the country. The perception of the Moriscos as an 'enemy within' that was collectively hostile to Christianity was fuelled by the emerging battle for supremacy between the Hapsburgs and the Ottoman Turks in the western Mediterranean, and Spanish fears of a Turkish invasion. Once again, these suspicions were particularly focused on the Moriscos of

Granada, which was seen as a particularly vulnerable link in Spain's defences by virtue of its geographical proximity to North Africa.

All these developments contributed to the 1567 pragmatic. In a stroke, Philip II issued what amounted to a charter for the complete eradication of Morisco culture from Granada, which demanded that the Moriscos disappear as a distinct and recognisable group. The task of enforcing this decree was given to Pedro de Deza, a hard-line former Inquisition official and an ambitious henchman of the fervently anti-Morisco Cardinal Espinosa, the most influential cleric in Spain.

In November, Deza was appointed president of the Granada Royal Audience and Chancellery. On arriving in Granada he informed the Morisco elite of the king's decision, and the news caused immediate consternation. One group of Moriscos in the Albaicín district of the city of Granada refused to disseminate its contents, on the grounds that they would be stoned if they did. Others lobbied Deza in an attempt to get him to change his mind, and an elderly Morisco named Fernando Nuñez Muley was entrusted with this mission.

Nuñez Muley was by no stretch of the imagination a crypto-Muslim. A former page of Hernando de Talaver who had been converted to Christianity as a boy, he had accompanied the archbishop in his attempts to evangelise Muslim villages in rural Granada, and had worked closely with the post-conquest regime in Granada since the late fifteenth century. Nuñez Muley would certainly have been considered a 'collaborator' by Osama bin Laden, but the honorific title 'Muley' suggests a man of some substance and influence within the Morisco community, which is presumably why he was chosen to act as its representative.

Like many Moriscos, Nuñez Muley believed that the pragmatic was unjust and unworkable, and likely to drive the already-beleaguered Morisco population to armed revolt. He therefore attempted to reason with Deza and wrote his arguments down in an impassioned memorandum of which various versions have been published. Nuñez Muley's *Memorandum for the President of the Royal Audiencia and Chancery Court of the City and Kingdom of Granada* is one of the key historical documents of sixteenth-century Spain, it provides a rare insider's perspective on the cultural world of the Moriscos – and the cultural prejudice and incomprehension that converged on them. His memorandum also raises issues that are not without relevance to our own era.

Nuñez Muley did not contest the pragmatic on the grounds of religious pluralism – a notion that had little purchase in sixteenth-century Spain. Instead, he attempted to establish a distinction between Morisco cultural traditions and Islamic religious practices, in order to show that the pragmatic's prohibitions were misguided, irrelevant and unachievable. Thus he insisted that Morisco dances were a folkloric rather than a religious custom that was anathema to pious Muslims; that the clothes worn by Granadan Moriscos were merely a form of regional costume without religious significance; that Arabic had 'no direct relationship whatsoever to the Muslim faith'.

Nuñez Muley also attempted to refute some of the assumptions behind the pragmatic's prohibitions. Contrary to Christian belief, he said, Morisca women did not wear the *almalafa* as a cover for illicit romantic liaisons, but out of modesty. He also refuted the notion that bathhouses were used by women for sexual encounters, and rejected the Christian associations between public bathhouses and Islamic religious ablution, insisting that they were only intended for hygiene and health.

He also criticised the pragmatic on practical grounds. How could Moriscos learn Castilian with no one to teach them? What would happen to those who could not learn it? How could Moriscos conduct their everyday business if they were not allowed to write in Arabic? How could Moriscos leave their doors open without being robbed? He attacked the idea that the pragmatic was designed to promote the integration of the Moriscos into Christian society, and reminded Deza that 'for the past thirty-five to forty years, the men here have worn Castilian-style clothing and footwear with the hope that His Majesty might show them the mercy of granting them certain liberties, relieving them of their tax burden, or giving them permission to carry arms. Well, we have seen nothing like this. With each day that passes we are in worse shape and more mistreated in all respects and by all manners, as much by the secular as by the ecclesiastical arms of justice, a fact that is well known and not in need of further elaboration.'

Nuñez Muley warned Deza that the pragmatic would lead to 'the destruction of the kingdom and its natives' and pleaded with the king to change course. His patient and reasoned attempt to deconstruct Morisco customs for Deza and the king's benefit were never likely to have much impact on men whose minds were already made up, and his arguments fell on deaf ears, as he probably suspected they would be.

In January 1668, the pragmatic was officially proclaimed and announced throughout the kingdom, and the population of Granada was given one year to prepare for it. Over the next twelve months Moriscos across the kingdom began to secretly arm themselves. In December that year, Moriscos in the Alpujarra mountains rose up and massacred priests and the local Christian population. This uprising degenerated into savage and brutal civil wars, in which Moriscos fought bloody battles with a succession of Christian armies and militias, aided by a contingent of North African and Turkish volunteers.

In 1570 the 'War of the Alpujarras' ended with a crushing Morisco defeat, and the majority of the Morisco population of Granada was ruthlessly dispersed to other parts of Spain, where many of them died en route due to cold, disease and violence. It is not known whether Nuñez Muley shared their fate, or whether he was already dead by the time the deportations took place. Nothing more was heard from him.

But the revolt that he had anticipated confirmed all the worst suspicions of Spain's rulers, and fuelled a new pessimism regarding the viability and desirability of assimilating the Moriscos. For the next four decades, Spain's rulers continued to pursue a fitful policy of assimilation that oscillated between repression, negligence and inactivity, while clerics and statesmen debated more extreme solutions to the 'Morisco question' that included extermination and expulsion.

In the 1580s, Philip II agreed in principle to expel all Moriscos from Spain, but it was not until 1609, after much vacillation, that the decision was finally implemented by his son Philip III. In the space of five years, nearly 350,000 men, women and children were expelled from Spain in what was then the largest forced population transfer in European history. Though it was not as comprehensive as Spain's rulers imagined, this brutal exodus nevertheless completed the destruction of the cultural legacies of al-Andalus. The anti-Morisco clerics and officials who had lobbied the Crown for this outcome celebrated what they regarded as a great act of religious cleansing, but within a few years leading Spanish statesmen were expressing regret at the economic cost of Spain's two expulsions.

The impact of the destruction of Spanish Jewry and Islam was not only felt in economic terms. The expulsion of the Moriscos was a triumph of bigotry and reaction over the more tolerant traditions that were also part of Spanish society. More than four hundred years later Nuñez Muley's eloquent memorandum suggests a counterfactual alternative to the Morisco tragedy, in which Spain's rulers acknowledged and accepted Morisco cultural difference as a permanent feature of Spanish society, and allowed integration to take place gradually and through negotiation rather than repression.

Nuñez Muley's attempt to differentiate between religion and culture, and his insistence that integration did not require complete absorption into Christian society, also has some resonance in contemporary Europe. Today, the distinctions between religion and culture are frequently blurred in the depiction of Europe's Muslim minorities as the alien antithesis of European civilisation – regardless of whether that civilisation is defined as 'Christian' or 'secular'. While culturally-specific practices such as female genital mutilation are perceived as inherently 'Islamic' and further proof of Muslim incompatibility with European values, female dress codes are variously stigmatised as an expression of cultural backwardness or even as evidence of a secret conspiracy to transform Europe into an Islamic colony.

Such perceptions have moved closer to the political mainstream, as governments across the continent adopt increasingly coercive assimilationist policies, which demand that certain categories of 'immigrants' in Europe become 'like us' – or leave. In some countries Muslim immigrants are subject to Muslim-specific cultural 'tests' to determine their compatibility with European liberal values. Others have introduced prohibitions on mosque building and the wearing of the burkha and the hijab. The cultural meanings associated with these prohibitions are not the same as they were in sixteenth-century Spain, but the underlying dynamic behind them is not entirely dissimilar.

Across Europe, culturally powerful and dominant majorities are allowing fear, chauvinism, prejudice and incomprehension to dictate a new emphasis on enforced assimilation rather than integration. More than four centuries later, the memorandum of Francisco Nuñez Muley contains a simple message which too many of Europe's politicians have forgotten; that the process of *convivencia* ('living together) is the result of negotiation, mutual understanding and mutual respect; that attempts to promote it by force are likely to prove counter-productive and generate bitterness, resentment, and conflict rather than integration, and drive communities further apart even as they attempt to fuse them together.

SEPHARDIC JUDAISM AND THE LEVANTINE OPTION

David Shasha

When my grandfather came to the United States from Syria in the early twentieth century, he brought with him the mores and values of a Middle Eastern Jewish culture that has not been protected and secured for his descendants. The literary texts as well as the documentary history of his world have been almost completely forgotten amidst a sea of adaptation to a very different way of seeing things. My grandfather was heir to many traditions that were to him a very intimate and organic part of the world in which he grew up: a world that was increasingly collapsing and falling prey to new modes of identification.

My grandfather was, as I am, a Sephardi Jew. We are the descendants of Spanish and Portuguese Jews who lived in the Iberian Peninsula before the great expulsion of 1492. In the wake of the expulsion Jewish families like that of my grandfather moved east, back into the Ottoman-Arab world where they remained part of the Muslim civilisation that had once flourished in Iberia.

Sephardim wrote the first page in American Jewish history, even though they now seem to have been written out of that very history. In 1654 the first Jews who stepped on the shores of America were Sephardic while the first synagogues of colonial America, Touro Synagogue in Newport, Rhode Island and Shearith Israel in New Amsterdam, were also founded by Sephardim.

Perhaps the most outstanding rabbinic figure that ministered in the United States was the now-forgotten Sabato Morais (1823-1897) of Mikveh Israel in Philadelphia. Morais brilliantly exemplified the Levantine Religious Humanism of the Sephardim, whose rich legacy was subsequently occluded by the emergence of an Ashkenazi immigrant majority. The Ashkenazim hail from Christian Europe. Their roots are from the Jewish communities that settled along the river Rhine in Germany and Central Europe during the early medieval period. They brought many of their internal schisms to the United States; schisms that have haunted Jews and the Jewish faith to this very day.

In our day, the Sephardic community lacks a firm academic foundation from which to learn and absorb the culture and values of its past. Having made the transition to the history and culture of another community, that of the Ashkenazi, Sephardim today lack the most basic and rudimentary means of understanding who they are and where they come from. Increasingly, the elders of the community, those who grew up in a world that was very different from the one that we as Sephardim now inhabit, are dying out. If this were not enough, the Sephardic community has developed in such a way as to make the necessity of understanding and processing this past an inconsequential matter. The most basic elements of the Sephardi identity are therefore contested and often transformed.

Sephardim and Ashkenazim have developed historically within different cultural milieux and have traditionally espoused divergent worldviews. Occidental Jews have taken traits of Western culture, while the Oriental Jews, many of whom continued to speak Arabic and partook of a common Middle Eastern culture until the mass dispersions of Jews from Arab countries after 1948, have preserved numerous folkways and traits of Arab civilisation.

However, the manner in which Judaism is presented in contemporary public discourse is mediated through the Ashkenazi Jewish tradition and its experiences. The Jewish religion is filtered through the ways in which Ashkenazi rabbis understood the classical biblical and rabbinical texts, which is very often different from the ways in which these same texts were read and applied in the Sephardic community.

Sephardic Judaism is characterised by a religious humanism that preserved the parochial Jewish legal and literary traditions under the rubric of a much wider sense of universal ethics and morality. These two components, particularistic religion and universal humanism, often seen by religious people as contradicting one another, were soldered together in the Sephardic worldview and played a crucial part in the harmonious development of religious scholasticism at the heart of the Middle Ages.

Sephardim

The term 'Sephardi' came into common usage in the wake of the efflorescence of Jewish cultural life in Islamic Spain. Though Jews had lived in the Visigothic-ruled Christian Spain, there was in this early period of Sephardic history no unique Hispano-Jewish culture. But with the development of Jewish intellectual and cultural life after the Arab conquest of Spain, a sense of something special was noted and identified. The movement of Jews from the eastern Mediterranean to the western Mediterranean and back was fairly fluid between the ninth and fifteenth centuries and the moniker 'Sephardic', Biblical in origin, spread throughout the Middle East. When, for example, the celebrated Rabbi Moses Maimonides, whose family was prominent among the Spanish Jewish elite, moved to Egypt he proudly continued to use 'Sephardi' when signing his name.

Arab Jews took on the great load of translating classical Jewish culture into a new language and into a new system of cultural values. The adoption of scientific principles and a new form of rational ethics led to the development of the conception that would remain at the core of Sephardic civilisation for centuries: that of Religious Humanism. At the centre of this tradition is the value of charity which is defined as love of humanity, as we can see in this passage from *The Law of Sinai and its Appointed Times* by the Victorian educationalist Moses Angel, who served as Headmaster of London Jews' Free School and is seen as a major figure in Anglo-Jewish religious and secular education:

> Then, charity, which in the doctrine of abstract faith, means love for universal mankind, shall cease to be what concrete religion made it, love only for self and self's imitators. Then, man shall acknowledge that true God-worship consists not in observance of any particular customs, but in the humble, zealous cultivation of those qualities by which the Eternal has made himself known to the world. The members of one creed shall not arrogate to themselves peculiar morality and peculiar salvation, denying both to the members of other creeds; but they shall learn that morality and salvation are the cause and effect of all earnest endeavours to rise to the knowledge of revelation.

Having affirmed the primacy of universal love and charity, Angel then goes on to recognise the need for ancient custom to be maintained – but in a manner that allows for diversity of worship and a respect for the values of pluralism:

> Men shall cease to attempt the substitution of one set of forms for another set of forms; they shall satisfy themselves with being honest and dignified exponents of their own mode of belief, and shall not seek to coerce what heaven has left unfettered – the rights of conscience.

The Sephardic ethical tradition had absorbed and transmitted the values of classical Judaism in a way that extended its hand to all the peoples of the earth. These values include honesty, selflessness, discipline, loyalty, graciousness, humility, a reverence for knowledge, an aversion to sin and immorality, and a deep and abiding faith in God and in the traditions of Judaism. This sense of morality is brilliantly defined in one of the central ethical texts of the classical Sephardic tradition: *Al Hidaya ila Fara'id al-Qulub* (The Duties of the Heart) by Bahye ibn Paquda, who flourished in Zaragoza, Spain, during the first half of the eleventh century:

> Humility in all worldly affairs, open and secret, in words and actions, when moving or at rest. In all these, a man's conscience should be at one with his conduct, and his private behaviour should not be different from his public behaviour. On the contrary, all one does should be equally measured and in due proportion, full of humility and submission to God and men, according to their various degrees and the benefit one gets from them in the world and in religion, as it is said: "Well is it with the man that dealeth graciously and lendeth, that ordereth his affairs rightly" (Psalms 112:5); "Be lowly in spirit before all men" (Mishnah Avot 4:9); "Be submissive to a superior, affable to a junior, and receive all men cheerfully." (Mishnah Avot 3:12).

This moral philosophy is equally evident in other literary texts of Sephardic tradition, such as Judah Alharizi's *Sefer Tahkemoni*. Alharizi was a poet and a rational philosopher; and *Tahkemoni*, composed between 1218 and 1220, was written in Hebrew in the Arabic literary genre of rhyme prose known as *maqama*. Like *The Assemblies* of al-Hariri, the eleventh-century poet from Basra, *Tahkemoni* contains a series of witty and humorous encounters each with a particular moral. The Spanish poet Don Santob de Carrion, who flourished towards the end of the thirteenth century, re-cast the venerable tradition of Jewish Wisdom literature in the lexicon of Andalusian-Sephardic Religious Humanism in his *Proverbios Morales* (c. 1355). The ground-breaking poetry of Judah Halevi (c. 1075–1141), who is said to have been born in Toledo, and Solomon ibn Gabirol (c. 1021–1058), who was born in Malaga, have their accents firmly on religious humanism. Ibn Gabirol is one of the most original and innovative poets of the Andalusian-Sephardic school, whose epic poem *Keter Malkhut*, The Royal Crown, is one of the most astounding accomplishments of the Hebrew literary heritage. He also wrote a highly original treatise on ethics, *The Principles of Moral Qualities*, which served as a guide for generations. *Sefer ha-Qabbalah* (The Book of Tradition) by the astronomer and philosopher Abraham ibn Daud (1110–1180), who was born in Toledo, is a rich example of the intellectual and philosophical Jewish history of the Andalusian period. Indeed, the Sephardic tradition is overflowing with ethical and moral classics like Abraham bar Hiyya's *Hegyon ha-Nefesh ha-Azubah* (Meditation of the Sad Soul), written in the early twelfth century, a work akin to Boethius' Latin classic *The Consolation of Philosophy* (c. 524); and important rhetorical and linguistic achievements such as Moses ibn Ezra's *Kitab al-Muhadara w-al-Mudhakara*, which is composed along the lines of Arabic *adab* literature, and Jonah ibn Jannah's (990–1050) seminal studies of Hebrew grammar and lexicography which were written in the Arabic language, but became a central part of Hebrew culture in the Middle Ages.

The vast production of the Andalusian Jewish poets alone could fill dozens upon dozens of volumes. An excellent single volume anthology of the Sephardic school, the only one of its kind currently available, has been published in English translation by Peter Cole in his comprehensive *The Dream of the Poem: Hebrew Poetry in Muslim and Christian Spain 950–1492*. It is important to note that the Hebrew originals of the poems remain relatively inaccessible to all but the most devoted students of this tradition, collected in out-of-print and hard-to-find academic editions – a telling indication of how this valuable Jewish culture has become inaccessible.

The Jewish thinkers and writers of Andalusia aimed to unite the spiritual values of monotheistic religion with the great advances in the sciences and philosophy that embraced the humanistic disciplines. Religious Humanism sought to understand the commands of God by making use of the intellectual resources of the human mind in all its workings. It combined sublime faith with rigorous scholastic analysis. So what is the historical significance of the literary legacy of the Jews of Spain? Ross Brann, one of the most important scholars of Sephardic-Andalusian Jewish culture, provides an apt answer:

With respect to the richness of its cultural productivity, the career of Sefardi Jewry is without parallel in Jewish history at least until the Italian Renaissance, perhaps even until the German Jewish Enlightenment. Indeed, the cultural values, texts and verse forms produced by the Jews of Spain were subsequently preserved, studied, imitated and transformed during the Middle Ages and Renaissance by Jews of every other Mediterranean land. And the production of Hebrew literature itself continued unabated until 1492, some 350 years after the end of the "Golden Age." In all their varied activities the Hebrew literary intellectuals demonstrated a self-confidence and an openness to the wider Arabo-Islamic society without compromising their personal piety, devotion to traditional learning, and what we would call today their "Jewish identity". By composing their poems in classical Hebrew, in reviving the language of the Bible as a medium for the description of diverse experiences and the expression of personal feeling, the poets emphasised the significance of the individual and revitalised the Hebrew literary tradition.

The Jewish experience in Muslim Spain was not without problems. The harmony was somewhat disturbed in the twelfth century when Spain was being overrun by the Muslim fanatics known as the Al-Muwahidun ('the monotheists'), who belonged to the Almohad dynasty of Morocco. The Almohads were Berbers who had established a state in the Atlas Mountains around 1120. The movement was started by ibn Tumart (1080–1130), a puritan religious scholar who studied under the great al-Ghazali at his academy in Baghdad. Ibn Tumart, much like contemporary Wahhabis and Salafis, accused other Muslims of lacking faith and ascribed polytheism and anthropomorphism to many of their beliefs and practices. His solution: to beat them into submission. This episode of Spanish history is recounted in Anthony Mann's Hollywood epic '*El Cid*' (1961) which features a ripped Charlton Heston taking the side of his Andalusian Muslim compatriots who were just as threatened by the Berber fundamentalists as were the Christians and Jews.

The Almohad invasions forced many notable Jewish scholars to flee Andalusia. Rather than leave Andalusia by travelling north to the Christian territories, the family of Maimonides elected to leave through the south and settle in Almohad Morocco where in all likelihood they were forced to convert to Islam for a short time. Maimonides himself probably hid this conversion while working in the court of the Egyptian Sultan given that reversion to Judaism after converting to Islam was deemed a capital offence. We know through the peregrinations of many Andalusian Jewish rabbis that the preferred route of escape from the fanatic Almohads led through the Christian north. A figure such as the polymath Abraham ibn Ezra (1092-1167), author of one of the most penetrating medieval Bible commentaries, travelled northward until he ended up in Europe proper. Ibn Ezra was keenly aware of having been exiled from his Andalusian home as he complained bitterly until his dying days over his lost homeland.

But ibn Ezra was not the only Andalusian Jew to move into the world of Christian Europe. The early years of the Christian victory over the Andalusian Muslim forces, culminating in the destruction of the last Muslim stronghold of Granada in 1492, was a good time for the Jews. Embracing the exiles from the south, the Catholic kings incorporated Jews into their courts as well as making ample use of the new intellectual and scientific advances of the Muslim civilisation that had been developing on the Iberian Peninsula. This great synthesis is reflected in one of the seminal documents of the Spanish Golden Age; Cervantes' *Don Quixote* (1604–1614). As is not so well-known, Cervantes uses the literary ruse of presenting his epic tale as a Castilian translation of an Arabic text composed by one Cide Hamete Benengeli. Cide here, just like Heston's legendary on-screen character, being the Arabic honorific for Sir, al-Sayyid. Spanish history is thus a struggle to some extent between the Arabic and the Latin – where the Arabic was the primary substrate of culture and civilisation.

In the Muslim world, the situation was very different. Jews were able to make their mark on Arabic culture in a number of different ways: with the adoption of Arabic as the language of culture, Jews found themselves immersed in the scientific and philosophical educational system of the Arab world. Figures like Maimonides, Moses ibn Ezra and Solomon ibn Gabirol, and so many others, marked this transition into a Judeo-Arabic cultural universe that quickly established itself as the cutting edge of Jewish self-expression. Even when the poet Judah Halevi composed a biting critique of this Judeo-Arabic culture in his classic book *The Kuzari* (written in Arabic, its original title was *Kitab al-Radd w-al-Dalil fi al-Din al-Dhalil*), he did so using the same Arabic language and couched his arguments in the same academic terms as would only be intelligible to a student well-versed in the philosophic rationalism of the time. And it should be well-noted that Halevi continued to produce Arabic-style verse until the very end of his life; never relinquishing the profane themes of the erotic and sensual that typified this cultural school.

Sephardim and Ashkenazim

We can thus see that the Sephardim for many centuries practised a form of Judaism which sought a creative engagement with its outside environment. In the Mediterranean world this meant an acculturation to classical Islamic civilisation. Prominent Sephardic rabbis, such as Maimonides and Abraham ibn Ezra, embraced the new Greco-Arabic synthesis, disdaining clericalism while espousing humanism and science, and composed seminal works on Jewish thought and practice. Sephardic rabbis were not merely religious functionaries, they were poets, philosophers, astronomers, doctors, lawyers, accountants, linguists, merchants, architects, civic leaders and much else. Samuel the Nagid, the famous polymath of Granada, even led troops into battle in the eleventh century to fight off the Christians.

In contrast to Ashkenazi Judaism, which preferred to live a world apart, utterly disconnected from European civil society, traditional Sephardic Judaism provided for a more tolerant and open-minded variant of Jewish existence. The Hatam Sofer, one of the most prominent Ashkenazi rabbis of the nineteenth century, boldly reformulated the Talmudic slogan for modern Orthodox Ashkenazi thinking: 'He-hadash asur min ha-Tora' – 'The Torah prohibits the new'.

The Ashkenazim of Christian Europe lived in a relatively hostile environment where accusations of deicide marked them as the penultimate 'Other' in a society that saw Jews and Judaism as antithetical to Christianity. In this difficult environment, the Ashkenazi Jews created a form of Judaism that was, I would argue, insular and deeply hermetic. Life in the ghetto was conducive to mystical ideas and influence of authoritarian forms of rabbinical authority. In Ashkenazi Jewish culture rabbis emerged as dominant figures and their religious rulings reflected deeply anti-rational tendencies.

To understand the profound differences between Sephardim and Ashkenazim, we need to look at the foundational casuistic approach, known in Talmudic parlance as 'Pilpul', which allowed Ashkenazi rabbis to frame Jewish law in a manner that suited their ghetto culture.

Pilpul describes a rhetorical process that the Sages used to formulate their legal decisions. The word is used as a verb: one engages in the process of Pilpul in order to formulate a legal point. It marks the process of understanding legal ideas, texts, and interpretations. It is a catch-all term that is translated in English as 'casuistry'. The term is understood differently in the classical Sephardic and Ashkenazi traditions.

The Sephardic tradition, emerging out of Babylonian academies and finding its definitive form in the many legal works of Moses Maimonides, held the Talmudic texts to be oral literature. Using mnemonics, technical terms, and other rhetorical devices to aid memorisation and transmission, Sephardim understood the Talmud to be a colloquy of discussions that were drawn from the proceedings of the great rabbinical academies of Babylonia. The Babylonian Talmud became the basis upon which the Jewish law would be constructed.

This was a process grounded, as the Muslim hadith literature, in tradition and the chain of transmission. Laws were transmitted in the name of rabbinical authorities. It was this chain of tradition, known in Islamic tradition as *isnad*, that drew clear lines between the formal authority of what has been passed down to us, and the process of codifying these laws. The ultimate purpose of the legal process was to elevate the law above personal and political concerns so that members of the community would be completely equal and not live at the whim of arbitrary judges. In order to maintain the distinction between the written Torah – the Hebrew Bible – and the oral law, the Talmudic Sages conceived of the idea of Pilpul as a means to join each law to its biblical proof and text. Rabbis would debate what in legal terms would be the formal 'title' of each law. Differences would arise regarding these legal titles that a court must use in a criminal charge.

The Talmudic formalism of Maimonides in his encyclopaedic legal compendium, the Mishneh Torah, was strongly contested by the Ashkenazi rabbis of France and Germany. In the Mishneh Torah, Maimonides famously eliminated the rhetorical discussions of the Talmud and simply presented the final ruling; a process that replicated the methodology of Rabbi Isaac Alfasi, Maimonides' precursor in Lucena. The Ashkenazi rabbis saw Pilpul as a substantive debate over the content of the Law rather than simply as a rhetorical matter. Their understanding of Talmudic Pilpul took the form of a radical reinterpretation of the law. As the Jewish scholar Haym Soloveitchik notes this was not a 'reinterpretation'; rather they 'read the Talmud, to perceive the Talmud, in a fashion which could be construed as a justification of the status quo'. This reformulation of the Talmudic discourse betrayed an authoritarian strain that underlay Ashkenazic Judaism. Custom took on an unquestioned force and the anti-rational tendencies created a deep well of antagonism to science and philosophical learning.

These two models of Jewish discourse allow us to see Judaism in radically different ways: the vertical, authoritarian model of the Ashkenazim reflects an atavistic, anti-modern approach that relies on superstition to express Jewish values and rejects outside influences; and the horizontal, dialogical Religious Humanism of the Sephardim, which encapsulates the wisdom of Maimonidean tradition in a form of critical inquiry that seeks to promote rationality and empower human beings.

When the Enlightenment came in the eighteenth century the Sephardim were able to make a seamless transition to the new culture (the Sephardic chief rabbi of London David Nieto was the first Jew to examine the scientific works of Isaac Newton while Isaac Abendana taught Newton Hebrew at Cambridge University) while European Judaism was torn by deep internal schisms, many of which continue to play out in the modern Jewish community through movements such as Zionism and Orthodoxy – each practising a form of cultural exclusion that is predicated upon a narrow interpretation of the Jewish tradition.

While Ashkenazi Jews in the modern period broke off into bitter and acrimonious factions, Sephardim preserved their unity as a community rather than let doctrine asphyxiate them. A Jewish Reformation never took place in the Sephardic world because the Sephardim continued to maintain their fidelity to their traditions while absorbing and adapting the ideas and trends of the world they lived in. We can point to the rabbinical figures of Sabato Morais and Elijah Benamozegh, two Sephardim born in Italy, who typified the Sephardic ability to construct a Jewish culture that preserved the parochial standards of Jewish tradition while espousing the science and humanism wrought by the massive changes of the nineteenth century.

Until the founding of the state of Israel in 1948, Arab Jews created a place for themselves in their countries of origin by serving in government, civic affairs, business, and the professions. James Sanua, an Egyptian Jew who wrote for the theatre and press, was at the forefront of the nascent Egyptian nationalist movement at the turn of the twentieth century. The last chief rabbi of the Ottoman Empire and then of Egypt, Haim Nahum Effendi (who died in Cairo in 1960), was elected as a member to the Egyptian Senate and was a founder of the Arabic Language Academy. By request from the Egyptian civil authorities Rabbi Mas'ud Hai Ben Shim'on composed a three-volume compendium of Jewish legal practice written in precise classical Arabic, *Kitab al-Ahkam ash-Shariyyah fi-l-Ahwal ash-Shaksiyyah li-l-Isra'ilyyin*, which served as a primary source for Egyptian Muslim lawyers dealing with Jewish cases. Elijah Benamozegh of Livorno composed his seminal work *Israel and Humanity* in the spirit of nineteenth-century European modernism as a work that promoted the universal religious values of Noahism; a faith that could unite all humanity under a single compassionate framework.

Despite the long record of accomplishment in the Sephardi world, the Ashkenazic tradition was able to dominate Jewish life the world over, marginalising the more open and rational tradition. The antagonism against Sephardi Judaism is best expressed by the Orientalist Bernard Lewis. In his *What Went Wrong?* where he reaffirms his infamous 'Clash of Civilisations' thesis, Lewis argues that the primal battle between Judaism and Islam is also reflected in miniature by the cultural split between Ashkenazim and Sephardim:

> The conflict, coexistence, or combination of these two traditions [i.e. the Judeo-Christian and the Judeo-Islamic] within a single small state, with a shared religion and a common citizenship and allegiance, should prove illuminating. For Israel, this issue may have an existential significance, since the survival of the state, surrounded, outnumbered, and outgunned by neighbours who reject its very right to exist, may depend on its largely Western-derived qualitative edge.

The Levantine Option

What if the future of the Middle East, contrary to Bernard Lewis and his partisans, lay in the amicable interaction of the three religions: Judaism, Christianity and Islam? What if there was a symbiotic relationship between the three faiths that emphasises commonalities in culture and politics rather than the deep-seated differences that are rooted in the Ashkenazi experience? If such a symbiosis can be achieved, the cultural memory of Moorish Spain where the three religions were able to coexist and produce a civilisation of great worth, would take prominence. The Sephardic voice would be central in articulating *convivencia*, the creative cultural dynamic that fired medieval Spanish civilisation, until its untimely destruction in 1492, but which continued through the glorious epoch of Ottoman civilisation, until its degeneration in the nineteenth century. The Sephardic tradition could unfold the delicate strands of the Levantine memory and construct a cultural model that would be more appropriate to the current situation than the spurious binaries promoted by the concept of Israel as an outpost of Western civilisation.

The model of Levantine Jewish historical memory would serve to collapse the alienating cult of persecution harboured in classical Zionist thought and omnipresent in the rituals of the state of Israel, replacing it with a more positive view of the past that would lead us into a more optimistic present. The nihilistic 'realism' of the current Israeli approach, filtered through the rigid orthodoxies of American Jewish institutional discourse and centred on the institutionalised perpetuation of the twin legacies of the Holocaust and European anti-Semitism, would then be countered by memories of a Jewish past that was able to develop a life-affirming and constructive relationship with its surrounding environment.

Current models of the conflict and ways to resolve it, from the Left as well as the Right, ignore the very valuable fact of the centuries of Jewish nativity in the Middle East. We see right-wing settlers imposing a romantic version of Jewish history on the conflict that has precious little to do with the organic realities of those who have lived in the region over many centuries. And left-wing groups, such as Peace Now, promote a resolution from within the same Western mind-set and construct ineffective 'peace' programmes that have historically done very little to engender a stable set of relationships between Jews and Arabs.

Both positions, firmly rooted in Ashkenazi Jewish culture, have failed because they have not seriously engaged the traditional ethos of the Jewish and Arab inhabitants of the region. They have merely adopted Western models of conflict resolution, violent and non-violent, arrogantly assuming that Jews are culturally different from Arabs. The Levantine option, if adopted, would be a means to create a shared cultural space for Jews and Arabs rather than the establishment of walls and barriers that are endemic to these Ashkenazi approaches.

Sadly, Jewish progressives, despite the rich history and tradition of Sephardi Judaism, tend to continue on their own Ashkenazi trajectory as that is the standard operating language of the institutional world in which they work and live. While Sephardic music and food are seen as quaintly exotic, the ideas and texts of the Sephardi tradition are resoundingly ignored. Internal to Jewish organisations there is a publicly unspoken yet privately understood belief that Sephardim are less capable and not as intelligent as Ashkenazim.

The most urgent problem that now faces the Jewish community does not come from the outside – it is the very internal repressive mechanisms that have served to sever the Sephardic Jews from being involved in the process of articulating their own voice within the larger framework of Jewish discourse.

The silencing of the Sephardic voice, internally by the self-censoring mechanisms imposed by Zionism as well as by the cultural blindness and insensitivity of the Western media, makes little sense at the present moment. We should be seeking new and more creative ways to identify what has gone wrong in our world rather than continuing to insist on the same conceptual mind-set that has led us to recycle the same options. We hear a constant stream of repetitive rhetoric that has done little to break the impasse that enslaves Jews and Gentiles to lives of mutual incomprehension and a seemingly endless reserve of ethnic hatred.

Until we develop ways of talking to one another in a substantial and civilised way – from within a shared cultural space that exists for those of us (becoming fewer and fewer) who still espouse the Levantine option – the questions surrounding Israel and Palestine, as well as the endemic violence that is a malignant cancer in the region, will continue to haunt Jews, Arabs and the rest of the world. The promotion of such a discourse is the most urgent and the most progressive need of our time – for Jews and Muslims alike.

A MUSICAL INTERLUDE

Cherif Abderrahman Jah

Sometime during 821, an elegant man disembarked at the port of Algeciras. He was accompanied by his wife, eight sons and two daughters. The inhabitants of Algeciras were surprised and a little amused to see the arrival of this gentleman, who was clearly distinguished, with a carefully trimmed henna-dyed beard, his eyes lined with black, wearing a leather hat, and playing an instrument. An intense aroma of flowers emanated from him and his wives and children. His name was ibn al-Hassan ibn 'Ala ibn Naffa, and he had arrived from Tunis on the invitation of the Umayyad Emir, al-Hakam I of Cordoba. The locals ran to give him the news: the Emir had just died. For a few days ibn Naffa did not know what to do. He had had to leave Tunis, where he played in the Aghalbid court, in some haste. Apparently, he had sung a song that offended the Sultan. Fortunately an emissary soon arrived from the new Emir, Abderrahman II, to say that his father's invitation would be honoured, and ibn Naffa was invited to live in Cordoba. He accepted the invitation. Ben Naffa came to be better known by his nickname: Ziryab, the singing blackbird, either because his music resembled a bird's, or for his dark complexion.

Although Ziryab's origins are disputed, he was probably Kurdish. We know that he played at the court of the Abbasid Caliphs during the reigns of Harun al-Rashid (766–809) and his son al-Mamun (786–833). In the eighth century Baghdad had a thriving musical culture. The courts of the Abbasid Caliphs had developed a custom (which didn't please everyone) of playing music in a hall that was adjacent to the court of the Caliph, separated only by a veil. This music hall was managed by the guild of the palace musicians, known as *sitara*. Baghdad was endowed with a number of schools of music, but without doubt the most prominent was that of Ibrahim Al-Mausili (742–804) and his son Ishaq al-Mawsili (767–850). Besides being one of the most renowned musicians of his time, Ishaq also wrote a book that collected a large number of songs of the era, *The Compendium of Songs*, which became an indispensable guide for his successors. The dispute between Ishaq and Caliph Harun al-Rashid's brother, Ibrahim al-Mahdi (779–838), an exceptional musician, gives us an idea of the intellectual liveliness of the period. For Ibrahim there were no musical rules, only free interpretation and creation. He was heavily criticised by Ishaq and other musicians for the innovations and simplifications he introduced to the rhythms. But despite their differences, the two men remained friends and exchanged a lengthy correspondence, each arguing for his particular point of view.

The musical culture of Baghdad was a product of frequent contact and cultural exchange with other civilisations. One of the main characteristics of Arab culture during the pre-Islamic and early Islamic period was the primordial importance accorded to poetry as the basic support system for the music. The Arabs had always given enormous importance to their complex and conceptually rich language, and admired literary and oral expression, the principal vehicle of their culture. But their music was elementary, had no harmony, and was exclusively homophonic. The primitive metric of the Arab Bedouins was enriched and acquired melodies through Persian and Byzantine influence. The rhythm went through a series of transformations, and gradually the music was intrinsically infused with poetry. A new and distinct form of music appeared from this amalgam of Arab, Persian and Greek components.

In Damascus, during the Umayyad period, the royal court employed numerous singers, poets and musicians. Initially, the enterprise of singing and music was an elite activity, limited to a few: rulers, court officials and the wealthy. But soon popular musical forms began to reach a much larger audience. Amongst the most common forms was the *thaqil*, a slow, heavy rhythm that soon gave way to the *haza*, a happier and lighter cadence. Music acquired mass popularity during the Abbasid period in Baghdad. The Pythagorean musical scale was adopted; and the classic *qasida* composed of a series of verses of a balanced structure and rhythm, conferring a certain monotony, made room for the *ghazal*, a genre of love song widely embraced. As music became popular, it started to play an important part in the lives of Muslims, not only as entertainment but also as a religious vehicle. Hymns to the Prophet Muhammad were set to music; and music was played during the birth of a child and at major feasts, and accompanied the troops on the battlefield. Music was also used for therapeutic purposes, to improve psychological wellbeing and adjust emotional mood.

Not surprisingly, scholars and philosophers began to develop theories of music. The first philosopher to undertake a serious study of the subject was Al-Kindi (801–873), a prominent figure at Baghdad's House of Wisdom. He is said to have written fifteen books on the theory of music, although only five have survived. He regarded music as a vehicle for connecting man to the cosmos and he encouraged its use in therapy. He was followed by al-Farabi (872–950), who in his *The Great Book of Music* explores the emotional power of music, provides a comprehensive study of intervals and their combinations, and gives an account of the main melodic instruments in use in his time and the scales produced by them. Ibn Sina (980–1037) developed musical theory further, providing a detailed and elaborate treatment of rhythm. Even al-Ghazzali (1058–1111), a staunch critic of al-Farabi and ibn Sina, conceded in *The Revival of Religious Sciences* that music is an important vehicle for reaching mystical union with God. He made a distinction between the sensual and spiritual perception of music, and argued that songs (*ghina*), melody and rhythm had a beneficial effect on the soul.

Ziryab makes an appearance in Baghdad against this background of theoretical study and music's emerging popularity. After a brilliant debut recital before Harun al-Rashid, he became a prominent addition to the court musicians. He became a student of Ishaq al-Mawsili, and all went well for some years. Then something happened; Muslim historians give us different accounts. In one account, Ishaq became jealous of the quality of his performances and rapidly rising reputation, and threatened his potential rival. In another account, a performance provoked anger from his patron. Either way, Ziryab had to flee Baghdad in some haste.

Baghdad's loss was al-Andalus' gain. Ziryab revolutionised Andalusian customs, making his mark not only on music, but also in the culinary arts, fashion and aesthetics. He set a high standard in musical accomplishment as well as in elegant dress and etiquette. He founded an important school of music in which generations of students were trained. His five sons and both daughters became distinguished musicians, who, along with the students he trained, ensured that his school continued for centuries. Its legacy was a huge repertoire of compositions.

Ziryab is credited with many musical innovations. He established rules for classical music performances still followed to this day in, for example, the orchestral structure of the twenty-four nubes. He introduced to al-Andalus musical forms which had been codified by Ishaq al-Mawsili in Baghdad, and described in their complexity first by al-Kindi then al-Farabi. He is responsible for the emergence of the *nabwa*, the suite form characteristic of the classical tradition, in which lyrics of both classical and colloquial Arabic are sung by a soloist or in chorus – a musical genre still very popular in Andalusia. Besides being a singer, Ziryab also played the oud, the unfretted lute, the signature string instrument of Arab music and predecessor of the modern guitar. To the four existing strings of the lute, he is said to have added a fifth. He also made his own lutes, with the chords made of silk and even, legend has it, lion intestine. He substituted the pick, which until then had been made of wood, for one made from an eagle's feather; this is still used today in the countries of the Maghreb.

For Ziryab, music was an integral element of the cosmic scheme. He was greatly influenced by al-Kindi, who believed that the four strings of the lute corresponded to the four humours of the body in Greek medicine. The first corresponded to bile and was yellow; the second was red and corresponded to blood; the third, white for phlegm; and the fourth, black, corresponding to black bile. What was missing, according to Ziryab, was the string that corresponded to the soul. He therefore added an extra string in the middle and painted it red in the belief that the soul resided in the blood. The great musician attributed his talent to inspiration by Jinn, who, he claimed, came to visit him at night. He would be seen playing late at night, often into the early hours of the morning, surrounded by a group of students.

But Ziryab was not the only great musical figure, nor Cordoba the only city where great musicians proliferated. Other cities of al-Andalus – Valencia, Malaga and Seville – were also alive with music. Seville was particularly renowned for its craftsmen who refined or invented musical instruments. Muhammad al-Mu'tamid (r.1069–1091), the ruler of Seville, was himself a renowned poet, and two musicians from his court acquired great fame: Abu Bakr ibn Zaydun (1003–1070) and ibn Hamdis (c.1056 –c.1133). The latter, forced to flee from his native Sicily, settled in Seville and from then on was known as 'The Sicilian'. Other *taifa* (city state) rulers who fostered music included Muhammad al-Mardanis (1124–1172) of

Valencia and Murcia, al-Mutawakkil (r.1073–1094) of Badajoz, and ibn Razin (r.1012–1044) of Santa María (Albarracín).

While rulers provided patronage and promoted music, the polymaths and scholars developed musical theory. In his treatise *The Classification of the Sciences*, the great litterateur and psychologist ibn Hazm (994–1064) explained the existence of three types of music which provoked specific emotional states: one type offered valour to the fearful; another transformed the avaricious into the generous; and finally, a third type united souls. The celebrated mystic ibn 'Arabi of Murcia (1165–1240) developed a theory of musical mysticism in the *Book of Answers*. Even ibn Rushd (1126–1198), the great philosopher of al-Andalus, wrote about music. But without doubt the most distinguished musical theorist of al-Andalus is ibn Bajja of Zaragoza (1095–1138). Besides being a mathematician, psychologist, philosopher and natural scientist, ibn Bajja was an excellent musician and the composer of many songs. He combined Christian and Muslim songs to create a style unique to al-Andalus; his songs are sung even today. His exceptional theoretical works are said to surpass the writings of al-Farabi.

Al-Andalus witnessed a conscious effort to popularise music and ensure it reached all segments of society. Around the tenth century, when the original Andalusian caliphate splintered into smaller city states, two forms of popular poetry were set to music. The new strophic poems of intertwined rhythms were called the *muwassaha* and the *zejel*. The *muwassaha* (adorned with an embroidered girdle) was composed of six stanzas, each consisting of four or five mono-rhymed verses, the rhythm changing in each stanza. It was recited in classical Arabic, except the refrain or *jarcha*, which was recited in Romance dialect Arabic. The *zejel*, recited in Arabic dialect, was a popular version of the *muwassaha*; its best known exponent was the poet ibn Quzman (1078–1170), who lived the life of a troubadour.

These new musical forms gained a great following not only in al-Andalus but also in the Muslim East, in Aleppo, Damascus and Cairo. Centuries of cultural exchange ensured that the music of al-Andalus reached other parts of the Muslim world. During the eleventh and twelfth centuries, the transmission was largely carried out by the learned men of al-Andalus who travelled widely and were appointed to influential positions in Cairo, Baghdad and Fes. A typical example is the astronomer, chemist and physician Abu al-Salt (1068–1134), who travelled to Alexandra and Cairo, and eventually ended up in Tunis, where he introduced Andalusian music to the court. Indeed, all Andalusian musical traditions were taken up by the closest neighbours in the Maghreb. There were strong relationships between city-states in al-Andalus and major cities in Morocco, Algeria and Tunisia. Thus Seville influenced Tunis, where music of Andalusian origin is called Ma'luf; Granada influenced Tetuan and Fes, where Andalusian music received the name of al 'ala; and Cordoba influenced Algeria, where its music came to be known as al-Gharnati. Morocco also produced its own version of *muwassaha*, made of double couplets and called 'Rhymes of the City'. After 1492, when waves of exiles from al-Andalus arrived in North Africa, the impact of Andalusian music was even stronger. The Muslims and Jews of al-Andalus zealously guarded and preserved their musical traditions. Those who remained in Spain continued to make music in their own style until speaking and singing in Arabic were officially banned in the sixteenth century.

In these circumstances, music was not written down but orally transmitted, and there was always a danger that the tradition would be lost. Of the twenty-four *nubas* that existed in al-Andalus, for example, only eleven were conserved in Morocco. This was largely thanks to poet and musician ibn al-Hussein al-Haik, who was born in the Moroccan city of Tetuan and lived during the eighteenth century. Like other musicians, al-Haik depended on oral transmission instead of written scores. So he sat about compiling the eleven *nubas* he knew. *The Songbook of al-Haik*, the most important source of classical Andalusian music, contains the musical notations of the song, as well as the names of the authors of the poems and melodies. Written in 1789, the *Songbook* has been handed down to generation after generation.

By the eleventh century, al-Andalus was a centre for the manufacture of musical instruments and an exporter of musical and poetic ideas north into Europe. Its instruments spread to France to be played by troubadours, a class of musicians and lyrical poets of knightly rank, and *trouveres*, a school of poets which flourished from the eleventh to the fourteenth centuries, composers of such works as *Chansons de Geste* and the *Songs of Roland*. Europe adopted and adapted Andalusian musical instruments such as the *rebab*, ancestor of the violin, the *quitara*, which became the guitar in English, and the *neqreh*, naker, as well as numerous percussion and wind instruments. An extensive musical vocabulary of Arabic origin was adopted in European languages such as French and English: 'lute (*oud*), rebec (*rabab*) and nakers (*naqqara*)', writes British music historian Owen Wright, 'are only the most obvious of a whole series of linguistic borrowings demonstrating that a significant proportion of the medieval European instrumentarium was made up of instruments either directly of Spanish-Arab provenance or sufficiently affected by similar types used in Muslim Spain, for an Arabic name to be adopted in place of an indigenous one'. *Oud* became the principal vehicle for European music throughout the Renaissance. Other instruments, such as the drum (*al-tabal*), frame drum (*al-duff*), trumpet (*al-nafir*) and hornpipe (*al-buq*), were also adopted. 'Centuries of close contact', Wright says, made these instruments 'thoroughly familiar, and it is sensible to assume that along with them were adopted for the most part their characteristic sounds and playing techniques'.

The music of al-Andalus is alive today; classical Andalusian musical orchestras can be heard throughout the Maghreb, in Algeria, Morocco, Tunisia and Libya. Traditional instruments such as the *oud*, *rabab* and *darbouka* (goblet drums) are still used, but the piano, cello and clarinet have been added to the ensemble. While playing the *nuba*, the instruments revolve around the principal *oud*. However, the Moroccan lute is different from lutes used in other parts of the Muslim world; following Ziryab, it has five strings. Voice and instruments complement each other; each phrase (*bit*) is taken up in the same movement by the instruments, although at times the voice sings solo. An echo of a rich history, and a living history too.

EMPOWERING WOMEN

Brad Bullock

'The only new idea that could save humanity in the 21st century is for women to take over the management of the world. This reversal is a matter of life or death.'

Gabriel Garcia Marquez

Al-Andalus represents a pinnacle of Muslim social and cultural achievement commonly invoked in contrast to current Muslim predicaments. What is not acknowledged, or indeed widely known, is that the openness and tolerance of Muslim Spain applied equally to women. There were no barriers to restrain them; and, by tradition, empowered women were highly valued. Andalusian women were, like their noted male counterparts, polymaths, excelling in music, law, and languages. Their voices were present and often highly esteemed among men in spirited discussions about artistic and intellectual pursuits or issues surrounding public life. And they were totally unreserved in expressing their feelings of love.

Among the most remarkable was the Umayyad princes Walladah, daughter of a Caliph of Cordoba, an 'emancipated woman' by all definitions. In his book *The Fragrance of Perfume from the Branch of Green Andalusia*, the famous Moroccan historian and biographer al-Maqqari (1578-1632) describes her as 'unique in her time, endowed with gracious speech, lavishly praised and centre of attention'. Never married, Walladah played host to poets and artists in her Cordoba home, often engaging in poetic contests. 'By God', she declared in one of her poems, 'I am suited to great things, and proudly I walk, with head aloft.' Asma Afsaruddin provides a survey of dozens of notable female poets and literary figures from tenth- and eleventh-century Muslim Spain, offering evidence of 'the amount of freedom enjoyed by these women and the high level of accomplishment that distinguished them'. Afsaruddin's list includes Al-Arudiyyah, who learned grammar and philology from her patron and soon surpassed him; Hafsah bint al-Hajja al-Rukuniya, whose beauty and elegance impressed the ruler of Granada, but she preferred a fellow poet, the slave al-Abbadiyyah, a writer of prose and poetry who spoke several languages; and al-I'timad, the wife of a ruler in Seville who, while she was the slave of another man, so impressed him by her ability with verse that he purchased and wed her. But women in Muslim Spain were not just poets and artists, but also scientists and philosophers. And they were not just a handful but numerous – and during their time they were as famous as their male counterparts.

Some critics question the use of such Andalusian women as generalised representatives of 'the emancipated woman'. Maria Viguera, for example, argues that those who participated in intellectual and cultural events were a privileged fraction of women who owed their freedoms to powerful and indulgent men. She contends that freedoms enjoyed by these women did not essentially challenge or change Islamic power structures or the primary roles of women as mothers and wives. The free woman of Andalusia, then, was a woman who did almost no work from a position of privilege within what remained a fairly rigid society.

Viguera's well-taken call for acknowledging the limits of Andalusi female freedoms, though, is part of a debate that misses the larger point: to a consequential degree, those notable women were seen; they were public figures involved in open conversations taken seriously by those in power. Viguera admits that these high-profile women held property which they used to endow public foundations. And the freedom of at least some Andalusian women to speak frankly and openly about their intellectual interests, love and sexual desires – to use their voices in this way at all – stands in stark contrast to that which was possible even among the elite in comparable non-Muslim societies across Europe during that time. The women of al-Andalus provide a vision of the way forward. Rediscovering the spirit of Muslim Spain, I would argue, demands an unprecedented and urgent commitment by the *ummah* to empower women. The reward? A much brighter future.

What is Needed

Muslim countries are among the most developmentally challenged in the world. The UN's Human Development Index, a comprehensive measure of social development based on life expectancy, education and income for 187 countries ranks only six majority-Muslim countries among the top third. Without a doubt, understanding how legacies of colonialism contribute to their present developmental status is pivotal, including past and current policies of the US and its Western allies. Yet these critiques rarely move us closer to practical strategies for positive social change. The strategy championed here is hardly novel, but aspects of the new global context are, while other crucial pieces of the puzzle have faded into the background in favour of what seems more urgent. The gist boils down to this: as go Muslim women, so go their children, and as go their children, so goes the future.

Why focus on women first as the best way forward rather than, for instance, economic growth, establishing democracy, building infrastructure and a civil society, a reformulation of aid or even fighting poverty? Development scholars certainly don't agree about what is needed most for that brighter tomorrow. Economists usually start with the presumption of economic expansion through traditional engines of economic growth, such as production and trade. Political scientists tend to begin with establishing civil society, civil liberties, and rule of law; positive social change necessarily proceeds from there. Diverse organisations alleviate hunger or poverty on grounds that establishing some level of basic needs fulfilment is a precursor to real and lasting progress. These differences in focus often lead to debates about moving towards or away from capitalism or socialism, and inevitably get tangled up in arguments over the merits of democracy (which, despite claims to the contrary, does not require a particular economic system). Within a Muslim context, the substance of published arguments appear basically the same, whether the analysts are 'Western' or not, decades of criticism about Orientalism and 'Islamisation' notwithstanding. What is common is that 'starting with women' is not regarded as a prominent advancement strategy.

The best reason for starting with women is that this strategy promotes all other development goals: economic productivity and employment, a civil society with fewer conflicts, and sustainable levels of material decency. These goals are all laudable and those working toward them are doing vital work. But it is not just a matter of what comes first: first a workplace and then women workers. Rather, empowering women is arguably the best path to overall social progress. Start here: women constitute more than half of a population and their potential contributions to solving society's problems are wasted when they are prized only for making children and keeping house. Women are already the key to youth and the future both literally (fertility) and culturally (in their roles for instilling values or a moral education, but also for assisting in schoolwork). Lastly, women are less likely to propose force as a preferred means for resolving conflicts. Another important reason to invest first in women is the matter of social justice. It won't do to dismiss arguments here as merely feminist or Western. Social justice has always been a hallmark of Islamic thought and practice. Whatever else is debatable, a better Muslim society will be one that returns to social justice as its primary cause, and that cause cannot ignore Muslim women (the largest social group routinely denied social justice).

Empowered Women in Context

For Muslim societies to produce women who, as Walladah declared, are 'suited to great things', we must consider the wide variety of contexts in Muslim countries. The means and participants may look notably non-Western, and then there are the various schools of religious thought about Islam and levels of religious authority that suggest empowering women may ideally mean many things. Practically, however, some things rise to the top for every Muslim society, starting with the priority for improving female literacy (even if they are not reading *Lolita* in Tehran). Fully educating women, meaning an education that provides viable options for joining the workforce, necessarily addresses literacy but also includes skills for doing a wide variety of jobs. A third aspect of empowerment is giving women greater freedom to succeed (or fail) in public spheres: economic, political, intellectual, cultural and social. This includes more freedom to speak their minds before they become involved in protests, whether as politicians, entrepreneurs, housewives or artists. Finally, female scholarship, especially religious scholarship, must be encouraged and supported – not merely tolerated. Doing all these things simultaneously may not be possible, and Muslim analysts or policy experts must consider the proper calculus for applying them. There seems little value in spreading female scholarship, for example, if a vast majority of women can't read.

All this about empowering women is much easier said than done, of course. Even if one agrees, the list of potential obstacles is long and daunting.

Yet, there are reasons to be optimistic. Such efforts are more likely to be initiated and take hold these days than in any period of the recent past. Unavailable to Andalusian women were recent forms of social media that make it easier for a critical mass of voices to create a public conversation. The freedom of a well-placed few to speak candidly about their concerns could foster wider discussions about social and cultural issues leading to an ultimate form of social empowerment for all. As the Arab Spring shows, many countries already have a highly literate and educated female population and talented female activists who are using modern communication techniques to make themselves heard. The clear message from many of them is that 'freedom' goes beyond the freedom they gained from replacing one government with another to encompass the freedom to engage in creating a more open society and additional space for women. Besides, efforts to empower women have as much chance of being adopted as many other development strategies that already meet the resistance of established power. These reasons for optimism, however, have to be balanced against a sober reality: the convergence of an exclusive system of social organisation and some very modern problems that pose an unprecedented threat to progress, especially in Muslim countries. This convergence raises the stakes, making efforts to empower women more urgent and the failure to do so more costly by the day.

What is in the Way

There are two basic hurdles to empowering women, and thus rekindling the spirit of al-Andalus: patriarchy and population.

Economist Heidi Hartmann reminds us that patriarchy precedes capitalism. Patriarchy is essentially a very old system of social organisation that reserves power and privilege for men. Hartmann's point is that resolutions about reforming capitalism will not by themselves challenge the structure of patriarchy; should that remain intact, the economic and social potential of women, and by extension society, remains severely compromised. It is easy to forget that patriarchy also precedes religious fundamentalism. Efforts to understand, assimilate, or 'root out' religious fundamentalists will not, of themselves, dismantle the crippling social limitations of extreme patriarchy. Although now nearly universal, patriarchy is not the oldest or, historically, even the most widely practised form of social organisation; it arises only with the advent of agriculture, a period that just about coincides with the emergence of all the world's major religions.

All religious fundamentalisms share distinguishable features. For Abrahamic traditions, whether the fundamentalist brand is Christian or Jewish or Muslim doesn't much matter for the essential social implications. Among those common features, fundamentalists claim with absolute certainty that theirs is the only truth and that any opposition is necessarily in league with forces of evil. Fundamentalism affirms a form of religious authority that admits neither criticism, change nor a different interpretation. Religious fundamentalism is always led by men, often by 'secondary level' males who feel threatened, and it invariably promotes ideology that seeks to preserve a historical patriarchy in amber. Certainly, fundamentalism props up particularly intolerant forms of patriarchy; at its most extreme it is tied to varying levels of abuse against women: beatings, maiming, and honour killings backed by conservative teachings about male headship that sanction control over women. Plenty of Muslim scholars explain convincingly that fundamentalism does not represent Islam or its primary tenets, that it has evolved to become the tail that wags the dog. Yet the need for Muslims to critique and address aspects of entrenched, institutional patriarchy remains even without religious fundamentalism.

In contrast to patriarchy, the other primary obstacle to progress, population pressure, is quite new. The role of population pressure as a root cause of many other developmental challenges must be brought back into the foreground, and it is certainly tied to entrenched patriarchy. Since the publication of *The Population Bomb* in 1968, many pundits have rightly criticised the overly simplistic and exaggerated Malthusian projections for mass starvation then made then by the authors Paul and Anne Ehrlich. Excellent work by Amartya Sen, Frances Moore Lappé, and others uncovers alternative explanations for famine and hunger, and the failure of the Ehrlichs' dire predictions for world famine in coming decades had the unintended consequence of pushing concerns about population growth into the distance. But the world's ability so far to avert widespread famine is only a part of the picture. The tougher issues are the sustainability of food or other resource production practices and how much time is available for new technologies to address swelling needs, which continue to grow geometrically.

Economists usually compare countries by using the supply of something needed divided by population, and then suggest ways to maximise growth in the numerator so that a country can make 'progress'. But it takes considerable time to develop new strategies and technologies and to get around economic and political road blocks to put them finally into place. An alarming number of countries are currently set to double their populations in a single generation, about twenty years. In any case, to imagine that countries can forever expand their economies to address growing needs is simply folly. A country can also improve living standards by steadily reducing the denominator – that is, the number of new people who will need a modicum of resources to support a decent life.

Recent research indicates that rapidly growing populations are indisputably tied to food, seed, and water shortages and to rising food riots or other forms of unrest. Lack of water is fast becoming the biggest developmental problem – particularly for its role in sustaining agriculture – leading to the suggestion that importing food is perhaps best viewed as a market for importing water. The amount of energy and water required by the US food system, for example, is unsustainable, and it is the largest food exporting country in the world. High population growth rates place ever more pressure on employment, particularly for the young, and on those working to support the unemployed. High unemployment rates are a major ingredient for violence and conflict, even without religious and ethnic tensions, making all environmental challenges exponentially more challenging. More countries will face protracted periods of some sort of crisis and leaders are more likely to dismiss calls for redistribution or reform on grounds that the country is facing a crisis.

Why women are so fundamental to social progress is that their position in society is inextricably tied to fertility rates, and in modern times high fertility rates are associated with resource shortages, poverty, unemployment, class inequality, political instability and civil unrest. Availability of modern birth control methods and campaigns to publicise the advantages of smaller families are essential ways to bring down fertility rates, and high proportions of literate and educated women make the success of those campaigns much more likely. But the most effective way to reduce fertility is simply by incorporating women into the labour force. Women everywhere work long hours – commonly more than men. But when women's work includes an income, at least some of which they can use for themselves and their children, they are not just less dependent on men: they delay marriage and child bearing, often to contribute to the income of their birth families. In short, they become economic assets for their families, especially when living on their own is not a viable social option. Moreover, as sisters and later as mothers, they tend to prioritise spending on children more than do men. These positive effects are heightened when women are routinely educated beyond primary school and when education provides skills for desirable jobs. Schooling itself tends to delay childbearing and reduce fertility, while education also encourages knowledge about and use of family planning, contraceptives and purposeful child spacing that, in turn, improves the health and life expectancy of women and children. When such women are given broader opportunities they tend to make better personal decisions, including perhaps a decision not to bear children. Finally, educated women are an enormous social asset toward addressing on-going challenges. To the extent that patriarchal structures resist or prevent the expansion of education and social roles for women, they preclude the best means for wide-reaching and positive social change. Put another way, the social costs of preserving patriarchy are already exceedingly high, and will only increase.

Population and the Ummah

For all the ways humans fall short of God's commands, there is at least one we have kept faithfully: 'be fruitful and multiply'. All Abrahamic traditions endorse this message, in one form or another. But these traditions emerged at a time when humans were adopting plough agriculture and were beginning to settle. Resulting food surpluses are squarely behind the development of advanced civilisation, where cities and their populations burgeoned. And yet, even in the time of Prophet Muhammad, at the beginning of the seventh century, best estimates place global population at only 300 million people – less than the current population of the United States. People didn't live very long, women often died in childbirth, and infant mortality was high. Agricultural surpluses also encouraged warfare. Social strategies for increasing populations, including polygyny and social status tied to fertility, were sorely needed. In the mid-1700s, centuries after Islam had already established highly advanced civilisations, world population still stood at around 600 million – still less than half the current population of India. After 1800, about the time the Industrial Revolution began to forever alter human prospects, the number was one billion people. Then by the 1960s, only a century and a half later, world population had tripled to three billion. Fifty years later, October 2011 marked our surpassing the seven billion mark. It's hard to fathom that when I was a small child in 1960, world population was still under three billion, so that in my short lifetime over four billion people have been added to the globe. You get the picture.

One can explain that exponential population growth has been pulled to the level at which we can produce food and other resources, a tribute to human innovation. But this addresses neither sustainable practice nor the very short intervals by which we are increasing global population by yet another billion – about every thirteen to fourteen years at present (if all goes as projected, it might even be twenty years before we exceed eight billion). Nor does it explain the lopsided nature of population gains, since about 97% of annual net growth now occurs outside the West. Let me be clear: current consumption levels in the US, if not arguably unethical, are clearly unsustainable even if its population growth were to cease tomorrow. As countries like China and India aspire to comparable consumption levels, world resource shortages are going to be unprecedented, especially among the poorer and more populous nations. This is not just because of the sheer 'Malthusian' number of people who will need food and water and housing and education and jobs, but rather because of the speed at which already precarious economies and governments will become overwhelmed, combined with the inadequate time the world will have to respond. Without extraordinary efforts to bring down human fertility before the next generation, the corresponding misery, unrest, and environmental disruption will be a swiftly mounting global problem, but the troubles will be very unevenly distributed among nations.

So how do things look for the *Ummah*? First, we can safely say on the basis of statistical evidence, that the most conservative or fundamentalist states – those most committed to traditional patriarchal authority – fare consistently poorly in developmental comparisons even against other nations at their economic level. Second, these same nations, and majority-Muslim states generally, post comparably high population growth rates that will raise ever higher developmental hurdles for coming generations, making it increasingly difficult to achieve the goals of social and political stability. Third, a major reason for these poor showings is the relatively low rankings for developmental measures associated with women.

Comprehensive social development is commonly measured using infant mortality rate (infant deaths per 1,000 live births). The current average rate for high-income countries is below five; by comparison, the average is nine times higher for majority-Muslim states (the seventeen lowest have an average rate of seventy-eight, higher even than for sub-Saharan Africa). Perhaps even more relevant here is maternal mortality rate (women dying in childbirth per 10,000 live births): for high-income countries, the average is sixteen, whereas it's 282 for majority-Muslim states, about eighteen times higher. For those same seventeen 'low development' majority-Muslim countries, about 680 of every 10,000 mothers die in childbirth, well above the dismal average of 619 for sub-Saharan Africa (meaning, these rates are not merely a function of poverty alone). The *ummah* is hurting.

To understand both rapid population growth and the time needed to respond to the challenges stemming from it, analysts often turn to the number of years it takes a given population to double. By the latest average annual growth rate, majority-Muslim nations will double their populations in only twenty-nine years. In comparison, the European Union nations will not double their regional population for another 233 years. The growth rate for Arab states is exactly double the world rate; already struggling with some of the highest youth unemployment rates in the world, 34% of the population is under fifteen years old – double that of high-income countries. A person in the middle of a high-income population will be almost forty years old; in majority-Muslim countries, that middle person will be twenty-three.

What about fertility and its implications? Generally, in countries where women bear more children, and bear them earlier in life, they are less likely to achieve literacy or appear in columns marking educational achievement or presence outside the home (a scenario common in traditional patriarchal countries). The fertility rate for majority-Muslim nations (3.1 children per adult woman) is nearly double that of high-income nations, and functional literacy for women is still less than 70%. Again, when compared to other countries of similar development level, the worst rates tend to be among the most traditional majority-Muslim states. It is a positive sign that female literacy rates for youth are often higher than for adults, thanks to more recent efforts to keep girls in school. Yet for majority-Muslim countries at every level of development, the youth literacy rates are higher still for males (and often notably so) reflecting continuing male preference.

By comparison to a typical woman in a majority-Muslim country, women in high-income countries are about two-and-a-half times more likely to finish secondary school – a minimum requirement for better employment; and they are about twice as likely to enter the workforce or hold a seat in the national government. Consistently, differences in the life chances of women and girls are associated more with rigid ideology than developmental level per se. The quickest way to understand this is by consulting the Human Development Report's overall rankings of gender inequality, in which about half of majority-Muslim countries rank towards the very back of the 146 countries listed: Yemen enjoys the dubious distinction of being 'first' in gender inequality, ranking dead last at 146th, but among the high-income nations Saudi Arabia ranks 135th.

Beyond the Impasse

If 'reclaiming al-Andalus' requires empowering Muslim women, then entrenched institutions that reserve power only for men together with exclusive interpretations of Islamic religious texts that venerate patriarchy stand in the way of overarching social progress at a time when giving women more power over their lives could not be more significant. On the side-view mirrors of many automobiles in the US appear the words 'things may be closer than they appear'. From my position, those who encourage the status quo or, worse, seek to establish even more extreme forms of patriarchy, only heap coals on themselves and their children in the very near future. Recent stories about electronic tagging of women in Saudi Arabia, or the shooting of the courageous student and education activist Malala Yousafzai in Pakistan, and the persecution of women in Iraq, Afghanistan and the Gulf, are not encouraging signs. Given the evidence against patriarchy, one wonders how long any thinking person imagines this could continue.

Bright, resourceful women have always exerted power outside the margins when operating within a patriarchy. But if the freedom and opportunity of Andalusian women was limited by class, the new empowerment must involve all classes – not merely the educated or privileged. Women generally must be seen, their public voices mixed with those of men. Transformations occur the moment women participate in the public sphere. For example Parvin Paidar notes that the Iranian revolution depended on the support of traditional Muslim women and youth, so that 'although the Islamic Republic seriously undermined women's position relative to their human rights, it gave its female supporters the opportunity for social participation and a sense of righteousness and self-worth', opening new political space for common women in a way that resonated with their traditional beliefs. She argues that this set the stage for some notable gains later during Khatami's moderate reformist presidency. This new era is marked by a resistance to oppressive patriarchal practices within Islamic structures. For example, Muslim women may accept arguments emphasising biological differences between men and women without accepting that they must necessarily give rise to inequality of rights, or accepting the premise that feminism and Islam are inherently incompatible. They could, indeed should, revisit an essentialism found in theories about the roles and rights of women, whether from Islam or the West. Paidar concludes that successful feminist efforts will require 'an alliance between secularists and Islamic feminists over specific issues at specific junctures'.

Even if viewed as a devil's bargain by some, Paidar's point about new political space in Iran is still valid: more authentically Islamic, the 'pragmatic approach to issues of difference and multiculturalism' will be more fruitful than 'debates on "Islam versus feminism" or "universalism versus cultural relativism"'. Efforts to include low-income women, those with rural and urban backgrounds, those more adept at using social media with those awakened to civil participation, are potentially as revolutionary as the spirit of al-Andalus.

Consider the important role women played, and are playing, in the Arab Spring. Yet, as Fadia Faqir notes in *Critical Muslim 1*, their contributions have been largely ignored or under-appreciated; and Faqir squarely identifies institutionalised patriarchy as the primary problem. Ironically, after demonstrating on the streets women went home to archaic familial hierarchies. Convincingly, in case after case, she catalogues aspects of gender inequality and discrimination before concluding: 'the Arab Spring will not endure, the shoots planted will not grow, without liberating the "last colony": Arab women.' Merryl Wyn Davies effectively takes the same position on patriarchy and gender equality in 'On Saudi Women Drivers' even though she questions the significance of the 'day of rage' – a well-publicised media event where some forty Saudi women drove cars in defiance of Saudi Arabian law. Davies writes, 'there can be no question that the Saudi insistence on debarring women from driving is wrong headed ... In reality, it is an empowerment of male weakness.' Whenever any protest becomes a 'media event' the context and significance of it often gets lost in favour of entertainment. This protest may be less trivial than it seems, however, since it also represents the right of women to work.

A related protest very easy to trivialise is Reem Asaad's successful boycott of Saudi shops selling women's undergarments, analysed by Thomas Lippman in his essay 'Saudi Women Shatter the Lingerie Ceiling'. Law and custom have required that Saudi shops for intimate female apparel must be owned and run by men, so that even those women shopping in upscale malls are assisted exclusively by men (mostly from South Asia). When, in 2006, efforts by Asaad and her supporters pushed through a government decree to transfer sales jobs in the lingerie shops to women, the matter seemed settled. But the decree was not enacted over the objections of traditional males and mullahs: women weren't trained to do these jobs; men would have to drive them to and from work; the shop front windows themselves would have to be covered. Undaunted, Asaad and her supporters used Facebook to organise an effective boycott while also training women to do retail tasks. After King Abdullah put his personal support behind the decree, shop owners were given until June 2012 to transfer those jobs to women.

Reading this story, some may focus on the hilarity or absurdity of fully veiled women arriving to purchase bras and panties from foreign male sales clerks, or shake their heads at the backwardness of 'Islamic' norms and move on. Yet, consider what the story implies. Increasingly open ranks of Muslim women (and men) are speaking out, using modern tools of communication and strategies inclusive of more traditional women or potential allies. This sounds a lot like the Arab Spring. Women want and need jobs, partly in response to rapidly rising costs of living, and they will continue to press for entry into the labour force in a wider range of jobs. Even in conservative Islamic states such as Saudi Arabia and Iran, women have long been a force in professions like law, medicine, and education; but this story is about women gaining access to retail jobs in an economic sector previously unavailable. Reclaiming Andalusia means integrity and material decency as much as it means an open society. Their men and their families need their income. These working women will most likely delay marriage and bear fewer children to support. And, when they face obstacles, they are increasingly likely to respond with organisation and activism.

Lippman concludes: 'these changes will meet entrenched opposition, but the economic and demographic forces behind them seem irresistible. The transition would be easier if women were permitted to drive ... because growing ranks of employed women will build pressure for it. Thousands of Saudi women have driving licences issued by other countries; they will be ready when the day comes.' Such remarks reflect the heart of this essay: educating and training women to enter the work force, giving them more control over personal decisions, and expanding their roles in public life represents the best strategy for positive social change. It is likely the only strategy to bring the sort of developments that liberate not just women but everyone in a society, and to deliver them quickly enough to avoid a future dominated by hardship, conflict, and further global isolation.

Beyond the matter of what's right or fair, empowering women is a force for great transformation. Those who continue to support extreme patriarchy understand this. Is there room for a dialogue with those who see efforts to empower women as 'evil' and 'un-Islamic'? There must be. Efforts to exclude them entirely will be counter-productive. But, like it or not, despite the resistance of orthodoxy and establishment Islam, efforts to empower women must eventually happen. Fortunately, the *ummah* has rich and well-established traditions to push for changes that empower women, value them for their intellectual and practical skills, and fully honour their personhood – al-Andalus being the prime example, where even some non-elite women were employed as civil servants and participated fully in social and public life. Lasting change in Muslim societies can only come when all Muslim women, regardless of education or status, are accepted as rightful agents of change. When this happens, no amount of fundamentalist religion will put the genie back in the bottle.

IBERIA'S NEW MUSLIMS

Marvine Howe

One balmy evening last summer, hundreds of ecstatic Muslim teenagers, many in headscarves, throbbed and swayed to the lyrics of Islamic pop singer Maher Zain at the sedate Garcia Lorca Theatre in Madrid's working class suburb of Getafe. The Lebanese-born star sang mostly of peace and love in English and Arabic, and referred to 'my brothers and sisters' from Palestine, Morocco, Syria, but also Madrid and Barcelona. The evening reached its climax when a little boy presented a Syrian flag to Zain, who draped it around his shoulders and declared: 'I'm not political, but babies are dying there; this song is for Syria: "Freedom".' The audience, which included a sprinkling of Spaniards, exploded with cries of 'freedom, freedom'. Afterwards, the organisers carefully marshalled the wildly cheering crowd out of the theatre in small groups to avoid any clash with the crowds massed on the square for a traditional Spanish parade of *fallas*, or giant paper mache figures, and fireworks. The two worlds mingled happily without incident. It was the first ever such concert in the Spanish capital, sponsored by the local Muslim Youth organisation and Muslim Relief, the Spanish branch of a British-based Islamic charity. There were no special security forces, no protest demonstrations, not even right-wing media charges of 'Islamisation'. Yet as recently as 2010, one Muslim girl, who chose to wear a headscarf in a public school in Madrid, caused a national uproar, with angry right-wingers screaming against 'a second Islamic invasion', forcing the teenager to change schools. For Muslim and non-Muslim observers alike, the fact that the Getafe concert happened without polemics, in fact went unnoticed by the general public, is a positive step towards the normalisation of Spanish Islam.

Given its turbulent history, the return of Islam to Iberia is of special significance. But who are Iberia's new Muslims? How have they coped in this land, still haunted by the contradictory legacy of al-Andalus, as the peninsula was known under Islamic rule, with its dark phantoms of war and pillage and tangible reminders of the brilliant multicultural civilisation of Cordoba, Seville, Toledo, and Granada? How have the newcomers been received by a largely Roman Catholic population in the post-9/11 age?

It's best to begin with the small community of 'old Muslims', people of Moroccan descent, who inhabit two Spanish enclaves in northern Morocco. Ceuta was occupied by Spain in the fifteenth century and Melilla by Portugal at the same time, but turned over to Spain in the seventeenth century. Through the years, the large Muslim minority in the military outposts was relegated to second class status, much like other colonised peoples. Few Muslim natives of Ceuta and Melilla enjoyed Spanish citizenship. Then under Spain's 1967 law on religious freedom, Muslims in the enclaves were permitted to form associations and began to assert their identity. Initially, the associations were of a religious nature, but in the 1980s, they developed social and political characteristics and demanded access to Spanish citizenship and civil rights. Finally after strong protests against discrimination, many Ceutis and Melillans were granted Spanish nationality. The Muslims, who now consist of over half of the enclaves' total population of 160,000, began to form their own local political parties. They attracted national attention when two women, in their early thirties and wearing headscarves, were appointed to the regional parliaments. Salima Abdessalam, an economist and a parliamentarian for the *Coalicion por Melilla*, devotes much of her time to non-governmental organisations and is critical of the authorities for promoting community solidarity for 'purely electoral purposes'. Fatima Hamed Hossain, a lawyer, social activist and member of the Ceuta Assembly since 2007, belongs to the *Union Democratica Ceuti*, a political group engaged in the fight against social inequalities in the enclaves. When asked about Spanish opinions of Islam, she responded: 'Am I not as Spanish as any other citizen?' She pointed out that even second and third generation Muslims have been brought up as foreigners, yet 'they pay the same taxes and the same mortgages as any other citizen'.

The first foreign Muslims to venture back to Iberia after the peninsula had been ethnically and spiritually cleansed by the beginning of the seventeenth century were university students who arrived in the late 1950s to early 1970s. Those who headed for Portugal came from the country's former colonies, mainly Mozambique. The students who went to Spain were predominantly from the Middle East, and came as a response to Generalissimo Francisco Franco's overtures to the Arab world.

Some of these pioneers are still around and lead the modern Islamic communities. One of the most noted is Abdool Majid Vakil, who travelled from Mozambique to Lisbon to study economics in 1956. His father had left India in 1900 to seek job opportunities in Portugal's East African colony, where he eventually owned the leading department store. Upon graduation, Abdool Majid Vakil took a post as research assistant at Lisbon University's School of Economics, married a Portuguese woman, who converted to Islam, and they had three children. He moved back to Mozambique in 1973 to take up the appointment of Minister of Planning and Finance in the colonial government. He acknowledges that he had not anticipated Portugal's revolution of 25 April 1974, and subsequent independence of the colonies. But he readily accepted an advisory position in the new independent government of Mozambique. Vakil's wife, however, was alarmed at the increased insecurity and fled with their children to Portugal. He followed them. Vakil was a co-founder of the Islamic Community in Lisbon in 1966; he was elected its president in 1988, a post he still holds. He is apt to issue statements that urge calm and understanding. For example, when protest against the anti-Islamic video 'Innocence of Muslims' erupted in September 2012, Vakil appealed to people of different faiths 'to live in concord, harmony and mutual respect'. Calling on Muslims to be 'exemplary citizens' he urged them not give in to 'the wave of exaltation sweeping the world'.

Slight of build, with greying hair and impeccably groomed, Vakil insists that most Portuguese Muslims are better integrated than Muslims in Spain and other European countries. 'Probably because we live together, not in separate communities, and speak the same language', he says. When I met him in his office in downtown Lisbon, Vakil raised the need for more interfaith dialogue. He deplored the Portuguese public's lack of knowledge about Islam and stressed that the place to begin is with better religious studies in schools. He was optimistic about the future because of the growing interest in Islam, as more Portuguese schools send classes to visit the Central Mosque and hear talks on Islam.

Vakil's equivalent in Spain is the Damascus-born Riay Tatary. He came to Spain in 1970 to study Medicine at the University of Oviedo, and is today imam of the Central Mosque of Madrid and president of the Union of

Islamic Communities of Spain (UCIDE), the largest Muslim federation in the country. As head of UCIDE, Tatary signed the 1992 accords between the Spanish state and the Protestant, Jewish and Muslim minorities. The accords sought to regularise the situation of the main religious minorities. Tatary was named President of the new Islamic Commission of Spain (CIE), set up to represent all Muslims of the country in their dealings with the central government. Tatary's conservative leadership has been increasingly contested by a younger generation of activists and North African immigrants, who have formed new federations and demand that the CIE be opened to include their representatives.

Tatary is self-confident and conciliatory but always ready to fight his corner. At sixty-four, he does not look like a grandfatherly figure about to retire. The grandee granted me an audience at his office in Madrid's Central Mosque from where he runs the UCIDE empire. 'I have good relations with the state', the UCIDE chief asserted, adding that he has cooperated with both the former Socialist government and the current conservative administration. He pointed out that he has been given the Civil Merit by King Juan Carlos. He said he was working with the authorities to open the national commission to new members but stressed that many groups 'have no roots or have political aims' and must be thoroughly investigated. While praising Spain's constitution for granting immigrants the same rights as citizens, he emphasised that Muslims still faced difficulties over the implementation of these rights. A main problem is religious education – there are some 200,000 Muslim children in Spanish schools, but only 10,000 can go to Islamic classes. Difficulties in opening mosques in neighbourhoods controlled by the far-right, lack of enough cemeteries, the misrepresentation of Islam, particularly during elections, were other important issues. However, speaking as someone who 'spent forty-two years of my life here and raised five children', Tatary thought that 'Spain is one of the non-Muslim majority countries where Muslims are most accepted'.

The first mass immigration of Muslims to the Iberian Peninsula occurred in 1974-5, in the wake of Portugal's revolution and the decolonisation of Portuguese Africa. Nearly a million refugees flocked to Portugal – Portuguese colonials and Africans as well as ethnic Indians who had served in the colonial administration and army or feared insecurity in the newly independent nations. They were called *retornados*, regardless of their ethnic origin.

Thousands of these immigrants were Muslim who formed the nucleus of modern Portugal's Islamic community. They were people like Jose Amara Queta, son of a Sunni Muslim tribal leader in former Portuguese Guinea. Queta, who was educated in a Roman Catholic school, held a senior position in the colonial Department of Education until Guinea became independent in 1975. He was labelled a collaborator and spent three and a half years in jail. He managed to escape to Portugal where he began a new life in construction, and sent for his wife and five children. On retirement, he took a course in the hotel business and worked as chief steward at Hotel Ritz in Lisbon. Today, Queta is owner of a stationery store, president of the Neighbourhood Association and administrator of the mosque at Quinta do Mocho, a district of social housing north-east of Lisbon.

Portugal also received a wave of Ismaili immigrants from Africa in the mid 1970s. They had Portuguese nationality and spoke the language. Faranaz Keshavjee, a journalist and social anthropologist, was five years old when her family moved to Portugal as *retornados*. Her father had owned a prosperous furniture shop in Lourenco Marques, but had to leave everything behind. Initially, they lived with thirty other Ismailis crowded into an apartment in Lisbon's Bairro Alto neighbourhood. Faranaz, a tall woman with auburn hair, obtained a master's degree in social psychology from Lisbon University, attended the Ismaili Institute for Islamic Studies and Humanities in London, and obtained a PhD from Cambridge. Her family chose to live in Lisbon, she explained, because 'the Portuguese are more receptive to immigrant communities than other Europeans'. She stressed that relations between the Ismailis and the Sunni majority are good. 'We respect each other and do our best to bridge the differences, not make them a source of conflict.'

Another group of Muslims who appeared in the 1970s-80s were Spanish converts to Islam, who believed they had a special link to al-Andalus. Some were followers of the controversial Sheikh Abdalqadir as-Sufi, who called for the restoration of the Caliphate, advocated slavery, and spoke favourably of Hitler. Born Ian Dallas in Scotland in 1930, he wrote plays and television scripts and did some acting before embracing Islam. After establishing a Sufi centre in Norwich, England, he moved to southern Spain. In the early 1980s, he established the Murabitun World Movement with the aim of reintroducing the Islamic currency of the gold dinar and silver dirham. One of Sheikh Abdalqadir's more positive contributions was the construction of the

'Grand Mosque' of Granada. A community of Spanish converts to Islam flourished around the mosque. But after a few years, many converts left the sheikh's movement to form other organisations. The Sheikh himself abruptly moved to Cape Town, South Africa, where he built a mosque and a school for Muslim leaders. While retaining his links to the Granada Mosque, the sheikh has left many unanswered questions.

Over the years, I have come to know a number of Iberian converts to Islam. In Portugal, they were generally discreet, sometimes closet Muslims. Lisbon's Central Mosque organised classes to help them adapt to the community. In Spain however, they often assumed leadership roles in Muslim organisations because they had better knowledge of the country's bureaucracy and knew how speak to the authorities. These converts included people like Felix Herrero, the outspoken former head of the Federation of Islamic Religious Entities (FEERI), Amparo Sanchez Rosell, a dedicated leader, organiser and head of the Islamic Cultural Centre of Valencia, and Laure Rodriguez Quiroga, the charismatic president of the Union of Muslim Women of Spain. And then there was Mansur Escudero, one of the most respected leaders of contemporary Spanish Islam.

In June 2008, I made my way along the fertile Guadalquivir Valley west of Cordoba to the bucolic town of Almodovar del Rio to meet Escudero and his American-born wife, Kamila Toby. The couple ran the Islamic Junta, which organises Islamic events, publishes books on Islam and operates the first Islamic website in Spain, from their spacious farmhouse. At the time of our meeting, Escudero was troubled by what he called Madrid's 'discrimination' against Muslims. 'We informed the government that since Spain is now a secular state, we want the same level of cooperation as it has with the Roman Catholic Church', he said, citing the 'big discrepancy' in Spain's giving millions of Euros to finance Catholic schools and other institutions and just a few thousand Euros for Muslims. Looking more like a country doctor in slacks and polo shirt than an Islamic firebrand, Escudero related the story of his unconventional path to Islam. Born in a village near Malaga, he was raised by strict Roman Catholic parents, studied with Jesuits and as a medical student, became a Marxist. Graduating from Madrid's Complutense University, he specialised in neuro-psychiatry at Cordoba's Mental Health Centre and established the first Spanish Centre for Group Therapy. He finally 'accepted' Islam in 1979 during a visit to Norwich, England, where he met Sheikh Abdelqadir and the community of British-born converts. Escudero said he joined the Sheikh's Murabitun, which had started out as a Sufi movement, but he left three years later 'because it had become like a sect, based on the authority of the teacher'. In 1980, Escudero created the first association of Spanish Muslims, the Society for the Return to Islam in Spain, and, in 1989, founded the Junta Islamica. Elected head of FEERI, Escudero signed the 1992 accords of cooperation with the Spanish government and became co-secretary general of the Islamic Commission of Spain, along with Riay Tatary.

But his relationship with FEERI turned sour. On the first anniversary of the 2004 Madrid terrorist attacks, attributed to al-Qaeda sympathisers, Escudero issued a fatwa in the name of the Islamic Commission, declaring Osama bin Laden and his organisation 'apostates' for 'horrendous crimes'. It was the first time the leader of a major Muslim organisation had taken such a strong and unambiguous position on Bin Laden. Controversy followed. While many Muslim leaders approved of the fatwa, some argued that he had no authority to proclaim a fatwa. Escudero resigned from FEERI, which has been plagued by leadership problems ever since. I saw Escudero several times before his untimely death from a heart attack on 3 October 2010, and was impressed by his progressive view of Spanish Islam. A strong critic of gender inequality, he supported the Islamic Feminist Movement in Spain. A firm believer in inter-faith cooperation, he urged the Vatican to open the great eighth-century Cordoba cathedral-mosque as 'an ecumenical space'. He spoke in favour of a just, secular state as 'the best defence of religious freedom'.

Another member of the Almodovar del Rio group is Abdennur Prado, formerly head of the Catalan Islamic council. He has written eloquently about being a Muslim in twenty-first-century Spain and the difficulties of belonging to a religious minority, persecuted for 500 years and now under attack in the era of globalisation by those who equate Islam with violence, totalitarianism and misogyny. In a ground-breaking essay, he describes the emergence of new Islamic thought in contemporary al-Andalus, born in 'the struggle against the Franco dictatorship and for the consolidation of democracy'. In the essay, Prado presents some leading members of the movement: Abderaman Mohamed Maanan, fifty-two, a Spaniard of Moroccan origin from Melilla, author of the critical commentary and translation, *Tafsir of*

Quran; his disciple Abdelmumin Aya, a Spanish convert, known for studies of comparative religions; and another convert, Hashim Ibrahim Cabrera, an artist from Seville and an authority on Islamic jurisprudence.

The arrival of large numbers of immigrants during the boom years of the 1980s and 1990s expanded the Muslim communities of Iberia. In Spain, most of the newcomers came from Morocco and Algeria because of their proximity. They took jobs in construction, the services or as farm labourers. Abdel Rahman Essaadi, a Moroccan professor of Arabic, who travelled to Spain in 1992, is a typical example. He became a seasonal labourer, harvesting tomatoes in the fields of Badajoz, potatoes at Victoria, oranges at Valencia, olives at Jaen, strawberries at Huelva, and pears and apples at Lerida. Joining the Spanish migrant aid network (Acoge) as a volunteer, Essadi worked his way up as trainer, social worker and expert in inter-cultural development. When I met him at the southern port of Lepe in 2006, he had been appointed president of the Andalusian Federation of Acoges, the first Moroccan to achieve such a position. Other immigrants also received a boost from the Spanish trade union movement. Mohammed Haidour, a student dissident from Morocco, escaped to Madrid with a group of soccer fans in 1986. As an undocumented migrant, he held an assortment of jobs from waiter and apprentice carpenter to salesman of cleaning products. From the outset, he joined the Association of Moroccan Immigrants, supported by the Spanish trade union confederation, Comisiones Obreras, which itself had started out in exile in France and Germany in opposition to the Franco regime. Today Haidour is on the national executive board of Comisiones Obreras, responsible for the department of Immigration.

The economic migrants to Portugal came mainly from the former African colonies. Braima Djalo, a thirty-five-year old shopkeeper from Guinea-Bissau, is a good example. He arrived in 1999 and has worked on numerous construction projects around the country – so many, in fact, that he boasts of having 'built modern Portugal'. I first met the slight Djalo during the summer of 2006, at a café on Lisbon's Rossio Square, where Africans usually congregate to get their news from home. 'There was no stability in Guinea and it wasn't safe to stay in the region', Djalo said, explaining that he decided to emigrate after rebel militias invaded the province of Casamance and destroyed his store and all his belongings. Leaving his wife and two children with his mother, he joined a group of sub-Saharan migrants who sailed from

Mauritania in a fragile fishing boat, or *patera*, for Spain's Canary Islands. Detained on arrival, the boatpeople were flown to Madrid with an order of expulsion. Djalo managed to find work on a fishing boat that was headed for Portugal, where he got a job with a construction company which gave him a contract, enabling him to obtain residence and eventually bring his wife to Portugal. I visited Djalo a few years later in his comfortable two-room flat at Venda Nova, a working class suburb of Lisbon, popular with Africans. He introduced me to his Senegalese wife Assinatou, who was pregnant and studying Portuguese so she could get a job cleaning offices and residences. While he is a practising Muslim, he has advised his wife not to wear a headscarf in public as this might reduce her chances of finding work. They have decided to make Portugal their home and have applied to bring over their two children under the family reunion law. Although Djalo was able to purchase a second-hand Renault on his wages, he hopes to get out of construction and find a job that will let him live at home with his family.

At first, Iberians were unperturbed by this influx of immigrants. There was a demand for imported labour and immigrants filled that dire need. Like other Europeans, they viewed immigrants as temporary guest workers who would eventually return home. But in 1991 Europe closed its doors to most of the world, requiring visas from 110 countries, including all of Africa. This exclusion prompted the invasion of *sin papeles* or undocumented migrants along Spain's Costa del Sol, Africans' closest gateway to Europe. Many Spaniards showed compassion for the boatpeople in their rickety makeshift *pateras* and the thousands who lost their lives in the perilous crossing. Numerous non-government organisations, often linked to the Roman Catholic Church, devoted substantial resources to aiding the newcomers, a majority of whom were Muslims.

The stories of *sin papeles* are truly heart-rending. Aziz Darrai, a homeless orphan from Casablanca, stowed away in a ship for Marseilles, age fifteen. He was caught and sent back to Morocco. He taught himself several trades, as baker's assistant, carpentry, electrician and bus driver, but did not give up his European dream. He made three more attempts, hiding on ferries going to Spain – he couldn't afford the 2,000 Euro fare for a place in a *patera*. On Aziz's last journey, concealed under a truck, Aziz was accidently hit by the truck when they landed at Algeciras. He was helped to the local mosque from there he was taken to the hospital. He was diagnosed with a fractured pelvis, advanced kidney failure and other ailments. The local Parish of San Pedro y San Francisco Javier agreed to take in the Moroccan until a new kidney could be found. I saw Aziz several times in the parish, where he was highly appreciated as a general handyman. On my last visit, I learned he had received a kidney transplant, married a Moroccan immigrant and now has two babies. But he is still doing odd jobs because of the unemployment crisis.

As more and more boatpeople washed up along the shores of the Costa del Sol and Canary Islands, Spain realised it had an immigration problem. The occasional stowaways and boatloads of *sin papeles* had turned into a big business: a modern-day slave trade. Drug traffickers organised flotillas of *pateras* and *Cayucosi* (rudimentary long distance vessels) with their human cargo from all over Africa for prices ranging between 2,000 and 45,000 Euros. Curiously, neighbouring Portugal was not a target of this naval assault. Nevertheless, it received its share of irregular immigration, mostly Brazilians, but also Muslims from India, Pakistan, Bangladesh and Africa, who arrived on tourist visas, and stayed on in an illegal limbo. At first, the Iberian governments did what other Europeans had done before them, resolving the problem through mass legalisations. In fact, Spain achieved a European record of sorts, regularising some 700,000 immigrants in 1995.

At the same time, Spain and Portugal developed what came to be known as the most liberal immigration policies in Europe, and openly opposed the growing 'fortress' mentality in other countries of the European Union. Their socialist governments set out to establish a humanistic model of immigration and integration based on the principle of 'Interculturalism'. This was defined as the interaction of different communities with respect for diversity, within the national law. While the Iberian neighbours shared the same aims, the structure was very different. Portugal established a centralised authority, the High Commission for Immigration and Ethnic Minorities, whose job it was to inform immigrants of their rights and facilitate their integration by acting as a bridge between immigrants and government agencies. In Spain, the Secretariat for Immigration and Emigration was set up under the Ministry of Labour and charged with implementing a 'Strategic Plan for Citizenship and Integration'. Under Spain's decentralised system, it was the regional and municipal governments that assumed responsibility for the integration of immigrants through health, education and social programmes.

But as the invasion of African *pateras* continued unabated, fellow Europeans accused the Iberians of being 'soft on illegals' and pressed them to defend the continent's southern borders. The increasingly vocal far-right multiplied its warnings against 'the Islamisation' of Europe. Most Europeans were in no mood to welcome a new influx of Muslim immigrants, following the terrorist attacks by Muslim extremists in Madrid and London and the riots in Paris. Even Spaniards, who had reacted calmly to the deadly assault on Madrid's commuter trains in 2004, began to show the strain. In 2006, the peak year for boat people, Islamophobia reached its highest level, with 60% of Spaniards holding a negative opinion of Muslims, compared to 37% in 2005.

Faced with new signs of xenophobia at home, Madrid and Lisbon took tougher stands on immigration. The Iberian states participated more actively in the European Border Patrol (FRONTEX) and its Atlantic Patrol, tightening their own controls. Accords were made with several African states for the repatriation of irregular immigrants, migrant requests for residence were reviewed on a case by case basis and volunteer agencies focused more on assisting integration than on relief. The system appears to be working, with a noticeable decrease in the arrival of boatpeople. The migrant mafias simply diverted their traffic eastwards to Turkey and the border with Greece.

Then the worldwide economic crisis struck Spain and Portugal. Their new-found prosperity began to evaporate. Brutal unemployment rates, reaching a European record of 25% in Spain and over 15% in Portugal, changed everything. The Socialist governments, with their enlightened vision of the social welfare state, were voted out of office for mismanaging the economy. The conservative opposition which came to power in both countries was obliged to make drastic cuts across the board to curb the soaring national debts.

While both Spain and Portugal continue to pay lip service to immigrant integration based on the principle of interculturalism, many programmes for migrant integration have been drastically slashed or eliminated. Madrid has gone even further in cutting off free education and health care for undocumented foreigners, the hallmark of Iberia's progressive immigration policy. The decision to deprive *sin papeles* of these benefits stirred a furious public outcry. In regions like Catalonia with a large immigrant population, volunteer agencies and representatives of the medical professions have refused to follow the ruling.

Recession has forced many Muslim immigrants to leave Iberia. According to a Spanish report, in January 2012, the Moroccan migrant population was 783,000, a drop of 22,000 from 2011. There is a similar trend in Portugal. Sheikh David Munir, who heads Lisbon's Central Mosque, says that attendance at Friday prayers has dropped by 10 to 15 per cent from an average 1,000 faithful two years ago. Taslin Rana, a businessman who heads the Bangladeshi community in Lisbon, said members had plummeted from 10,000 in 2010 to 3,000 by 2012.

However, despite diminishing numbers and new hardships, it is clear that Muslims on the Iberian Peninsula are there to stay. In Spain, Muslims have assumed new visibility and become more assertive and conscious of their rights, while in Portugal, they are increasingly part of the national fabric.

In 2012, the twentieth anniversary of the accords regulating relations between Spain and its religious minorities, an agreement was reached to enlarge the Islamic Commission of Spain. It will be expanded from its original two federations to include representation of all recognised groups – over one thousand. In what has been called a coup d'etat, fourteen Muslim federations met in Madrid in late November to oust Riay Tatary, the historic leader of the Islamic Commission. There was only one dissenting voice from Tatary's UCIDE. The new interim President is Moroccan-born Mounir Benjelloun, the popular leader of the Islamic Federation of Murcia. His vice-president is the widely respected Spanish convert, Amparo Sanchez Rosell.

There is also a new solidarity among Muslims in Spain, more co-operation between the main communities, the Moroccans and Pakistanis and the Spanish converts. Increasingly, Spain's Muslim community is prepared to show a public face, heedless of emerging anti-Muslim attitudes, particularly in the heavily immigrant areas of Catalonia. Many mosques and prayer halls have outgrown their original space and seek new premises, but frequently encounter opposition from Neighbourhood Associations. It sometimes takes an extremely deft mayor to arrange a compromise between Muslim communities, aware of their rights under the law, and citizens, who complain of noise and congestion at Islamic prayer times. Mosques and Islamic groups frequently organise open door campaigns, holding cultural events in places of worship to win friends in the general Spanish public.

A new Muslim political party, Catalunya Omnium, was formed in Barcelona at the end of 2011 by fifty Moroccan and Pakistani Muslims. It will take part in regional elections in 2014. The spokesman for the group, Rachid el Attabi, said the party's aim was to win the votes of some 500,000 Muslim residents in Catalunya. 'It's time to defend our rights', said El Attabi, owner of a halal butcher's shop in Barcelona. The news was greeted with a typical tirade from Josep Anglada, head of the Islamophobic party, Plataforma per Catalunya. Anglada called the move, 'another step in the Islamist strategy to penetrate institutions and accumulate political power'.

Some Spanish Muslim organisations have made a mark beyond the country's borders. For example, in 2005, the Islamic Junta of Catalunya organised the first International Congress on Islamic Feminism, with the declared goal of 'developing activism in pursuit of the rights of Muslim women'. There have been four congresses since, grouping prominent Islamic feminists from around the world. Natalia Andújar, vice-president of the Junta, said that the conferences have shown 'the pluralism in which Muslim women live Islam, a diversity that we must respect and celebrate'.

Another landmark event in the development of Islam in Spain is the establishment of two new satellite television stations, funded by Iran and Saudi Arabia. While both stations broadcast in the Spanish language and are beamed to Latin America as well as Spain, they are in essence very different. Hispan TV's programme is more ideological and mainly produced in Iran. Its objective appears to be the spread of Shi'ite Islam in Spain and Latin America. Early in 2013, however, the Spanish government – apparently under pressure from the European Union – shut down the Iranian channel, and Tehran threatened legal action in the name of free speech. Cordoba TV, on the other hand, is produced in Spain and staffed mostly by local Muslims. 'We are a Spanish channel with an Islamic point of view', says Yusef Abajo, the Spanish Muslim spokesman for Cordoba TV.

Soeren Kern, a senior fellow at Madrid's Strategic Studies Group and a known Islamophobe, describes Cordoba TV as 'the brainchild of a radical Saudi cleric, Abdul Aziz el Fawzan'. He goes on to say that its aim is 'to propagate the extremist Wahhabi sect of Islam'. Emphasising that Iran is also promoting Spanish broadcasts in Latin American countries, Kern typically concludes that this is 'another indication of how radical Islam is advancing worldwide, fuelled substantially by what the West pays for their oil'. But in a detailed report on Cordoba TV, Muslim feminist Laure Rodriguez Quiroga points out that the station is directed at non-Muslims as well as Muslims and employs a number of women in key posts. She also notes that while there is some religious content aimed at correcting erroneous views of Islam, most of the schedule is focused on news, and social and cultural issues. Several friends who have joined Cordoba TV, told me of the open and relaxed atmosphere. Laila Rattab, a young Spanish Muslim of Moroccan parents, who has studied journalism at Madrid's Complutense University and hosts a women's programme, told me she has broad leeway to discuss women's issues. Her Moroccan husband, Houssien El Ouariachi, who holds a doctorate in History from the University of Granada and works for the Belgium-based Alliance for Freedom and Dignity, manages a news programme. He says he has total licence to report events from around the world, including human rights issues.

While Portugal's young Islamic community has been slow to participate in politics, Muslims are present in business, finance and the professions. Aside from a few exceptions like banker Abdul Majid Vakil, they are not very visible for the simple reason that Muslims have been generally well integrated into Portuguese society. One Muslim immigrant who has made a name for himself in politics and social causes is Mamadou Ba, a forty-one-year-old Senegalese citizen. Founder of the Associação Luso-Senegalesa in the mid-1990s, Ba is a leader of SOS Racismo, an international volunteer agency, and an activist in the left-wing Portuguese party Bloco de Esquerda. He received recognition for his advocacy work on behalf of immigrants in 2011, when he was named one of the ten 'Immigrant Activists in Europe' by Oldenburg University in Holland. Another well-known Muslim is Zeinal Abedin Mohamed Bava, the dynamic CEO of Portugal Telecom, who has become a role model for young Portuguese Muslims. Born in 1965 in Mozambique, Zeinal Bava and his family, business people of Indian stock, migrated to Portugal after the 1974 revolution. The Bavas opened a small furniture factory in Lisbon and sent Zeinal to England, where he studied Electronic Engineering at University College London. He began his career at Portugal Telecom as chief financial officer of the Pay-TV division in 1999, held key management roles in the company's main business units, and rapidly made his way up the corporate ladder. In 2008, at the age of forty-six, Zeinal Bava was appointed Chief Executive Officer of the telecommunications company, with interests not only in Portugal but also in Brazil, Africa and Asia. Named the 'Best CEO' in European telecommunications by the

'Institutional Investor' in 2010, he was re-elected CEO in April 2012 for the term ending in 2014. Although Bava's beaming face often appears in the Portuguese press, it is usually associated with advances of Portugal Telecom. Very little has been written about his family life, aside from a 2008 profile published by the Portuguese weekly Visao, which described him as 'a tireless worker capable of spending fourteen hours a day in his office, he only has two passions as far as anyone knows: his career and his family'. It notes that Bava's wife Fatima is a Roman Catholic, their three children go to a Catholic school and Bava is 'discreet' about his own Islamic faith. 'He doesn't talk about it and his co-workers don't ask him anything.'

Most of Iberia's Muslims are not obsessed with the legacy of al-Andalus. Some converts feel a special connection to the civilisation that flourished under Moorish rule. Some even go as far as to cite DNA studies that allegedly show that many Iberians share Muslim or Jewish bloodlines. Moroccans and other Muslim immigrants express special pride in Moorish architectural and scientific achievements dating from Medieval times. However, in my numerous conversations with Muslims of Spain and Portugal, no one has ever suggested the restoration of Islamic rule over the peninsula. Al-Qaeda militants who call on Muslims 'to recover al-Andalus' are dismissed as madmen. 'We don't reclaim land', says the Spanish-Moroccan union leader, Mohamed Haidour, but 'recognition' that Islam is part of Spain's past. Moroccan social activist and TV anchor El Ouariachi says that 'Spanish left-wing intellectuals hold that we are the same people on both sides of the Mediterranean' but the majority of Spaniards prefer to ignore their Islamic roots. The Spanish convert Mansur Escudero told me shortly before his death in 2010: 'Al Andalus is a paradigm for *convivencia* among the three great monotheistic religions. What appeals to Muslims is the model of civilisation, the arts and sciences that were developed here under Islamic rule. It has nothing to do with recovery of territory.'

RECONQUISTA 2.0

Jordi Serra del Pino

I am a fan of 'Sota Terra', a programme on TV3 in Catalonia. A few months ago, one particular show caught my attention. It was about an archaeological excavation in Balaguer, a town in the north-east of Spain. The purpose of the programme was to determine if Balaguer had been an important city of al-Andalus during Muslim rule. That struck me as a bit odd. Balaguer is in the province of Lleida in Catalonia. And Catalonia, I thought, had little to do with Muslim Spain. Indeed, I had always believed that the Muslim presence in the northern half of the Iberian Peninsula was short and not very significant. But as the programme developed it exposed my deep ignorance. The archaeological excavation revealed a totally different version to the one I thought was the accepted, dominant history of the region. Not only did Balaguer turn out to be one of the most important cities of the Andalusian North, what is known as al-Andalus Superior, but the presence and impact of Muslims in Catalonia had been longer and far more relevant than I had imagined. I only knew that the first Umayyad wave had gone as far as south ern France until they were stopped at the Battle of Tours (732), and that Cordoba and Granada were great Muslim cities. By the end of the programme, I had learned that the Umayyads not only conquered but had settled in most of Catalonia, irrigated vast areas and founded new cities. And there was something more. The programme argued that to describe the process of expelling people from the land they had lived and cultivated for several centuries as the Reconquista (to conquer back or to recover) was simply absurd. The process is more properly described as usurpation.

There was a reason for my ignorance. I was born in Barcelona, possibly the most famous city in Spain, but also the capital of Catalonia, which is an 'autonomous community of Spain' and has the official status of a 'nationality'. But when I was born Spain was still a totalitarian regime under Franco's dictatorship; at that time, Catalan names were banned, and my parents could not register me with my real name: Jordi. Instead, they had to use the Spanish translation of my name: Jorge. At school we spoke Catalonian but our homework and examinations had to be done in Spanish, and signed with our Spanish names. The lessons and subjects were also filtered according to the dominant ideology and al-Andalus, the prime example of diversity and *convivencia* in the history of Iberian peninsula, was hardly mentioned – a deliberate act of suppressing the history and heritage of Spain. Instead, we were regaled with the exploits of the Reconquista which, we were taught, forged modern Spain. One thing is true though, modernity came to Spain riding the Reconquista horse and both were here to stay. We were taught the features of the Reconquista as dogma and its main actors, the Catholic monarchs, were presented as legendary characters. Moreover, the Reconquista was a spiritual endeavour, led by Isabella and Ferdinand, who founded the nation that would rule the world in the forthcoming years. To reinforce the notion that all the good in Spain comes from the Reconquista, the previous times had to be presented as worse, darker, evil; hence, the need to wipe out any traits, features, remains, history and heritage of al-Andalus. Thus, very little was explained about the contributions of Islam to Spanish culture, the works of intellectuals like ibn Rushd also known as Averroes (1126–1198) who was instrumental in the preservation of the philosophy of Plato and Aristotle. Mosheh ben Maimon, commonly known as Maimonides (1135–1204) was also overlooked and yet his contribution to Jewish law, ethics and Jewish history makes him one of the top Jewish scholars of all times. Of course, talking of figures like those would have shattered the cliché that Moors were barbaric, it would have required an acknowledgement of the fact that al-Andalus enjoyed substantial periods of peace and prosperity in which arts, science and philosophy were fostered regardless of its origin.

So it is not surprising that I grew up knowing little about al-Andalus; even worse, what I thought I knew was largely propaganda. As they say, winners write history. And I should have already learned this lesson: as a Catalan I have had to fight for my heritage (I still have to work on my Catalan writing), my identity (I had to follow a judicial process to get my name translated into Catalan) and my country. To be a Catalan in the nation-state called Spain is not easy. To people who ask me why do you want to be Catalan if it takes so much work, I can only repeat the words of the poet Joan Sales: 'I am Catalan just as the apricot is an apricot and not a peach'. Yet the most disturbing part in the reflections generated by 'Sota Terra' was the realisation that even defeated nations can hide and diminish the relevance of those they subjugated at one point in time. I had always thought that I had made an honest attempt to uncover the real history of my country (Catalonia), but the TV show proved that I had also fallen victim to stereotypes and prejudices. The true nature of what was the Reconquista also forced my gaze in another direction. And all these considerations are even more poignant now, because I have the inescapable feeling that the current Spanish conservative government wants to engage in a second Reconquista, what we could label as a Reconquista 2.0. This time it is not the Moors who will be expelled, but the Catalans who will be subdued. The right-wing People's Party, led by Mariano Rajoy, has devoted a great deal of effort to recovering the Reconquista imagery. For example, El Cid, a Castilian nobleman who was one of the fiercest and most victorious Christian leaders of the Reconquista, has made a big comeback. As has Queen Isabella, who is depicted in a new television series as a modern woman ahead of her time. In the show, Isabella has to conform to the limitations of her position and epoch, but it is also clear that it is not what she would actually like. Thus, Isabella becomes not only the spiritual mother of Spain but a feminist avant la lettre! The zealous determination of the Castilian Catholics to purge Spain of its diversity is reflected in the conservative drive to homogenise the state.

Of course, Spain is not a homogeneous entity but an amalgam of many nations within a nation state. Indeed, we cannot speak of Spain as a political entity until the eighteenth century; before that what existed was a variety of kingdoms, counties and other entities that exerted their authority over portions of a territory with the geographical label of España or Hispania. That is to say that before the Succession war (1701–1715) which placed a Bourbon king, Philip V, on the throne (the first truly Spanish king), Hispania referred only to a place, a geographical category like Scandinavia, the Maghreb, or the Balkans. It was not a kingdom or a state, a political and legal category. This is important as it is very often ignored or even denied. When the Catholic monarchs married they did not forge a new realm but a dynastic union between the kingdoms of Castile and Aragon; both, however, kept their distinctive rule, government and even customs. Even during the Habsburg dynasty, when Spain was the biggest empire in the world, it was not a single state. Thus Philip II, the most powerful monarch of his time, was not the king of Spain but the king of Castile, Portugal, Valencia, Aragon, Naples and Sicily, the Count of Barcelona, the Lord of the Seventeen Provinces and some other minor titles. Only after the Succession war when the Bourbon candidate defeated the states of the Aragon crown (present day Aragon, Catalonia and Valencia), depriving them of all the traditional laws and rights, was Spain transformed into a centralised, absolutist state. Yet, in many senses, this moment, rather than a turning point, was merely the continuation of a trend that had started with the Reconquista several centuries before. For much of its history, Hispania has seen the rule of different nations, of different ethnic or cultural origins, and with a variety of religions. I would suggest that Hispania was better off only when the rulers managed to accommodate its internal diversity, which is where al-Andalus comes in. The Muslim invasion was, aside from some battles, quite bloodless. After their defeat at the battle of Guadalete (711), the Visigoth kingdom of Toledo negotiated a treaty that traded land for privileges and eased the instalment of the first Umayyad wave. What followed was, culturally, one of the most vibrant and, religiously, one of the most tolerant periods of Spanish history.

The Reconquista was a result of two factors: the desire of Christian lords to gain territories and the progressive decline of Muslim strength. The tragedy here is that the Christian onslaught implied the loss of most of the progress and development brought in by the Muslims. For instance, in Urgell, a county within the Marca Hispanica in northern Catalunya, the execution and expulsion of the Muslims left the new conqueror with a large amount of land with no one to irrigate or look after it. Naturally, it became impossible to sustain even a fraction of the population it had fed before. Of course, not all Christian rulers were so antagonistic to the Muslims. Alfonso X, the thirteenth-century King of Castile, León and Galicia, called the Wise, founded the Toledo School of Translators, creating a sanctuary for many scholars who wanted to learn from others regardless of their origin, race or faith. Unfortunately, such cases were the exception rather than the norm.

So part of what I learned at school was correct. The Reconquista and modernity are handmaidens. The Reconquista gave modernity a forging origin and, in return, modernity conferred to the Reconquista a mythical character. A new credo was born that became the criteria for determining who could live under the new regime and who could not. Modernity's emphasis on uniformity perfectly matched the Reconquista-inspired new rule. Homogeneity was promoted vigorously as an instrument to shape the adherence of growing ranks of citizens to a new, centralised and unified power. No one has put more emphasis and passion on the removal of difference than Castile – either then, during the period of Moorish Spain, or now, in our times.

It is important to realise that Spain has at least four cultures, each with its own language. Three have a Latin root (Castilian, Catalan and Galician); the fourth, Basque or Euskara, is pre-Roman and one of the oldest languages in Europe. All these languages have survived and enjoy some degree of recognition and protection; all give voice to their particular culture and worldview. While all of them are 'Spanish', they also demonstrate that Spanish culture is not monolithic. Yet what is commonly known as Spanish is only Castilian. It could be argued that since the Catholic Monarchs, Castile has striven to represent, to become, to embody, what it means to be Spanish and what constitutes Spain. Even the Habsburg dynasty, relatively open and tolerant, was essentially Castilian; but it was the House of Bourbon, the royal family of French origins that ruled Spain from the eighteenth century, that delivered a fatal blow to Spanish diversity. Castile was the only kingdom that supported the Bourbon King Philip V (r. 1700-1746) in his claim to the Spanish throne. Indeed, Castilians have always been on the winning side in most of the internal fights and wars in Spain. One could be tempted to conclude that the discrimination against non-Castilian languages could just be a question of revenge over the losers. But then we should have to ask why the longest democratic period in Spanish history has not changed the modern notion of what is Spain and what it means to be Spanish.

The 1978 Spanish constitution is probably the last genuine attempt to build a more inclusive Spanish identity. Enacted at a particularly complex moment when Franco followers were still many and powerful, the constitution is an exercise in balance: it declares the unity of the Spanish nation, but it also acknowledges the existence of other peoples and nationalities within its territories; it makes Castilian the official language of all the states, but it recognises the other languages as Spanish too. All in all, it was welcomed as the harbinger of a new epoch. For instance, it opened a way for some territories, such as Catalonia and the Basque country, with aspirations of self-rule. Unfortunately, it soon became evident that old ideas die hard. So now we face the following paradox: the non-Castilian languages are in danger of disappearing precisely at the time when they are enjoying the greatest protection in decades. Spain has devoted, and is still devoting, enormous resources to eroding the presence, scope and projection of non-Castilian languages and cultures. The Instituto Cervantes (paid for by the taxes of all Spaniards, Castilians or not), does not spend a cent in protecting any culture that is not Castilian. Spain has also systematically prevented the enactment of any European rule that could give official status to any non-Castilian languages (do take into account that, for instance, the Catalan speaking community could be around 11 million people, more than that of many official European languages). Furthermore, Spain has systematically impugned autonomous laws that establish some degree of positive discrimination for non-Castilian languages in their own territories.

But to complain about this situation only reveals a weakness in the character of whoever is complaining. We are supposed to be proud of being in Spain. To be Spanish is to be modern, progressive, European, and patriotic – one of the best sentiments a person could have, or so we are told. But being proud of being Catalan, Basque, Galician, Andalusian or any other non-Castilian affiliation is an almost pathological sentiment, since these identities are old fashioned, provincial, excluding, and against any progressive notion. In other words, it is normal to feel or to want to be a Spaniard; it is abnormal to feel close to your regional language and culture. That is why Catalan nationalism is considered and projected as sick. One only has to look at the main newspapers published in Madrid, or listen to Spanish radio or watch national television stations to confirm this. I am not sure whether this hatred is worse for Catalonia or for Andalusia. It is true that Andalusia does not have to endure such harsh criticism. But one can argue, on the one hand that this is because, overall, Spain feels sympathy towards Andalusia. But on the other hand, that is surely because Andalusia has been more successfully assimilated.

The root of the problem is that Spanish identity has been constructed as a zero sum. For Castilian Spain, identity is like a box with a limited capacity; the more non-Castilian identity you add to the box, the less Spanish you become. And from a Spanish point of view, anything but a total and complete adherence to the Castilian-Spanish identity is unacceptable.

Economically, the situation is no better. Spain was modernised without any consideration of the non-Castilian regions. However, despite all the historical misfortunes, Catalonia and the former territories of the Aragon Crown have managed to become the economic engine of Spain. Yet, Madrid punishes them with a severe fiscal deficit. In Catalonia alone this deficit is estimated to be between 15 to 20 billion Euros per year. Since 1986, an estimated 200 billion Euros have been transferred from Catalonia to Madrid. The situation is made worse by the fact that Catalonians pay more tax and enjoy fewer social benefits than some Castilian territories. Catalonia is now losing its locally generated wealth at a rate that compromises its own economic viability. In short, for the kingdoms of the old Aragon Crown it is a bad business to be in Spain. The tragedy is that Spain seems ready to bleed its more prosperous territories to death even if that would surely imply the collapse of the Spanish economy as a whole. Not surprisingly, the Catalonians are now challenging the old motto: 'rather broke than diverse'.

In the age of Reconquista 2.0, Catalonia is set to follow in the footsteps of al-Andalus. It faces economic stagnation and cultural obliteration if it remains in Spain. Most Catalonians see it as a simple equation: if Spain does not allow them to be Catalonian, they cannot be Spanish. Hence, as the polls show, the majority is now in favour of independence. On 11 September 2012, I joined over 1.5 million people in the streets of Barcelona in a pro-independence rally – one of the biggest demonstrations in Europe.

And what about Andalusia? I would argue that it is in a worse shape. One of the most advanced, prosperous, and culturally refined territories in Spain has become one of the most subsidised European regions. Even though Andalusia is rich in resources, it still suffers from an archaic property distribution that concentrates great portions of territories into the hands of a few landlords (some of them received obscene benefits from European Union funds). The public sector is the main employer of the region, helping to create a neo-subsidised caste: the public servants. Moreover, the rich Andalusian cultural heritage has been reduced to banal folklore for the consumption of tourists: the bullfighter, the flamenco guitarist and dancer have become global references for Spain, perverting the deep meaning and relevance that these cultural forms hold for Andalusia. Andalusians are told they are good at looking after the tourists and entertaining them with flamenco, great at parties, but not very good at working hard.

Many Andalusians, particularly the young, are fighting to recover their heritage, culture, and identity. But this is a doomed project within the current nation state. Spain could tolerate Andalusia as a regional folk culture but it will never accept a fully-fledged Andalusian nation.

With Spain facing grim economic prospects, the main concern of the Spanish government is to purge any political sub-state autonomy and cultural difference. For Madrid, the solution to Spain's problems is ... more Spain! The alternative answer, less Spain, cannot even be imagined. The idea that the spirit of al-Andalus can be recovered, in a sort of al-Andalus 2.0, and the internal cultural diversity of the state be allowed to blossom is anathema. Like the Christian lords during the Reconquista, the Castilian-Spanish government is obsessed with defeating the enemy of diversity and suppressing the national aspirations of the regions, to push it over the cliff – regardless of the consequences. However, Spain may have survived the first Reconquista, it is doubtful it could survive a second.

So Spain finds itself at a historic juncture. It can press on with Reconquista 2.0 and face the collapse of Spain as a country, when the state would break up into several smaller nations. It can try to introduce some internal reforms such as correcting the fiscal deficit, which may provide the current system with some time, but without a real change in the Spanish worldview, the problems would only multiply and lead to a more abrupt and violent collapse in the long run. Or, it could introduce some real, deep changes and move forward to al-Andalus 2.0. Whatever course is adopted, it will determine the future of Spain for many years.

There are two prerequisites for Spain to move forward in a spirit of al-Andalus. First, Spain must free itself from the notion that Castilian equals Spanish. This concept of Spain has little meaning for most non-Castilians because there is nothing in it for them, beyond further aggravation and impoverishment. Diversity cannot be maintained by imposing Castilian as the canon of the state for the other cultures, identities or nations to follow and adopt. This can only lead to injustice, resentment and conflict. However, if Spain wants only to be Castilian, then it should be content with being Castile and let go of those non-Castilian cultures, identities or nations that do not want to be Castilian.

Second, Spain must abandon its outdated concept of equality, that it is only a myopic and reductive notion of uniformity. Even Aristotle accepted that fairness has as much to do with treating equally what is alike as it has do to with treating differently what is diverse. Uniformity was a product of the modern obsession with surpassing cultural diversity. It certainly made it easier to rule a large state. But uniformity, even in the guise of equality, is dangerously obsolete in post-normal times. Today we understand that diversity is wealth, we measure the richness of an ecosystem by its biodiversity, and we consider that an economy is more affluent if it is diverse. Yet, we still seem reluctant to foster diversity in the social domain. The diverse nations of Spain – the Catalan, Basque, Galician or even the Andalusian – have diverse needs and requirements that cannot be met with imposed uniformity, or with some standardised notion of equality.

I would argue that cultural diversity would be best served if Spain become an Iberian or Hispanic confederation in which the different nations or territories could negotiate the kind and intensity of its bond with the other members of the confederation. Such an arrangement would allow its members to act together in issues that demand unity but would also permit a high level of internal flexibility. In most respects, the confederation would just be an interface; in an increasingly interconnected world, with a growing number of issues that require a global approach, it would be foolish to conceive the confederation as a border to protect its interior from the rest of the world. Instead the confederation would act as a cell wall, not just holding the integrity of the cell but allowing it to connect with the rest of the global organism.

There may be other ways and arrangements to preserve and encourage the diversity of Spain. But one thing is clear: Castilian Spain must choose between Reconquista 2.0 and al-Andalus 2.0. Meanwhile, we the non-Castilian people of Catalonia are making our own preparations for independence.

REIMAGING THE CORDOBA MOSQUE

Zara Amjad and Gulzar Haider

O, the ever-flowing waters of Guadalquivir,
Someone on your banks
Is seeing a vision of some other period of
time.

Standing in front of the Cordoba Mosque, Muhammad Iqbal, the celebrated twentieth-century poet and philosopher of the Indian Subcontinent, had a transcendental experience. It was January 1933; Muslims and Jews were still forbidden from visiting Spain, and Iqbal had to get special permission from the British government. He was transfixed by the 'aura' of the mosque , which sits near Guadalquivir, the river that runs through Cordoba. As he gazed at the mosque, his soul was 'kindled' and his heart 'illuminated'. He was moved to write. The 'Mosque of Cordoba', a poem of sixty-four couplets, is seen as one of his best poems. Indeed, it has been suggested that it summarises his philosophy. The poem talks about our unending quest for Divine love, our constant search for knowledge, our perpetual desire to be creative. It dwells on the endless chain of life and death, where everything – man, nature, buildings, cultures, art and stories – dies only to re-emerge in different shapes and forms, just as day inevitably follows night. Total immersive dedication and individual attachment to a higher purpose is what Iqbal saw in the mosque. As always, he mines the past to create hope for the future.

He was one of the first Muslims to be allowed to pray in the mosque, which he considered not just as a place of worship but as a work of art that reflected God's own beauty:

Your beauty, your majesty,
Personify the graces of the man of faith.
You are beautiful and majestic.
He too is beautiful and majestic.

Your grandeur calls to mind
The loftiness of His station,
The sweep of His vision,
His rapture, His ardour, His pride, His humility.

For Iqbal, the mosque seemed to define time itself. It is a place and space of and for stories; the stories of Abraham and Moses, Jesus and Muhammad, a building that witnessed the rise and fall of cultures and civilisations. The mosque radiated with 'Godly love', 'the essence of life', 'which death is forbidden to touch'. In the final analysis, 'Mosque of Cordoba', like all mystical poems, is a poem of love:

To Love, you owe your being,
O, Harem of Cordoba,
To Love, that is eternal;
Never waning, never fading.

After praising the foundations, columns, arches and terraces of the Cordoba Mosque, Iqbal ends up describing it as 'Mecca of art lovers' that elevates a parochial place called Andalusia 'to the eminence of the Holy Harem'.

The Mosque of Cordoba was built in 785 by the Prince Abd ar-Rahman I, the founder of the Umayyad Caliphate of Spain. It is located at the south edge of the historic city; there is a Roman bridge that connects the two banks of river Guadalquivir. The mosque creates a mysterious impression of space: there is a forest of colonnades; standing in one position a person would have multiple views of the two storey arcade, making the space seem nearly weightless. The boundless horizon creates a sense of infinity. The space has the desire to draw a person in every direction; the domed areas hold the visitor in one place. The mosque responds to the sky and the cosmos but the sky itself is not visible. One feels the presence of the absence in the mosque.

The most notable feature of the building is its arcaded hypostyle hall, with 856 columns of jasper, onyx, marble and granite, described by Iqbal as 'countless pillars like rows of palm trees in the oasis of Syria'. The mosque was crafted by Byzantine craftsmen and the material, including complete columns, was taken from existing Roman buildings. The columns branch up to become double horse-shoe arches with alternating coloured stones. The mosque was built on the site of a Roman Temple which was turned into a church that lasted some six hundred years. Abd ur-Rahman I purchased the Church of Saint Vincent, demolished it, and constructed the mosque on the same site.

Over the years, the mosque has been subjected to numerous extensions. It was expanded over a period of two hundred years (785–987) under Muslim rule. The *maqsura* (screen which encloses the area of the *mihrab* and *minbar*) was added during the caliphate of Abd ur-Rahman III (r. 912–961), whose reign marked the height of the Umayyad power. It is the jewel of the mosque. Its purpose was to protect the Caliph from assassination attempts. The Caliph prayed under a sea-shell-shaped domed *mihrab*, with the cosmos above him in the form of a beautiful cross-vaulted dome. The *maqsura* was visible from the main entrance of the mosque across the courtyard but was never accessible to the general public. When the mosque was further extended, in 986, on the eastern side, the *maqsura* became off centre in the basic layout. Even in these extensions, the rhythm of the double horseshoe arches was maintained and the new columns were made to look like the old ones.

What is unique about the mosque is that the *mihrab* (which indicates the direction of *Ka'abah*) is due south whereas the actual *Qibla* is south-east. A possible reason for this could be that Muslims followed the layout of the city which followed a strict Roman grid. They did not disturb the rest of the city's layout and utilised the foundations of the Church of Saint Vincent. Another hypothesis is that Abdal Rehman I kept the same solar orientation as that of Umayyad Mosque in Damascus, therefore re-enforcing the memory of his homeland. It is difficult to believe that the architects and builders were unaware of the actual direction of the *Qibla*. What is more likely is that the Cordoba Mosque is situated at different junctures within larger architectural history. As Nuha Khoury, the American architectural historian notes, the mosque's 'connections to the past make it the culmination of an older Umayyad tradition, while its particular creative location in al-Andalus makes it the point of inception for a new tradition with different subsequent histories in Spain and North Africa.'

The building remained static until 1236 when, following the conquest of Cordoba by Fernando III of Castile in the Reconquista, it was consecrated as a cathedral. A Villaviciosa Chapel and the Royal Chapel were constructed within the mosque. Further Christian features were added in the fourteenth century, and the minaret of the mosque was converted into the bell tower of the cathedral. Perhaps the most significant alteration came in 1523 when a Renaissance cathedral was built within the expansive structure. The cathedral was dropped right in the middle of the mosque and sits in an east to west direction. It destroys the harmony and delicacy of the double horseshoe arches. Some sixty-three pillars had to be removed from the mosque so that the cathedral could be made exactly in the centre. The space at the centre of the mosque, which was originally flooded with light, became extremely dark due to the monumental cathedral, which itself has light coming in from its huge windows. The rest of the mosque has several domed areas which pour light into the mosque. It is reported that when Charles V, who supported the building of the cathedral, eventually saw it in 1526, he exclaimed: 'You have built here what you or anyone might have built anywhere else, but you have destroyed what was unique in the world.'

The 'Mezquita', as it is known, now functions as a cathedral and a tourist site. There is Sunday Mass and there are tourists; it is not a mosque anymore. Muslims of Cordoba are not allowed to pray inside the mosque, and a petition to the Pope in 2002 was rejected. Even as a cathedral it functions as a place of worship only on Sundays. Nonetheless, the building still echoes the stories of its origins, displays the burden of its changing roles throughout history, narrates the entire story of the rise and fall of Muslim Spain, announces itself to the world, and has the quality that Iqbal captures in his poem.

Suppose we were to reimagine the Cordoba Mosque as Iqbal saw it. Not as a mosque for Muslims, but as a universal space for all religions, an invitation to the children of Adam to gather in a special place to reflect on the Divine. Not as a cathedral, but free of the Christian attitudes of the Reconquista and the architectural re-assertion of the return of the Christian power. As a place that is an ode to the Heavens and the Earth, and to God and His mercy which is not bound to any religion. What would Cordoba Mosque look like, to use Iqbal's words, as 'the reverberation of the symphony of Creation'?

This, then, is a theoretical re-imagining of the Cordoba Mosque, and Andalusia, in the present time.

We begin with re-locating the Renaissance cathedral to its metaphorically equal place across the river. The cathedral is moved stone by stone so that it can continue to function but now has a more clear identity of itself, with an opportunity to reflect on itself and focus on the previously occupied mosque across the river. The cathedral leaves a huge void in the mosque. This void, which appears like a missing tooth, is to be developed and inhabited as a centre which is sacred to more than one religion. The mosque will not resume its status of a mosque. It will, instead, offer a space for everyone to gather.

The void left by the cathedral is 138 feet wide and 240 feet long. Some area is to be returned to the mosque; and only 60 feet is used from the 138 feet of width. The void will expand itself underneath the floor which will be utilised and made into library. From the floor of the mosque, the ground will be dug down to about 30 feet so that there is minimum intervention on the ground level, maintaining the infinity created by the colonnade. Amongst the forest of palm trees, this void will be like an oasis, where the wanderers of this world can stop for the shade under the trees to quench their spiritual thirst. It will be transformed into an area for congregation or self-reflection. The void will announce its presence to the sky, but it will be deeply rooted into the nave of the earth. It is like digging back into the foundation of one's existence to discover and release one's ego from all desires.

The void is re-inhabited in such a way that the memory of the cathedral's insertion is imprinted in it. The new intervention respects and acknowledges the absence; it is a carved out courtyard in the vertical axis of the cathedral. Ramps take you down in the carved spaces and invite a circumbulation (*tawaf*) around the courtyard.

The descent into the memories of the mosque and the cathedral is gradual. The ramp is between a set of glass columns that light the path till the ramp ends. These glass columns fan above you, like a ghost from the past or a faint memory slowly revealing itself. They are rendered weightless by the light which strikes them, illuminating their surroundings and taking this light to where the path ends. During the day, the columns take the light from the punctures right above them on the roof; during the night, they are giving off light. In their second cycle, the ramps are resting between the pilasters that are frozen memories of the cathedral. Thus from the start, the ramps are held by the mosque's memory and are passed on to that of the cathedral. The ramps spiral from the lowest level of the courtyard moving outwards into and under the open sky.

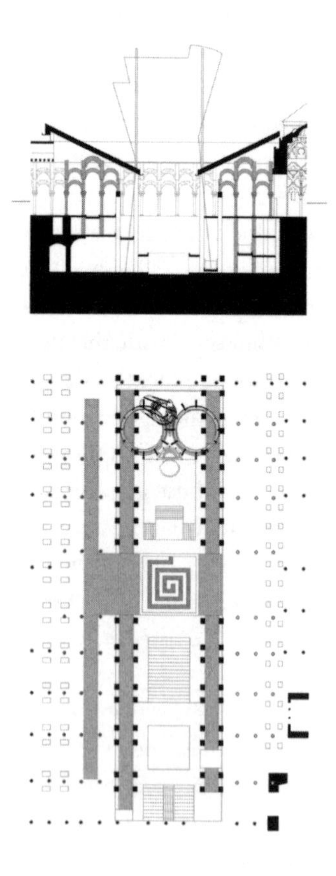

The void in the axis of the cathedral

The courtyard is a sitting arena of steps facing east. This well of stairs faces the altar and leads to the body of water that reflects the altar and the sky. The body of water is under the pre-existing memory of the dome of the cathedral, symbolically bringing the sky in its place. It is to keep a portion of the sky or God's mercy in this place; the hands are raised towards the sky receiving the rain water, which is fed to the pool. Water is channelled from the roof to the pool, which in turn gives it back to the life-giving river Guadalquivir. It is as if Cordoba is shedding tears of happiness and providing nectar to the river that has, for centuries, been keeping this place alive. The water flows to the river via an underground channel. The body of water itself has a passageway that can be accessed only when there is no water in the pool. There is another passage that opens up on the bank of the river from the mosque. It is at the south side of the courtyard and at the lowest levels. This new '*Haram*' or centre pays an ode both to Iqbal and Guadalquivir. The breeze from the river brings fresh songs of Cordoba or narrates stories of the world. The tunnel can be accessed from the river to bring people directly into the re-inhabited void so they can take a journey back upwards to the palm trees of Cordoba.

The re-located cathedral not only leaves a huge void in the centre of the structure but also several punctures or marks in the floor created by its columns and buttresses. The pilasters are in the place where the columns were; around every column, four pilasters are made to demarcate their boundary. The punctures left by the buttresses are approximately 20 feet in length and width. The floor of the Mosque of Cordoba varies because during different extensions new floors were added; the floor holds all the marks of the history of this building. The new floor is dug from the void left by the cathedral; the punctures that have been left by the buttresses are encased. A glass slab is added as a lid for the punctures so that the continuity of the floor is not disrupted; it also adds a visual disparity that serves as a reminder of the history of the building.

The pilasters on the immediate periphery of the courtyard stop at a certain height; steel columns shoot out from them to the original height of the courtyard. They present themselves as the skeleton of a large body: incomplete, barren, just staring or reaching out to the sky. The cathedral on the other side of the river can look back at the place where it once stood, to the height that it was against the gentle horizon of the double horse-shoe arches. This harp-like colonnade shoots out light to the heavens declaring its presence.

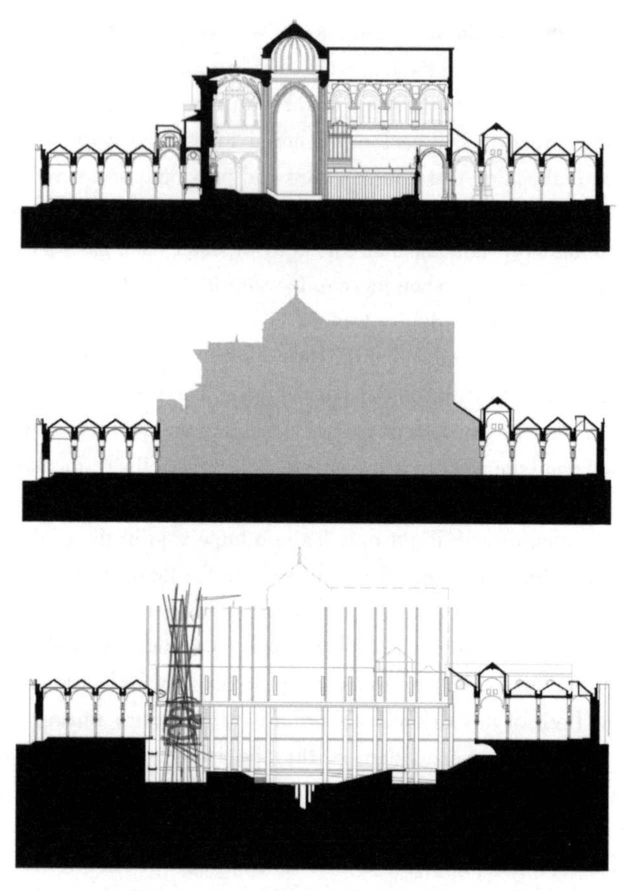

Transition towards inhabiting the void

From within the altar

The front view of the altar

Courtyard and sea of steps from within the altar

The altar here is paying an ode to the light, to the wind and rain and to the heavens above. It goes up to the height where the dome of the cathedral was located, and is made up of glass cones that are supported by steel rods and rings. On certain special days (solstices and equinoxes), the cones bring in light through its punctures. The altar is like an organ which plays the music of the winds and collects rainwater that is fed to the pool. The cones are hollow and they intersect each other at various junctures. The steel rings demarcate different levels and heights in this building but, more importantly, they employ symbols of different religions.

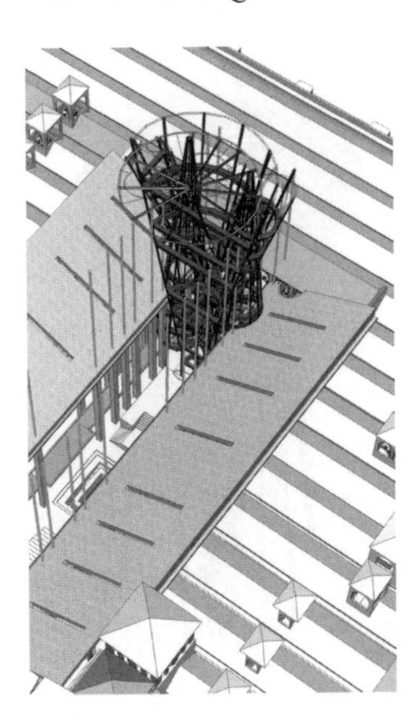

Rainwater collecting roof and altar

View of the pool and the altar

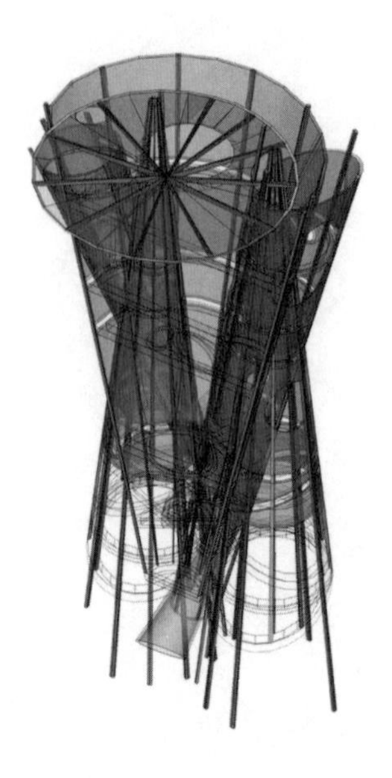

The ecumenical altar

From beyond the altar

Entering the ramp under the glass arcade

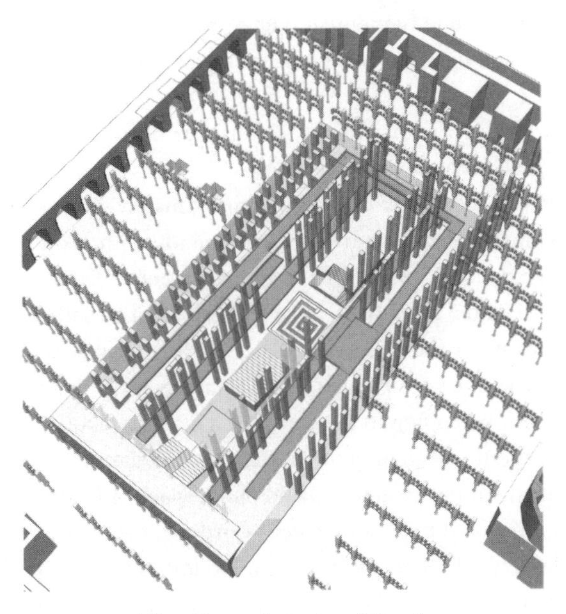

The Circumbulation (*Tawaf*)

The re-imagined Cordoba Mosque now has:

~ a carved out courtyard framing the base of the vertical axis of the cathedral;
~ a series of pilasters that are in place of the columns of the cathedral to accurately freeze the memory of the cathedral;
~ steel columns that are left open to the sky at the height of the columns of the cathedral;
~ an arcade of glass columns that serve as memories of the mosque columns;
~ ramps that take you down in the carved spaces while performing a *tawaf* around the courtyard;
~ a library that is under the floor of the mosque, it runs in line with the pilasters;
~ a new altar that employs spiritual signs and religious symbols of all religions and is an ode to light, sound, and water;
~ a pool '*mandala*' that is in place of the dome of the cathedral, it collects rainwater which is circulated back to the river;
~ an underground tunnel that opens onto the river to let in the breeze and the music of the wind from the river.

But there are still two other things to consider: the minaret and the islands on the Guadalquivir.

The minaret has base dimensions of approximately 40 by 40 feet and has two symmetrical staircases moving to the top with a solid dividing wall between them. With a height of approximately 200 feet, it will serve as a residential place for scholars. These scholars and students will meet and encounter the Cordovan scholars who are present in the tower at all times. The journey upwards in the minarets is divided into four residences each belonging to the legacy of a historic scholar. The base of the minaret and the beginning of the journey is dedicated to ibn Rushd, undoubtedly the most notable son and philosopher of Cordoba. The next apartment is devoted to another son of Cordoba, the Jewish philosopher Maimonides, one of the most prolific and followed scholars of the Torah. The third apartment is for Thomas Aquinas, the Roman Catholic philosopher and theologian who had a long-running argument with ibn Rushd.

The final level or stage is given to Iqbal. The minaret represents an architectural allegory in which three scholars of Abrahamic traditions continue their dialogue and discourse, mediated by the universal insights of Iqbal, where all learn to co-habit with each other.

The Guadalquivir, 'The Life Giving River', has small islands where a few water mills from the Muslim period of Cordoba have survived, a symbolic reminder of the richness of this place. On these islands, there will be pavilions dedicated to different religions of the world. Each pavilion will show the essence of the religion it is representing in context with nature; together they will provide a space for the common goal of our different spiritual traditions - a symbolic journey from a place of one individual differentiated religion to a place, the Inhabited Void, the Courtyard, that is for all.

The journey that starts from the newly relocated cathedral, through the pavilions in the islands to the philosophers in the minaret and the previously existing mosque, is a celebration of the different appreciations of the Divine. This re-imagined Cordoba Mosque aims to invite everyone to a historically religious site, to link religion to humanism, in pursuit of the shared goals of humanity. It is 'a vision of some other period of time', where the wounds of history have been healed with 'the essence of life' and where pluralism and humane futures flourish.

The Re-imagined Cordoba Mosque

ESSAYS

GANDHI AND PALESTINE by *Vinay Lal*

MUSLIM DOGS *by Barnaby Rogerson*

GANDHI AND PALESTINE

Vinay Lal

I

On 26 November 1938, Gandhi published in his journal *Harijan* a reasonably lengthy statement entitled simply, 'The Jews'. 'My sympathies,' he candidly stated, 'are all with the Jews', and yet he could not be blind 'to the requirement of justice. The cry for the national home for the Jews does not make much appeal to me. The sanction for it is sought in the Bible and the tenacity with which the Jews have hankered after return to Palestine. Why should they not, like other peoples of the earth, make that country their home where they are born and where they earn their livelihood?' Gandhi had penned these reflections on 20 November in response, as he wrote in the opening paragraph, to 'several letters' asking him to declare his 'views about the Arab-Jewish question in Palestine and the persecution of the Jews in Germany'. Earlier that month, in a single night of terror crystallised as *Kristallnacht*, SA storm troopers, often joined by German civilians, went on a systematic and unchecked rampage in Nazi Germany and parts of Austria against Jewish homes, shops, businesses, and synagogues, thereby signaling their determination to put into place a policy of annihilationist horror that would lead eventually to the 'Final Solution'. A quarter of the Jewish male population of Germany was, on the single night of 9–10 November, dispatched to concentration camps.

Gandhi's statement of 20 November has had, barring its contemporary reception, a largely fugitive existence – until recently, that is. A number of prominent theologians and Zionists, among them Judah Magnes, Hayim Greenberg, and Martin Buber, sought to engage Gandhi in a dialogue on his interpretations of Jewish history and Jewish aspirations for a homeland, but the events of World War II and the Holocaust appeared to have vastly outpaced Gandhi's views. Even many of Gandhi's admirers perforce had to admit that he was incapable of understanding the nature of evil, and his two letters to Hitler, both of which begin with the salutation 'Dear Friend', are generally construed as unmistakable evidence of his naivety and an outlandish idealism hopelessly at odds with the unforgiving world of realpolitik. Neither letter ever reached the intended recipient; both were suppressed by the Government of India, exercising its prerogative of wartime censorship. In his missive of 23 July 1939, Gandhi urged Hitler, the one person capable of putting an end to the madness that was on the horizon, to listen to the appeal of someone who had 'deliberately shunned the method of war not without considerable success'. His second letter, written on Christmas Eve 1940, begins with an acknowledgment of the fact that the very salutation with which Hitler is addressed was likely to provoke consternation among Gandhi's friends and ridicule among his adversaries: 'That I address you as a friend is no formality. I owe no foes. My business in life has been for the past thirty-three years to enlist the friendship of the whole of humanity by befriending mankind, irrespective of race, colour or creed.' Gandhi did not believe that Hitler was the monster he was made out to be, but nevertheless many of your acts, he tells Hitler, 'are monstrous and unbecoming of human dignity' – among these acts are the 'humiliation of Czechoslovakia, the rape of Poland and the swallowing of Denmark'.

A man may not be a monster, but his acts may be monstrous: that Gandhi held to such a view should come as no surprise to those familiar with Gandhi's insistence, in Christian parlance, that one is enjoined to hate the sin, not the sinner. British rule in India was abominable, but Gandhi was prepared to believe that there were Englishmen to whom the cause of Indian freedom was dearer than it was to many Indians. What should surprise us, however, is that the British proscribed Gandhi's letters to Hitler: if non-violence is as impotent in the face of fascism as is universally believed, why cower in fear of a non-violent activist? If truth alone triumphs, why shouldn't Gandhi's letters have been allowed to test the mettle of a man made out to be a monster? Or did the British find unpalatable, even sinister, Gandhi's claim, in his second letter to Hitler, that the difference between 'British Imperialism' and 'Nazism' was only one of 'degree'. Did Churchill suppose that this assessment from the man he once mocked as a 'half-naked fakir' was calculated to embolden Hitler? If so, one must suppose that the power of Gandhi's word was feared far more than the British were ever willing to admit.

Interesting as are all these considerations, there is the matter of Gandhi's statement on 'The Jews'. It is not only Gandhi's supposed naivety, and the brute but still unproven fact of Hitlerism and fascism triumphing over non-violent action, that would condemn his statement to obscurity for some years. There has been for some time a relatively widespread view that Gandhi was not a particularly learned man. By this it is meant not merely that he had neither the time nor the inclination for intellectual or artistic pursuits as such, but also that he was uninterested in scholarly debates and was wanting in intellectual curiosity. On the related subjects of Judaism, Jewish history, and the history and politics of Palestine, Gandhi is thought to have been alarmingly ignorant. Once before, as the Ottoman Empire was being dismembered and Gandhi was to become the spokesperson for the ill-fated Khilafat campaign, he had ventured to voice briefly his opinion on Jewish claims to a homeland in Palestine. From early 1921 until the second half of 1937, however, there was barely a squeak from Gandhi on the question of Palestine, though the Arab revolt of 1936 had put the country into a state of acute unrest. The revival of his interest in the question of Palestine in 1937 owed much to circumstances to which I shall allude in due course.

In very recent years, however, Gandhi's statement of November 1938 on 'The Jews' has found a fresh lease of life: if the Mahatma has had to be assassinated repeatedly, he also continues to take rebirth in the most unexpected ways. Nathuram Godse, a staunch Hindu and Gandhi's assassin, would not have been amused. Indeed, it would not be too much to say that, in varying intellectual circles, Gandhi's pronouncement on Palestine has now been crowned as a model of judicious reasoning, intellectual perspicacity, and moral probity. In part, this has to do with the general reassessment of Gandhi that has been taking place over the last decade: if every constituency loved to hate him at one time or another, many of those same constituencies have now declared their admiration for his principled adherence to moral standards amidst the ruins of politics. Even analytical philosophers, who were wont to treat vexed debates on secularism, religion, and the public sphere as cognitive puzzles, have turned to Gandhi. But the resuscitation of Gandhi's views on Palestine owes at least as much to the fact that, in the more than six decades since the founding of Israel and the *nakba*, the dispersal and dispossession of the Palestinians, all competing views have been tested and found severely wanting. When asked by Reuters' special correspondent in May 1947, 'What is the solution of the Palestine Problem?', Gandhi replied: 'It has become a problem which seems almost insoluble.' That Gandhi had arrived at this estimate so early into the dispute is, if disconcerting, equally a sign of his awareness that the conflict could not be resolved within the ambit of what we might call 'normal politics'. Here, as has happened so often, many of the advocates of non-violent resistance have appealed to various publics with the argument that, since all other remedies have failed, it is time that non-violence was given its just dues in the market-place of opportunity.

II

It is, however, far more than weariness with the unending cycle of violence that should compel us to turn to Gandhi's pronouncement on 'The Jews'. Let this much be said as well: just as it is doubtful that news of the atrocities of Kristallnacht had reached Gandhi in Segaon, an obscure village in the heartland of India where he had ensconced himself a few years before, so it is reasonably clear that he would have, while deploring the oppression to which the Jews had been subjected, seen little reason to alter his views. His statement was written with full awareness of the extent of the depravity to which the Nazi regime had sunk. One must not suppose that, writing in November 1938, Gandhi had a premonition – any more than did others – of the gross evil that was about to unfold, and that consequently he may have been more receptive to the Jewish case had he written his article when the mass slaughter of Jews had commenced in the concentration camps at Auschwitz, Treblinka, Bergen-Belsen, and elsewhere. Quite to the contrary, Gandhi had condemned the Nazi regime in the strongest possible terms in his article: the 'German persecution of the Jews', he wrote, 'seems to have no parallel in history. The tyrants of old never went so mad as Hitler seems to have gone. And he is doing it with religious zeal. For he is propounding a new religion of exclusive and militant nationalism in the name of which any inhumanity becomes an act of humanity to be rewarded here and hereafter.' Gandhi's article of 1938 should, then, be taken as the summation of his views on Jewish claims to a homeland in Palestine, and the case for or against him, for those who are invested in the zero-sum logic of adversarial politics, rests with this article.

Gandhi commences his article, as I have noted, with the observation that his 'sympathies are all with the Jews'. His closest European associates and friends in South Africa were nearly all Jews, and it is only with a touch of exaggeration on his part that he describes some of them as having become his 'life-long companions'. Gandhi's at one time flourishing legal practice in Johannesburg was ably managed by Sonia Schlesin, a Jewish woman of Lithuanian origin. The journalist Henry Polak, who had arrived in South Africa from Britain and had begun to work on the *Transvaal Critic*, a newspaper entirely typical in its open display of racism towards Indians and Africans, was slowly drawn to Gandhi. Their friendship blossomed, and Polak would go on to serve as editor of *Indian Opinion*, the first of several newspapers founded by Gandhi; he moved into Phoenix Settlement, similarly the first of Gandhi's several extended experiments in communal living, and the two lived, so Gandhi wrote in his autobiography, 'like blood brothers'. It is Polak who effected one of the most transformative moments in Gandhi's life when he slipped a copy of Ruskin's *Unto This Last,* into his hands as he was about to commence a train journey; Gandhi would later render it into Gujarati as 'Sarvodaya', or 'Welfare for All'. Hermann Kallbenbach completed the all-important Jewish triumvirate: an architect of Lithuanian German stock, he was an unlikely candidate as a disciple or even friend of Gandhi. Well built and athletic, Kallenbach was devoted to sports; but his distinction resides perhaps in the fact that he was the first of many men and women of substantial means who felt mesmerised in Gandhi's presence. They shared lodgings together in Johannesburg, and the intimacy of their friendship can be surmised from their long and unusual correspondence, where Gandhi was signified as the 'Upper House' and Kallenbach as the 'Lower House'. The onset of World War I, which saw Gandhi leave for India and Kallenbach interned on the Isle of Man as a German citizen, led to an agonising separation that would last until May 1937, when Kallenbach arrived in India as an emissary of the Jewish Agency charged with garnering the support of Gandhi and the Congress leadership for the aspirations of Jewish people in Palestine. When Kallenbach died in 1945, the *Indian Opinion* declared that among Gandhi's associates he was known as 'Hanumana': 'As Hanumana was to Shri Rama so was Mr. Kallbenbach to Mahatma Gandhi.'

'In South Africa', as Gandhi had once remarked in 1931, 'I was surrounded by Jews.' His statement of November 1938 establishes his credentials in this respect, and at once points to two considerations that Gandhi sought to bring to the attention of his readers. First, no one could say that Gandhi had no proximity to Jews, or that he was unaware of the peculiarities of their history. 'Through these friends,' Gandhi writes, 'I came to learn much of their age-long persecution. They have been the untouchables of Christianity.' Let us leave aside for the present the parallel, which Gandhi describes as 'very close', that he draws between the treatment of Jews by Christians and the treatment of Untouchables by Hindus. The history of Jewish suffering, Gandhi appears to be suggesting, is not known to him merely as an abstraction, as a factotum gleaned from some encyclopaedia; rather, this suffering is, so to speak, writ large on the faces of his Jewish friends. And, yet, since friendships can be blinding, it is perforce necessary that 'the more common universal reason' should also nudge him towards 'sympathy for the Jews'. Secondly, to the extent that Gandhi had close friendships with Jews, he was duty bound to subject his sympathy for them to the rigorous test of justice. Sympathy should not be confused with partiality; and so we come to that formulation which we have encountered before: 'The cry for the national home for the Jews does not make much appeal to me.'

In advancing a case against Jewish claims to a homeland in Palestine, Gandhi dwells on the ethics of 'belonging'. Thus he argues, 'Palestine belongs to the Arabs in the same sense that England belongs to the English or France to the French.' This does not appear to be a morally compelling argument, particularly in view of Gandhi's recognition of the Jewish invocation of a biblical sanction to claim Palestine for the Jews. Does priority of arrival or origin confer unqualified and exclusive rights of possession to land? We know, to take one example, that native Americans were invariably stripped, one should say robbed, by white Europeans of their lands, but the same white Europeans have, for generations since then, used the priority of their 'arrival' to disenfranchise later immigrants and draw up hierarchies of true-blood 'Americans'. On the other hand, how would Gandhi have assessed the postcolonial rejoinder, encountered among formerly colonised immigrants to England or France who were confronted with the ugly face of racism, that 'we are here because you were there'? If Gandhi might now appear to be in some difficulty, he at once puts a different inflection on the notion of belonging. 'It is wrong and inhuman to impose the Jews on the Arabs', he writes, adding: 'What is going on in Palestine today cannot be justified by any moral code of conduct. The mandates have no sanction but that of the last war.' Palestine can only be turned into a 'national home' for the Jews by reducing the 'proud Arabs' to nought, which would be 'a crime against humanity'.

If one had to ask how precisely the Jews were being imposed on the Arabs, the answer lies, in the first instance, in that torrid history which commences with a promise made by a now obscure British foreign official, known only as the author of the Balfour Declaration, that the British Government viewed 'with favour the establishment in Palestine of a national home for the Jewish people' and would rightly endeavour to 'facilitate the achievement of this object, it being clearly understood that nothing shall be done which may prejudice the civil and religious rights of existing non-Jewish communities in Palestine, or the rights and political status enjoyed by Jews in any other country.' That the Balfour Declaration promised not Palestine to the Jews, but a national home in Palestine, was a distinction which would be overlooked. But that any declaration was at all possible owed everything to the prerogatives that Britain and France, triumphant nations at the height of their power and ambition, exercised in carving out spheres of influence in the Middle East. Much later, Nehru echoed the idea already implicit in Gandhi's suggestion that a Jewish homeland would be an 'imposition' on the Arabs: 'British imperialism played its hand so cleverly that the conflict became the conflict between Arabs and Jews, and the British Government cast itself in the role of umpire.' (Some might contend that the role of Britain in the creation of Israel has been exaggerated: anti-Semitism was rampant in the British Foreign Office, to be sure, but one can just as convincingly argue that American Protestantism accommodates both deep-rooted anti-semitism and unstinting support for Israel as an oasis of Western democracy and civilisation in the desert of Muslim-dominant states.) Jewish immigrants, pouncing upon the Balfour Declaration as a licence to stake a vigorous claim to a Jewish homeland, would begin to pour into Palestine. 8,000 Jewish immigrants had arrived in 1923; two years later, the number rose to 34,000. The numbers might have been sustained in the second half of the 1920s but for the worldwide depression; however, the economic recovery of the 1930s, and the onset of anti-semitism, led to a resurgence of Jewish immigration into Palestine. In 1935 alone, 61,800 Jews arrived in Palestine; and from constituting less than one-tenth of the population at the eve of World War I, the Jewish community numbered about one-third of the population at the eve of the World War II. In contemporary times, the parallel that comes to mind is the reterritorialisation of Tibet, as a matter of deliberate state policy, by the Han Chinese.

Having declared his opposition to a Jewish 'national home' in Palestine, even as he characterises Germany as a country that has shown 'how hideous, terrible and terrifying it looks in its nakedness', Gandhi proposes what appears to be an anodyne if indisputably reasonable solution: 'The nobler course' of action, he argues, 'would be to insist on a just treatment of the Jews wherever they are born and bred. The Jews born in France are French in precisely the same sense that Christians born in France are French.' That this is not a sentiment Gandhi had struck upon at a moment's notice is amply clear from his statement on Zionism released to the Jewish Agency a year earlier, where he gives it as his opinion that 'the Jews should disclaim any intention of realising their aspiration under the protection of arms and should rely wholly on the goodwill of Arabs.' Jews were to wait for a home in Palestine until such time as 'Arab opinion' was 'ripe' for that possibility: 'And the best way to enlist that opinion, is to rely wholly upon the moral justice of the desire and therefore the moral sense of the Arabs and the Islamic world.'

If mere insistence on just treatment were enough, the world would have had no need for liberation movements, anti-colonial struggles, or agitations for social justice. How does one calibrate the difference between insistence, persuasion, and coercion? And if 'insistence' is to be more than insistence, as a persistent, forceful, and articulate expression of sentiments, then we have to question the measure of insistence. Gandhi's own life amply suggests that he had an expansive conception of the insistent struggle for rights, and his *satyagraha* campaigns, especially in India, went well beyond what is ordinarily understood by the term 'insistence'. But there were mitigating circumstances that, in Gandhi's judgment, had diminished whatever moral case could be advanced on behalf of Jewish aspirations. Jewish dependence on British arms had greatly eroded the credibility of Jewish nationalists, who had nothing but the naked strength of British imperialism to press their demands. What impressed Gandhi even more was what he took to be a distinct and salutary aspect of Jewish history, one that should have emboldened rather than demoralised them. Who else but the Jew could claim the world as his or her own? If Jews were desirous of having a national home, were they willing to disavow their rightful claims over all the lands where they had put down some roots? Balfour himself had given it as his firm opinion that the creation of a Jewish home in Palestine was not to be construed as a signal that the rights of Jews in other states could as a consequence be abrogated. 'If the Jews have no home but Palestine,' Gandhi asks, with perhaps a greater awareness of the xenophobia and exclusivism that informs nation-state politics than he is commonly granted to have displayed, 'will they relish the idea of being forced to leave the other parts of the world in which they are settled? Or do they want a double home where they can remain at will? This cry for the national home affords a colourable justification for the German expulsion of the Jews.' That the demand for Palestine as a national homeland would make Jews vulnerable was, even then, the lesser part of the problem. The supreme tragedy of Jewish history, Gandhi might well have argued, was that the Jews seemed incapable of recognising that they alone could will an escape from the tyranny of the nation-state narrative.

III

At this juncture, before entering into a consideration of the response to Gandhi's statement on 'The Jews' by enlightened Jewish opinion, it would do well to probe the reasons that may have informed Gandhi's thinking on the notion of a Jewish homeland. He treasured his long association with numerous Jewish friends, and in the concluding part of his statement, invoking Cecil Roth's book *The Jewish Contribution to Civilisation*, he called to mind the innumerable ways in which the Jewish people had enriched 'the world's literature, art, music, drama, science, medicine, agriculture', and the like. On the other hand, while he could not claim similarly close friendships among Arab intellectuals or public figures, he commanded a large following in the Arab world where developments in India were closely monitored. When Gandhi was set free on 25 January 1931, an editorial in *Al-Ahram* invited Egyptians to celebrate the occasion as 'the day of Gandhi, the day of India, the day of freedom'. A few weeks later, on 10 March, another editorial in *Al-Ahram* posed the questions that were on the nationalist agenda in the Arab world: 'India and Egypt: does the Indian question affect the Egyptian question?' The query was answered unequivocally in the affirmative: 'At close inspection one finds that British policy in Egypt and India is the same. As a result, the events in Egypt in 1919 affected India and British reaction here is the same as there. Similarly, just as the British course of action was contingent upon our course of action, so too does the same apply to India.' The editorialist opined that the British were inclined to 'look at the Orient as a single entity'. We should not be surprised, then, that when Gandhi halted in Suez on his way to London in the fall of 1931 to attend the Round Table Conference as the emissary of the Indian National Congress, a committee was there to receive him when his ship docked at Port Said. The 7 September edition of *Al-Ahram* gave over the entire front page to Gandhi's visit with these headlines: 'An hour with Gandhi on board the ship. Gandhi's message to Egyptian nationalists. Gandhi warns that the Civil Disobedience campaign will resume if conference fails.'

It is reasonable to assume that, given the supreme importance that Gandhi attached to the question of Hindu-Muslim relations in India, he would not have been unimpressed with the necessity of cultivating close ties with the 'Muslim world'. Indeed, nearly all commentators take it as axiomatic that his views on a Jewish national home were profoundly shaped by the imperative to sustain friendly Hindu-Muslim relations and even, as the demand for Pakistan began to gain adherents, keep India undivided. On 4 July 1937, Hermann Kallenbach, who had been reunited with Gandhi in India after more than twenty years, carried a message for the Zionist leadership at the Jewish Agency offering the services of the Congress in facilitating a 'direct conversation between Arabs and Jews only.' The 'Muhammadan population of India, being 70,000,000,' the letter concludes, 'is by far the most important in the world. The intervention of some of their leaders with a view to reach conciliation, may have far-reaching results. What do you think about it?' Once before, when it was put to Gandhi that his attachment to the Khilafat cause seemed to go well beyond his desire to see 'justice on the Khilafa', Gandhi had admitted: 'Attaining of justice is undoubtedly the corner-stone, and if I found that I was wrong in my conception of justice on this question, I hope I shall have the courage to retrace my steps. But by helping the Mahomedans of India at a critical moment in their history, I want to buy their friendship.'

Had Gandhi, then, surrendered to political compulsions in opposing a Jewish homeland in Palestine, or at least, as shall be seen shortly, a homeland that apparently could not be brought about except as a consequence of the imposition of British imperial interests? Could it be that if the demand for a Jewish homeland, whether taken to be as contiguous with undivided Palestine or to be carved out of it, were to be conceded, it would strengthen the hands of those in India who clamoured for the vivisection of India? Of course, one could have argued from the other end of the political spectrum: if a section of Muslims in India were prepared to wage a struggle for the creation of a homeland where their interests would allegedly be better and more equitably represented, by what right could they deny the same privilege to Jews in Muslim-dominated Palestine? To Jewish leaders the logic of the Muslim position might have seemed inescapably pragmatic: while in India they professed to speak as a victimised minority, albeit a sizable minority, in Palestine, speaking from a position of strength, they rejected the claims of another minority.

Even a minimal familiarity with Gandhi's worldview suggests why the cold calculations that doubtless informed the views of many of his contemporaries and subsequent commentators are unlikely to have entered into his deliberations on the Jewish question. This is apart from the consideration that the Jewish minority in Palestine cannot be said to have an isomorphic relationship with the Muslim minority in India: not only were Muslims in India both numerically and proportionately a much greater part of the whole population, but they also had a significantly different relationship to 'Hindus' than did Jews among Christians. The language of 'majority' and 'minority' belongs to an enumerative universe rather than to the fuzzy world in which Jews were non-Christians but nevertheless not a statistical aggregate that we describe as a 'minority', much as the Muslims of India, even when they were not part of a ruling elite, were never simply a 'minority'. It is doubtful that Gandhi had any use at all for this modern form of political arithmetic; indeed, everything in his political and ethical views militated against those crass considerations that have led to the frightening, indeed ethically numbing, normalisation of politics. The confession that he had wanted to 'buy' the 'friendship' of Muslims was in fact an admission that he had once lapsed from his own standards of ethical conduct in politics, and Gandhi's other writings on the Khilafat affair point to the indubitably more apposite conclusion, namely that his support for the restoration of the Khilafat was not even remotely predicated on the idea that Indian Muslims were therefore obliged to reciprocate the favour, for example by supporting the ban on cow slaughter. If we are to understand why Gandhi found himself unable to support the idea of a national Jewish home in Palestine, we shall have to abandon altogether the easy comforts of the view that, try as he might, he could not overlook the political expediency of furnishing support to Indian Muslims, especially at a time when the demands for separation had greatly accelerated. True, Gandhi had often declared that no cause was as dear to him as the solidarity of Muslims and Hindus, and he had gone so far as to say: 'I do not want *swaraj* without Hindu-Muslim unity.' But Hindu-Muslim unity purchased through sheer submission to naked political calculations could not be the grounds for *swaraj* either.

Let me turn, then, to the considerations that, in my judgment, weighed heavily with Gandhi. However inconsistent this argument appears to be with his repudiation of Jewish claims to a national home, it must be recognised that Gandhi perceived himself as an advocate of Zionism. Not only is Gandhi's understanding of Zionism distinctly at odds with the predominantly political connotations carried by the term today, but he also framed his views around Zionism at a time when Zionist aggression, in the shape of the nation-state of Israel, did not exist. Gandhi differentiated between spiritual and material Zionism, not unlike the distinction made by Martin Buber between Prophetic Judaism and Jewish Nationalism. 'Zionism in its spiritual sense is a lofty aspiration', Gandhi was to state in an October 1931 interview with the *Jewish Chronicle*, and he went on to elaborate: 'By spiritual sense I mean they should want to realise the Jerusalem that is within. Zionism meaning reoccupation of Palestine has no attraction for me. I can understand the longing of a Jew to return to Palestine, and he can do so if he can without the help of bayonets, whether his own or those of Britain.' An unpublished statement on Zionism made by Gandhi to the Jewish Agency around 4 July 1937 sheds some further light on this matter, and stands as a reminder that the intervening six years, during which time Palestine — caught between an Arab revolt on the one hand, and, on the other hand, vigorous Jewish self-assertion which saw the Haganah transformed into a well-armed militia and the creation of a Jewish terrorist strike group, the Irgun Zvai Leumi — had been thrown into a state of extraordinary turmoil, did not occasion a change of heart on Gandhi's part. As Gandhi wrote, 'Assuming that Zionism is not a material movement, but represents the spiritual aspirations of the Jews, the introduction of Jews in Palestine under the protection of British and other arms, is wholly inconsistent with spirituality.' Renouncing the use of arms, Jews were to 'rely wholly on the goodwill of Arabs'; but Arabs were not to construe this statement as indicative of Gandhi's repudiation of the idea of a Jewish homeland. 'No exception can possibly be taken', Gandhi warned, 'to the natural desire of the Jews to found a home in Palestine. But they must wait for its fulfilment, till Arab opinion is ripe for it.' As for the Jews who were already settled in Palestine, their abandonment of arms was calculated to earn them the goodwill of the Arabs and render their position safe. Anticipating that his position would be brushed aside as the wishful thinking of an idealist committed to non-violence, Gandhi concluded: 'My opinion is based purely on ethical considerations, and is independent of results. I have no shadow of doubt that the existing position is untenable.'

Their spiritual aspirations, Gandhi advises the Jews, need not be manifested in the shape of a nation-state in Palestine, even if their desire to live for this fulfilment is understandable. Taken in summation, however, Gandhi appears to summon some further reasons for his inability to support the Jewish case. If Hindus, Muslims, Sikhs and others were to be left to resolve their differences amongst themselves, precisely the same position had to be advocated apropos Jews and Arabs in Palestine. Zionism as a material movement, backed to the hilt by the force of arms and sustained by an imperial power, could only exist in an adversarial position vis-à-vis the Arabs. 'As the idea of Muslim nationalism was fabricated with British encouragement in India,' Nehru had once written, 'so also the idea of Zionism was fabricated by British Imperialism in Palestine.' Gandhi was unlikely to ever put the matter so starkly, but nevertheless he shared the view that Jewish claims would crumble without British support. Gandhi's long experience of British rule in South Africa and India had made him deeply suspicious of imperial powers, and he was convinced that Jewish aspirations for a homeland were morally untenable if they could not be sustained without the massive militarisation of Palestine. More than seven or eight decades after Gandhi shared his reflections with his readers, one is struck by the prescience with which he seems to have anticipated the relationship that Israel would forge with the United States, Britain's successor as the dominant imperial power in the region.

We should deliberate, as well, on Gandhi's understanding of social relations between religious communities in India and his invocation of the history of non-violent resistance in South Africa. In his attempt to explain the plight of Jews and the course of action open to them, he draws on two, perhaps tendentious, parallels. First, in commencing with a brief account of his life-long association with Jews, he adds this characterisation of them: 'They have been the untouchables of history. The parallel between their treatment by Christians and the treatment of untouchables by Hindus is very close.' One might, of course, legitimately question Gandhi's understanding of how precisely 'religious sanctions' were used to suppress untouchables in India and Jews under Christian rulers; one might also point to the fact that, unlike the Jews, the untouchables were not in search of a homeland. Indeed, the Jews were an eminently diasporic people, but Gandhi would not have been unsettled by the many differences that underlie the histories of the Dalits and the Jews.

In 1932, Gandhi had resisted, with a fast unto death, an attempt, as he saw it, to provide Dalits with a corporate political identity that placed them outside the fold of Hinduism; and as he had drawn a parallel between Dalits and Jews, one might understand why he would have been similarly resistant to attempts to cast Jews as possessed of a distinct political identity that could only find its expression in a national homeland in Palestine. The far more interesting question to ask is whether Gandhi read Judaism through the experience of Christianity, and whether he may not tacitly have accepted some of the assumptions that historically shaped Christian interpretations of Judaism.

Whatever the merits or otherwise of the parallel that Gandhi was to draw between Jews and Dalits, I cannot but believe that he would also have had in mind the larger history of social relations between religious communities in India and, in particular, the unusual history of Jews in India. 'The Palestine of the biblical conception is not a geographical tract', he says in his statement of 1938. 'It is in their hearts.' Some Jews, he stresses, 'claim to be the chosen race', and they are to prove it so 'by choosing the way of non-violence for vindicating their position on earth.' Yet perhaps they were also the 'chosen race' because it was their singular experience to claim the entire world as their own: 'Every country is their home including Palestine not by aggression but by loving service.' Scholars of Jewish history are struck by the near singularity of India in the worldwide Jewish experience, but Gandhi would have embraced their history in India as a model for Jews around the world. We may underscore these words, 'Every country is their home', and turn to their history in India, one country where they faced no persecution; moreover, much as adherents of many other religions have found, Jews could openly practise their faith and signal their own distinct contributions to the making of Indian civilisation. Perhaps the leading scholar of Indian Jewish history, Nathan Katz, has written that 'Jews navigated the eddies and shoals of Indian culture very well. They never experienced anti-semitism or discrimination.' He goes on to describe in what respect India could have served as a model for the world: 'Indian Jews lived as all Jews should have been allowed to live: free, proud, observant, creative and prosperous, self-realised, full contributors to the host country.'

The history of Jews in India apart, Gandhi took notice on more than one occasion of the travails of Indians in South Africa. Let me thus turn to that other parallel which surfaces in his pronouncements on Jewish aspirations, most emphatically in his statement of 1938: when Gandhi counsels the Jews to engage in mass non-violent resistance, he argues that Jews 'have in the Indian *satyagraha* campaign in South Africa an exact parallel. There the Indians occupied precisely the same place that the Jews occupy in Germany. The persecution had also a religious tinge. President Kruger used to say that the white Christians were the chosen of God and Indians were inferior beings created to serve the whites.' No one was persuaded by this comparison; equally, no one had a more poignant response to Gandhi than Martin Buber. Not only was Buber one of the most revered Jewish theologians of his times, he was held in high esteem as a humanist philosopher by his contemporaries. His principal biographer admits that Buber admired Gandhi 'more than any living person in public life', and consequently his copious response to Gandhi, a letter written from Jerusalem on 24 February 1939, takes on additional significance. For weeks, wrote Buber, he had agonised over his response, reading and re-reading every line in Gandhi's statement; he made repeated pauses, 'sometimes days elapsed before short paragraphs', in order that he might test his knowledge and way of thinking.

'Jews are being persecuted, robbed, maltreated, tortured, murdered. And you, Mahatma Gandhi,' writes Buber in a tone of equal parts astonishment and admonishment, 'say that their position in the country where they suffer all this is an exact parallel to the position of Indians in South Africa at the time you inaugurated your famous "Force of Truth" or "Strength of the Soul" (*Satyagraha*) campaign. There the Indians occupied precisely the same place, and the persecution there also had a religious tinge. There also the constitution denied equality of rights to the white and the black races including the Asiatics; there also the Indians were assigned to ghettos …' Nothing that Gandhi had said about Indians in South Africa seemed to have any bearing on the position of Jews in Germany. Was not Gandhi aware, Buber asked, 'of the burning of synagogues'? Did he know or not know what 'a concentration camp is like and what goes on there', of 'its methods of slow and quick slaughter?' Only ignorance could explain the 'tragi-comic utterance' that had emanated from Gandhi's mouth when he had dared to compare the two situations. Surely Gandhi knew that the 150,000 Indians in South Africa were nourished on the hope that there were 200 million of them in India, but how did Gandhi overlook the fact that the Jews had nothing like a Mother India to which they could look for succour, spiritual repose, and material assistance? Last, but not least, was Gandhi not able to comprehend that nothing in the experience of humankind could have prepared one for a regime of the type encountered in totalitarian Germany? 'And do you think perhaps', asks Buber, 'that a Jew in Germany could pronounce in public one single sentence of a speech such as yours without being knocked down?'

An indefatigable letter writer and master of the epistolary art, not one to flee or wither from criticism, Gandhi never replied to Buber's letter; and he did not do so for the simple reason that it never reached him. Nevertheless, we can be certain there is nothing in Buber's letter that would have taken Gandhi unawares, or over which he had not already pondered a good deal. I have argued that Gandhi remained singularly unimpressed throughout his life with arguments that hovered around ideas of majority and minority, and similarly he would have found it impossible to agree with the suggestion that Mother India was even remotely a guarantee of political or social entitlements to Indians in South Africa. Evictions of Indians from Kenya and Uganda in the late 1960s and early 1970s, or the repeated coups that have driven out Indians from Fiji in the last two decades, are only a few instances that one can summon of the sheer impotence of India on the world stage – and that at a time when India has been a sovereign power, not a nation living under the impress of colonial rule. But such arguments would be churlish, given the moral gravity of Buber's charges; the more compelling task is to see in what manner Gandhi may have anticipated Buber's criticisms. Thus, from Gandhi's standpoint, the parallel is not exact – but only because, contrary to Buber's reasoning, Indians in South Africa were uniquely handicapped. The 'Jews of Germany', writes Gandhi in his statement of 1938, 'can offer *satyagraha* under infinitely better auspices than the Indians of South Africa. The Jews are a compact, homogeneous community in Germany. They are far more gifted than the Indians of South Africa. And they have organised world opinion behind them.' This is not the voice of anti-semitism, pointing to the Jews' alleged 'control' over world banking, financial institutions, or influential policy-making institutions; rather, Gandhi was speaking from his awareness that Germans Jews were highly educated, capable of mobilising public opinion, in every respect a 'compact, homogeneous community'. The Indians in South Africa, as Gandhi would narrate at length in *Satyagraha in South Africa*, were largely uneducated and hopelessly divided. Buber himself was inclined to see German Jewish culture as the apotheosis of

Western civilisation, and Gandhi was not amiss in wondering how poor and unlettered Indians, many of them indentured labourers, could stack up against members of a community disproportionately influential in the world of letters, arts, and the sciences? Why had people with vision, courage, and tenacity not arisen from within the community of German Jews to lead their people? If the experience of Indians in South Africa was no Sunday picnic, Gandhi was also quite clear that a non-violent response, well before anti-semitism would be transmuted into organised killing on a mass scale, might have mobilised opinion in Germany against the rise of National Socialism.

Other Jewish commentators, all admirers of Gandhi but troubled if not tormented by what they took to be his inexplicable injustice to the Jewish people, would step into the debate. These rich exchanges do not call for a vindication of one position or another. They can be read, perhaps more productively, as contributions to an eloquent, ethically informed, and philosophically subtle disquisition on the multiple meanings of home and dispossession. We often make a home and dispossess others by our act. The home that we long for, when realised, suddenly loses all its attractions. Our home might come to burden or haunt us, creating other forms of dispossession. Our actual home may well be elsewhere than the home in which we live. We may be at home in not being at home at all, and the home that we call home may have no relation to the home that is in the heart. The home that we turn over to our guests at long last begins to look and feel like a home. The home that is not ours takes shape as a home in the mind of the honoured guest. That home with which we draw a boundary to keep out others becomes more than a marker of territory, helping shape conceptions of the outside and the inside, the other and the self, the alien and the familiar. That home which keeps out others is evidently a home to some and not a home to others. We may, like the reluctant exile, gain a political home and lose our cultural home. We may have several homes, and yet feel dispossessed; or we may have no home at all, and feel that the world is at our fingertips. The only home truth is that the politics of home and dispossession is not to be unravelled by the homilies with which nationalisms are created, nurtured, and exploited.

IV

One of the many ways in which Gandhi's life might be interpreted is to view him as a man who, in the last analysis, felt himself at sea in the world. In this respect, though he was not in the quest for a homeland, he most likely saw himself as akin to the Jews. His life offers fleeting impressions of someone who, even as his feet were firmly planted on the ground, was curiously unmoored. For much the greater part of his adult life, Gandhi was bereft of a family home, sharing not even an extended family type home that was overwhelmingly the norm in his lifetime. He shared his life not merely with Kasturba and their sons but with dozens and often hundreds of inmates in communes and ashrams. If, for instance, the notion of home implies the idea of a private sphere, Gandhi displayed not merely indifference to the idea of privacy but was inclined to see it as a species of secrecy and thus deception. Again, though his life in both South Africa and India is associated with cities such as Durban, Johannesburg, and Ahmedabad, as well as cities such as Delhi and Bombay which he visited on hundreds of occasions, he never felt at home in the city. The worldview of cities remained distant to him until the very end, and it is surely apposite that a city took his life. It cannot be an accident that, having vowed not to return to Sabarmati Ashram until India had been delivered from the shackles of colonial rule, Gandhi went on the Dandi March and then drifted around for a few years until he settled upon Wardha in central India. In early April 1936, he set himself up in the desperately poor and mosquito-infested village of Segaon, which then had a population of less than 700. Segaon was without roads, telephones, and postal service; no medical clinic graced this village where typhoid and malaria were rampant; and it is from here that Gandhi plunged body and soul into what was dearest to him, namely the constructive programme. Segaon had the virtue only of being, it is said, the dead centre of India, home to everything and nothing. Moving beyond the family, the village, and the city, we must contend with the ultimate irony: if Gandhi was the chief architect of the Indian independence struggle, it is also, to my mind, indubitably the case that he was never at home with the idea of the nation-state. No nationalist was less invested in the nation-state that he had helped to forge.

The fate of the Jews interested Gandhi for all the reasons – the persecution of a gifted minority, the nature of pluralism in modern societies, the accommodation of religious difference – that others might have been animated by in their narrative, but also because the story of this great diasporic people brought home to Gandhi with visceral intensity the problems of being at home in the world, of feeling at home while being dispossessed, and of being homeless while possessed of a home. It is fitting, as I have argued, that his intellectually most engaging interlocutor on the 'Jewish Question' should have been Martin Buber, a Zionist who was a dissident within Zionist circles, a devout Jew who migrated to Israel but was never entirely comfortable with Jewish nationalism. There have, however, been in more recent times other extraordinary Jewish lives which appear to exemplify Gandhi's idea of a spiritual Zionism that cannot be fully reconciled with the idea of a Jewish national homeland in Palestine, and in closing I would like to point to the illustrious, indeed luminous, life of Marek Edelman. Deputy Commander of the ill-fated Warsaw Ghetto Uprising, and a true inheritor of traditions of Jewish radicalism bequeathed by the likes of Rosa Luxembourg, Edelman passed away in 2009 – on 2 October, the birthday of Mohandas Gandhi. Poland had, before the war, the largest Jewish population of any state in Europe. Few of its three million Jews survived the concentration camps; fewer still were those who offered opposition to the Germans and lived to tell the tale. Edelman was among that singularly microscopic minority.

Poland was overrun by the Germans within days; and so commenced World War II. Within months, the Jewish neighbourhood of Warsaw had been transformed into a ghetto, bounded by barbed wire and brick walls; and something like 480,000 Jews were confined to that space. The ghetto, Edelman wrote in a pamphlet marking the forty-fifth anniversary of the uprising, increasingly felt the 'breath of death'. Reports of mass executions of Jews circulated, but as Edelman put it cryptically, 'The ghetto did not believe'. The stories were too horrible to be plausible. On 19 April 1943, the day the Warsaw Ghetto Uprising commenced, only 60,000 Jews were left alive in the ghetto. Many years later, Edelman would contest attempts to elevate the number of resistance fighters beyond 220: while it might have been comforting to believe that more of the ghetto's residents had been prepared to enter into a struggle that was doomed from the outset, pitting young, emaciated, hungry, poorly equipped and ill-trained men against a much larger force of German soldiers armed with artillery and machine-guns, Edelman's own resolute fidelity to the truth would not allow him to enhance the numbers. In the three weeks during which the resistance fighters held out, Commander Mordechai Anielewicz was killed; Edelman made good his escape, living to take part in the equally futile Warsaw Uprising of 1944.

Having survived the war, Edelman went on to have an eminently successful medical career, becoming one of Poland's most renowned cardiologists. I would like to believe that it is no accident that he treated diseases of the heart. His fellow survivors of the Warsaw Ghetto made their way to Israel, but Edelman alone found himself unable to abandon one of the most tragic homes of European Jewry. To leave Poland would have been tantamount to cutting away a piece of himself. In later life, Edelman was among the most prominent Jewish figures, and a survivor of the Holocaust, to embrace the view that Israel's conduct towards the Palestinians was uncomfortably reminiscent of the Nazi repression of Jews. Edelman became a vigorous critic of the occupation: thinking, no doubt, about the massively unequal forces that were pitched in battle during the Warsaw Ghetto Uprising, he recognised as well the enormous disequilibrium of power between the Palestinians and the state of Israel. But, as his letter of August 2002 addressed to 'all the leaders of Palestinian military, paramilitary and guerrilla organisations', and 'to all the soldiers of Palestinian militant groups', makes amply clear, Edelman was equally critical of their easy and heady embrace of violence. 'We were fighting with a hopeless determination,' the letter states, 'but our weapons were never directed against the defenceless civilian populations, we never killed women and children. In a world devoid of principles and values, despite a constant danger of death, we did remain faithful to these values and moral principles.' It is men such as Marek Edelman who, Gandhi would have said, are the true repositories of Jewish history, and whose lives provide an intimation of what it will take to resolve the question of Palestine.

MUSLIM DOGS

Barnaby Rogerson

It was a packed London underground train, so social interaction was already set at a glacial minimum – the standard non-communication of a late-morning English commuter crowd. In through the sliding door strolled a caricature from Hollywood central-casting of a potentially threatening Muslim male – a tall, big youth, with a thick beard, black boots, camouflage trousers and a vest with big swirling Arabic calligraphy tattooed all over his rippling biceps. There was a noticeable intake of breath and a scattering of nervous glances between neighbours, as if to mime 'bomber alert', and various glances which seemed to be sussing out the chance of subtly moving into a different carriage at the next stop without looking too offensive.

Then suddenly I noticed a total mood change. Even the pair of uptight middle-aged ladies, sitting rigidly beside the door with their blue-rinsed hair, silk shirts and cardigans, were smiling and their heads were bobbing about in happy animation. They even seemed to be greeting this man – an unheard of action in an English train and especially bizarre to a stranger, let alone a bearded Muslim. What could possibly have happened? Then I saw what had caused this dramatic sea-change. The young man was very gently coaxing a dog onto the train. Most of the passengers moved over to make room (which they would never have done for a mere human) and then they began to talk, even to ask direct questions of the young man. For his well-groomed dog Husky had a damaged back leg. Within minutes the story of the dog and its 'nice young owner' was buzzing around the carriage. The two of them had just returned from a veterinary clinic where he had been told that the operation to correct the dog's leg – which was a genetic fault not an accident – would cost hundreds and hundreds of pounds. I am pretty sure that if anyone had started a collection then and there, there would have been some handsome contributions, especially when the young man explained to the old ladies that the tattoo on his forearm meant 'in the name of God the most merciful and ever compassionate'. By now the whole train had become interested in Islamic calligraphy and I was certainly not alone in wishing the two of them good luck when I left the carriage. Later that day, I realised that this chance event had been the most impressive example of an instantly friendly connection between the indigenous British and a Muslim male that I had ever witnessed – and I am talking as someone who has spent a lot of time attending various state-sponsored, but largely fatuous, interfaith conferences.

It also got me thinking, how doomed are all the natural crossroads of social interaction between the Christian host nation of these islands and the British Muslim community. Close your eyes and think of typical British everyday food: a pork pie, a bacon sandwich, a sausage on a stick, a hotdog in a bun – all no good for sharing with a Muslim neighbour. Try again and imagine some typical British after-work activity like a pint in the pub, a drink at the club and maybe a flutter at the bookies – also no good for interaction with Muslims. That these differences also extend to two very different social attitudes to dogs was almost comically absurd. And there can be no doubt about this. By and large, the Muslims of Britain dislike dogs. They do not hate dogs, they do not want to stone them, they do not want to harm them, indeed they might even respect them at a distance, but they do not want to touch one, let alone allow themselves to be licked, which is the dog equivalent of a kiss.

To be British and a self-confessed dog-disliker is to admit to a serious character failing. To own a dog is the easiest possible way in which to meet your neighbours in any parish in Britain, be they the highest or the lowest citizens of the land. To go out of your way to greet someone else's dog, to know their name and give them a pat, is an instant doorway into the owner's affection. To give a local example, the old house-keeper for the priests at our local Roman Catholic church never travels anywhere without two bags of dog-treats in her pockets – and is now treated a bit like St Francis by the whole community. I also remember the tension of introducing a radical Irish friend to my deeply conservative parents. The issues they could have come to blows over (be it race, class, religion, politics, nationalism – not to mention Northern Ireland) were legion – but his first social action was a stroke of genius, for he rolled on their lawn and played with their three bloodhounds, and instantly became in their eyes such a good man that all possible bones of contention dissolved in an instant. This is a very unlikely course of action for any of the Muslim friends that I know. I walk my dog through a number of small parks and street markets in central London, and have learnt to recognise a Muslim at about a hundred yards by their adverse reaction to an approaching dog. I am aware of this, especially amongst young mothers, and take early avoidance action. I might slip on a lead if she had been trotting at my heels, or tighten her chain, whilst giving them some extra space as we walk by. Now and then I add a mischievous *salaam aleikum* to see their reaction. Muslim men tend to hold their ground, but I can see that they are keeping a sharp eye on the polluting distance between my dog and their leg.

Similarly when I get off the train from London to Winchester and try to get a local taxi to take me to an isolated cottage, I'm now used to a bizarre ritual of rejection. The taxi rank of this Hampshire cathedral town has been effectively monopolised by hardworking Bengali-Muslims who work all hours, including our traditional holidays (when you need a cab most), drive carefully, give scrupulous change and do not drink. But none of them will ever allow my dog into their vehicle, even when I suggest that she is obedient and will sit neatly on the floor. They are very polite and try to avoid any offence but draw a veil over their real feelings by inventing excuses, such as customer complaints, allergies, asthma, you name it – while effectively operating a dog ban. So I go down the taxi-rank (it being ill-mannered not to try any of the taxis who had lined up in such an orderly queue) all the time knowing I will not get a lift until I come across a white face, who will typically be the only driver who will welcome a dog into his car. This is my own experience. Once you delve into the pages of the more right-wing press in Britain, you will come across more extreme stories: of Muslim bus-drivers refusing to allow dogs onto their vehicles, of Muslim prisoners refusing to have their cells searched by security dogs and Muslim travellers refusing to be sniffed-over by the dogs of the drugs patrol. To compound this already awkward social arena, I have been told by Asian Muslim friends that in their experience the most aggressive breeds of dogs (rottweilers, alsatians, bull-terriers and dobermans) are often owned by racists with a can of beer in their hands and a belligerent turn of phrase on their lips, which turns a casual stroll through a park into a nightmare ordeal of alienation, rather than one of the pleasures of life.

So what is at the root of it all? And is there anything that can be done to defuse this curious situation?

The first obstacle to be considered is a series of hadith of dubious origin which rightly or wrongly continue to underwrite the cultural consciousness of the modern Islamic world. Their authority and their veracity may have been questioned by contemporary textual scholars of Islam, but they are still deeply embedded. The one I have heard most often, and with the most conviction, is that 'angels will not enter a house in which there is a dog', followed by 'the company of dogs voids a portion of a Muslim's good deeds', though a third hadith, 'dogs, donkeys and women, when they cross in front of a man at prayer, negate its worth', seems to be taken less seriously.

If these sayings were all that underpinned the Muslim attitude to dogs, a full-scale assault could be launched against the nature of these hadith. But it is not as easy as that, in part because the nature of dogs, their loyalty, stupidity and obedience, have for thousands of years led them to be associated with the police. In the coded word-game of animal stories and jokes beloved in both the ancient and modern Islamic world as a safe method of discussing politics, the lion represents the current ruler, the wolf a minister, the fox a politically ambitious servant, whilst the bulk of humanity is dressed-up in the powerless role of a flock of sheep or a herd of cattle. Dogs are the police - stupid, greedy, randy and loyal to the powers-that-be. Just like the police, they have to be fed, but they should never be loved or trusted or brought in to meet your family, and now and then, when they overstep the mark and get out of control, they have to be slaughtered. By the same bloody token the only cure for a rabid dog is mythically supposed to be to drink the blood of kings. At times of political turbulence, one of the first signs that public dissatisfaction is on the cusp of turning violent is when street dogs start getting attacked. It's a coded message to the informers and secret police embedded in the community that it is their turn next, unless they clear out. It also gives an even sharper edge to that traditional Islamic insult, son of a dog.

In recent years, the image of a dog-lover has acquired another negative twist. It has become associated with Muslim urban elites who have become too westernised and lost touch with local values, feeding their pampered pets on the best cuts of meat whilst the poor starve. A well-connected Pakistani journalist recently told me in all seriousness that he thought that

President Pervez Musharraf's known devotion to his dogs (a pair of Pekinese) was one of the root causes for his rejection by the electorate. It is just as well, he went on, that they didn't know that his first dog, acquired as a boy in Ankara, had been named 'Whiskey'.

A more factual, historical bedrock for the Muslim distrust of dogs comes from the earliest and most trustworthy Muslim historians who record that the Prophet ordered that all the stray dogs in Medina be rounded up and destroyed. The only exceptions to this slaughter were those dogs that were being kept by families as guards, to hunt or to help with the herding of animals. It is widely believed that this order was given to control an outbreak of rabies, in much the same way that in animal-loving Britain there is currently a cull being organised of all the wild badgers in order to limit the spread of bovine tuberculosis. This historical view is supported by the second powerful dog-related tradition, Muhammad advised that any container that had been licked by a dog which might have potentially infectious saliva, be removed by a vigorous scrubbing with abrasive sand, followed by a succession of washes (some traditions specify seven, some five, some three) before the container could be considered clean. This is sound advice for stopping the spread of disease from dogs to humans. It is interesting to reflect that the Prophet did not order the destruction of either the dog or the dish, nor that dogs be kept away from human households, but merely that a container used by dogs should be cleaned properly and effectively before it was used by humans. Yet from this practical house-keeping advice, a whole layer of Muslim distrust for dogs was built by later generations of lawyers. The jurists of early Islam decided, on the basis of this, that dog saliva must be judged unclean. Thenceforth any pious Muslim who was touched by a moist dog's nose or tongue had to go through the ritual three washings, if he was to judge himself to be clean enough to pray. At a single stroke, one begins to appreciate why a modern Muslim might be anxious not to be touched by a dog's nose, knowing that they would have to undress and shower three times afterwards before they could go to the mosque or to pray in their home. And the Lord alone knows what a textually pious Muslim driver is expected to do, to ritually clean his taxi after he has permitted a dog in it.

This is from the mildest reading of the law, as espoused by the comparatively dog-friendly Maliki judicial tradition. They specifically argued that it wasn't the whole dog that was impure, just its saliva. For they argued that all nature must be considered pure, unless there were very clear instructions, in either the Qur'an or a reliable hadith, to counteract this basic assumption. Other jurists decided that urban dogs, who are always sniffing around human waste, as well as their own and other animals', were by their nature in a state of continual ritual impurity, but were more relaxed about rural dogs. Others ruled that dogs fed by humans were pure, but that wild dogs were impure but there was never any doubt that dog saliva was impure at all times. The worst legal moment for dogs was when wild and rabid dogs joined the list of '*khafstra*' (literally 'corrupt creatures') who are debarred from the merciful strictures of the Qur'an and can be killed at any time with impunity. This decision once again rested on that action of the Prophet, when he ordered the disposal of the rabid dogs of Medina. But as 'wild dogs' are often treated as potential 'rabid dogs', an un-owned dog could also be considered wild, and therefore be categorised amongst the gang of five vermin (scorpions, snakes, mice, vultures and rabid dogs) who are placed outside the frontiers of Islam. One doesn't have to look too far in history – to the late leader of Libya for instance – to see that the epithet 'rabid dog' has lost none of its power to evoke something beyond the pale. Gaddafi's propaganda machine attempted to paint his political opponents, especially those who had escaped into exile abroad, as 'rabid dogs' who should be shot down without trial or mercy. Curiously the dog imagery came back to haunt Gaddafi, when a reverse propaganda image of his regime emerged, with stories of police brutalising political prisoners in wired compounds before setting wild dogs onto them, which helped swing the international community towards intervention.

The Prophet's actions in attempting to rid Medina of rabies in the seventh century also gave some legal protection to dogs. He had spared the working dogs – those who guarded, those who herded and those who hunted – and this is not forgotten. In my experience a traditional Muslim family, especially one living in the countryside, will have no problem in keeping such dogs. But these dogs exist to work, and can never be treated as a household pet, or allowed into a house, tent or courtyard in a manner freely given to sheep, cats, horses, camels and cows. Dogs typically exist right on the edge of the domestic space, either tethered beyond the stables, on the flat roof of a house or guarding an orchard. They are fed and watered from their own dishes like a worker, but never pampered like a member of the family.

The Muslim tradition, where hounds are concerned, tends to favour speed and sight, rather than the long endurance game of keeping to a scent trail which is at the heart of the western tradition of hunting with hounds. So Muslim huntsmen prefer the graceful looking physique of a 'sight hound', most famously the Saluki and other breeds that look similar to greyhounds, lurchers or wolf-hounds, rather than 'scent hounds' like the archetypal western foxhound, bloodhound or beagle. In this Muslim tradition, a fast running huntsman aspired to take the game from the grip of the hounds and perform the ritual blood-draining throat incision immediately, reciting '*bismillah Allahu Akbar*'. But this was not always possible, and certainly not predictable, so it was usual practice to also pronounce the '*bismillah*' over the heads of the hounds the moment they were let off their leashes.

Another curiosity about dogs in the Islamic world is that they tend to be given not sold, for there is a tradition that the Prophet advised his followers in Medina 'not to trade in dogs'. Some scholars believe that this was an attempt to discourage the consumption of pit-roasted dog which was a traditional feature of the oasis harvest festival. Whatever the historical reasons, travellers should be aware that too great an admiration for a young puppy can often end up with it being bestowed as a gift – with the owner refusing to accept either money or a gift in return, just as they would not expect to pay for a puppy when they next require a dog. This removal from the cash economy adds another subtle slight to the status of 'Muslim dogs' which, without becoming too morbidly sentimental, helps give them that distinctive hang-dog look, for they know that they live on sufferance as the least loved of all animals in daily contact with man. They will be fed if they prove themselves loyal workers, but the moment they give into any temptation to go wild, they literally cross a legal frontier and are classified amongst the vermin.

Although a dog in the traditional Islamic world will not expect to be patted, he can expect to be well watered, for there are a number of sayings of the Prophet that strongly approve of caring for a thirsty dog. The best known of these traditions (listed by Muslim) remembers how a prostitute was seen dipping her stockings into a well in order to bring some water up to a parched dog. Her act of charity was observed by the Prophet who assured her that such acts of kindness were loved by God and that all her sins had been washed away. Another hadith, so similar in mood that it could almost be a different telling of the same event (this one recorded by Bukhari), remembers a man quenched his thirst at a nearby well, but upon seeing a dog suffering so badly from thirst that it was eating the dampened earth, he took off his slipper in order to fill it from the well and give the dog some water – whereupon the Prophet assured him that God thanked him for this deed and forgave him. This so astonished the crowd around the Prophet that they asked, 'O God's apostle, is there really a reward for us when we serve animals?' To which the Prophet replied, 'Yes indeed, there is a reward for serving any living being.'

This is where Islam and Christianity can converge, in their esteem for all creatures great and small, not just that higher ape, humankind. A Muslim might remember the Prophet's advice, 'whosoever is kind to the creatures of God is kind to himself', backed up by his much sterner declaration that 'there is no man who kills even a sparrow, without it deserving it – but God will question him about it on Judgement Day'.

A thoughtful Muslim might also inform their British neighbour that the Qur'an advises that all of creation is engaged in the act of praising God, even if this praise is not expressed in human language. Those who have the gift for hearing such harmonies believe that in the dawn and dusk chorus, we are listening to the times in the day when it is the habit of birds to sing their praises to God. It is also believed that the wisdom of Solomon was such that he understood the language of the ants, while another similar tradition records that the Prophet (who had worked as a shepherd from boy to manhood) was able to translate the complaints of a camel to its owners.

The Prophet forbade animals to be killed for anything other than eating and he called down a curse upon whoever shoots at a living animal for mere sport or as a live target, who imprisons animals without providing them with sufficient food, who sets them to fight against each other and also forbade any brand to touch the face of an animal or its body to be mutilated whilst it was still alive. If they chose the right moment, a Muslim could also tell their neighbours stories about the Prophet's favourite animals, such as his cat, Muezza, and his camel, Qaswa, and also give them the names of his horse and his mule. They could perhaps also remember the only dog referenced in the Qur'an (believed to be named Qitmir), loyally guarding the seven sleepers in the cave, 'and their dog stretched his forelegs across the threshold', or tell some alternative tales, perhaps about the Prophet's uncle Hamza who was a renowned huntsman, but expressed his love for God by respecting the sanctity of Mecca where it was forbidden to draw the blood of man or animal, though he made it his habit to decorate the wall of the Kaabah with trophies gathered from his hunting in the desert. Perhaps they might also remember the story of how the Prophet, at the very peak of his ten-year battle against the pagan Lords of Mecca, had the compassion to post guards around a heavily pregnant bitch so that she could give birth to her puppies in the desert and not be trampled underfoot by the marching columns of his army.

Perhaps the most all-embracing is that extraordinary Qur'anic verse [6; 38] which declares that 'there is not an animal that lives on the earth, not a being that flies on its wings, but forms a community like yours. Nothing have we omitted from receiving their own revelation, and they shall all be gathered to their Lord in the End.' This is glory for animal-lovers to exalt in, a basic understanding that all creatures are spiritual partners on this earth.

When I think back to that young Muslim man on the London underground giving advice to the concerned old ladies around him – I remember they were thrilled to hear that their cherished animals would go on to the Lord in the end. When I was able to speak to him, he cut to the quick about how easy it was to be a dog-loving Muslim, for he claimed that only a man who knew about dogs could have given such good advice about how to contain, then police, the spread of rabies. Just as Britain would later also be able to achieve a rabies-free environment, with its draconian quarantine law and alert-eyed customs officials posted at every port. From another dog-loving Muslim, I have heard about some practical house rules: his dogs do not sit on the sofa, the bed or on the prayer mat, and he also still strictly adheres to the Prophet's advice about hygiene. 'If my dog cleans up a bowl, it then gets a good scouring and at least three thorough rinsings.' From such a practical instruction as that, it seems clear to me also that the Prophet knew all about looking after a dog. For at the very least, we know that his wife, Maymunah had a puppy named Mismar.

I have always been intrigued by the back story behind that mischievous hadith that declares that 'angels will not enter a house in which there is a dog.' This is supposedly based on the archangel Gabriel refusing to enter the

Prophet's house to deliver a revelation after he discovered that everyone was playing with a puppy. This story, I have always thought, can be read two ways, either that archangels are allergic to dog hair and dog saliva like Muslim taxi drivers, or the archangel realised that a revelation of love and playful affection had already been delivered to the House of the Prophet through God's gift of a puppy.

ART AND LETTERS

THE WRITING ON THE WALL

Boyd Tonkin

Only on my third visit to the Alhambra did I really begin to understand the writing on the wall. The palace-fortress of the Nasrid rulers of Granada can be read – if you know Arabic – just like a book. The surfaces of its ornate interiors are plastered with religious mottos and secular poetry inscribed in the exquisite calligraphy that swirls around the rooms. Previously, I had to rely on tourist guides to decipher them. So I had grasped vaguely that, in the mid-fourteenth century, the sultans Yusuf I and Mohammed V had embroidered these walls with a dynastic slogan that now reads like a fateful warning about the dangers of false modesty: 'There is no conqueror but God.' In 1492, of course, the conquerors were themselves conquered. The Most Catholic monarchs, Ferdinand of Aragon and Isabella of Castille, occupied the hill of the Alhambra – the 'red fort'. Muslim al-Andalus, with Granada as its last redoubt, began to fade into glorious legend.

Then, during a literary weekend organised one blossom-laden April by the Hay Festival in and around the Alhambra, I toured the gorgeous, fragile labyrinth of brick and stucco again in the company of the exiled Palestinian poet Mourid Barghouti. In the Chamber of the Two Sisters, he gazed at the walls and began to read, translating with impromptu grace as he went: 'We would love the stars more if they were fixed to this wall, not floating in the sky....' Later, I found the author of those lines: ibn Zamrak, a fourteenth-century poet-politician of Granada who would have haunted these rooms – with their repeating figures of inscriptions and mosaics arranged into a hypnotic geometry – almost every day.

To anyone with a taste for history's own recurrent patterns, the irony felt almost too neat. Here, in the edifice that has come to symbolise the lost homeland of Islamic culture in Europe, a writer who represents the modern face of Arab dispossession traced the lines left by his ancestors. Not only from Israel-Palestine, but across a region still scarred despite its frail 'spring' by every stripe of unjust regime, luminaries of Arab poetry and culture have for decades had to drift in exile across distant skies. Combine this personal and artistic dislocation with the progressive urge in post-Franco Spain to reclaim the fabled tolerance of (some of) its medieval kingdoms and you can see why the ancient cities of al-Andalus have become a favoured gathering-place for many of these wandering stars. Festivals, conferences and symposia, all in various ways devoted to promoting a revival of medieval cross-cultural harmony or '*convivencia*', have flourished across modern Andalusia over the past twenty years, often boosted by funds from foreign governments such as Saudi Arabia, Kuwait and Qatar.

I have watched Emirati notables glide through the Great Mosque in Cordoba, the brilliant capital of al-Andalus under the Umayyad caliphs, on their way to yet another fiesta of inter-faith and inter-cultural dialogue. In 1999 the Kingdom of Morocco helped to create the Foundation for Three Cultures in Seville, one the prime movers behind these events. In 2011, the 1300th anniversary of the Arab conquerors' arrival in Spain via Gibraltar, the 'rock of Tariq', Cordoba itself became the first Spanish venue for the 'Averroes Encounters' – international debates named for the philosopher, jurist and scientific thinker ibn Rushd – 'Averroes' to Christian authors – who lived and taught in the twelfth-century city.

At Hay's Alhambra festival, however, it was the stirrers rather than the sheikhs who commanded the stage. Juan Goytisolo, the veteran Spanish dissident who, aghast at Franco's Spain, chose to 'adopt' Moroccan Sufi culture and settle in Marrakech, warned against the sort of high-minded talking-shop that feeds off vague platitudes. 'We can't generalise,' he insisted. 'The Arab world is like a patchwork. What applies in one country does not apply in another.' The Lebanese author Elias Khoury, who in *Gate of the Sun* wrote the epic novel of the Palestinians' tragedy, told me as we sat amid the pseudo-Moorish kitsch of the Alhambra Palace Hotel that 'I don't like this idea of putting writers into categories. … If I am to be read, it should not be because there are Arab elements in my work, but because it speaks to you as a human being.'

At that point, before the recent Arab uprisings, writers and thinkers from across the Middle East and North Africa did at least agree on the stifling corruption of the states that reluctantly hosted, or else expelled, them. 'The problem of the Arabic book is the problem of Arabic society,' Khoury affirmed. 'It is dictatorship and censorship. And this censorship isn't only against writers and books – it's against the whole society.' As he put it later, speaking under the walls of the Alhambra, 'the freedom of the writer is meaningless if he is in a society which is not free.'

As a venue for reflections on past glories, and for dreams of greatness restored, Granada surely has no peer. The nostalgic, elegiac element to its art and myth began long before the fleeing sultan Boabdil halted on the heights south of the city and looked back, so the story goes, over his lost domain at the place of 'the Moor's Last Sigh'. As the final bastion of Muslim Iberia, the Nasrid kingdom acquired a sort of sunset glow prior to the final coup delivered by Ferdinand and Isabella. In fact, thanks both to the centuries-long span of the Christian 'Reconquista' in Spain and the gulf between the pluralistic Umayyad rulers and their more austere Berber successors the Almoravids and the Almohads, the writers of medieval al-Andalus always seem to be looking back regretfully to a vanished golden age. 'On the morning they left/ we said goodbye/ filled with sadness/ for the absence to come,' runs (in Cola Franzen's translation) the famous lyric '*Leavetaking*' by ibn Jakh of Badajoz. He was writing early in the eleventh century, almost half a millennium before Granada fell.

For some later commentators, both Arab and European, the rot had already set in when the enlightened Cordoba of the Umayyads succumbed to the Berbers in 1009, and the Caliphate began to splinter into squabbling petty kingdoms. Surely no major culture – not even the Roman Empire in the West – has ever staged a longer goodbye than al-Andalus. One of the most famous elegies for its departed splendour dates from the middle of the thirteenth century, after Seville had fallen to the Castilian kings in 1248. Abu al-Baqa al-Rundi writes (in James T Monroe's translation) of ablution fountains that weep over 'dwellings emptied of Islam. ... Now inhabited by unbelief/ In which mosques have become churches wherein only bells and crosses may be found.' The first line of his lament strikes the plangent note that searchers for romantic Moorish Spain have often echoed: 'Everything declines after reaching perfection, therefore let no man be beguiled by the sweetness of a pleasant life.' Glory, in classical Arabic verse no less than in the post-classical poetic traditions of the West, always carries within it the seeds of its own decadence.

It's inevitable that wistful fantasies of a 'golden age' tell us more about the dreamers than about the dream. Golden ages always exist more tangibly in the imagination of the present than in the experience of the past. For the procession of cultural tourists and visiting artists who tramp through the Alhambra, al-Andalus often means the ideal of multicultural peace and amity that allegedly bloomed here in the past, and may now offer a template for future coexistence.

Of course, no golden age – Elizabethan England, Renaissance Florence, Periclean Athens, Mughal India – can ever stand close examination. No medieval society anywhere shared modern conceptions of equality and pluralism. To live as a Christian or Jew in al-Andalus would surely have been a preferable condition to minority status anywhere north of the Pyrenees. But the '*dhimmi*' remained second-class citizens in some ways, protected yet controlled. Yes, in the mid eleventh century, Granada had a Jewish grand vizier, Joseph ibn Naghrela – an utterly unthinkable appointment in Christian Europe. Accused of favouring the Berber elite at the expense of the long-established Iberian Arab population, he was lynched in 1066. A massacre of the city's Jews followed. Ibn Zamrak, whose lines Mourid Barghouti recited for me in the Chamber of the Two Sisters, practised assassination as part of his statecraft. In the manner of all medieval courts, he was dosed with his own medicine and murdered in 1393.

So, if every golden age hides a core of brass and iron under the gilt, why does the notion still appeal? For guests at a literary festival in the Alhambra, the prospect may beckon of an Arab – or at least Arab-influenced – cultural terrain where people of all faiths and both genders might speak and write in freedom and in fellowship. Nasrid Granada, don't forget, sheltered a notable school of women poets. For Emirati bigwigs at their five-star conference hotels, I suspect that the ideal of al-Andalus might have more to do with a hands-off respect for other people's cultural boundaries – and for the overlords' absolute sovereignty within them – than with unfettered free expression.

As fairy tale, dreamland or utopia, Moorish Spain has gone through as many revamps and renovations as the Alhambra itself. Cultural historian Robert Irwin depicts the palace as a kind of palimpsest that embodies the vastly divergent views of its successive proprietors – Muslim emirs, Christian kings, secular bureaucrats – about its role. As a symbol, its meanings and messages still multiply.

Plenty of the Arabian Nights fantasias woven around the Alhambra by nineteenth-century Orientalists had precious little to do with sober inquiry into Islam's past and future presence in Spain and Europe – the agenda for so many Andalusian evenings these days. In the English-speaking world, the cult of Granada got going in earnest in the 1830s, after the American writer-traveller Washington Irving published his *Tales of the Alhambra* in 1832. He had lived in the dilapidated palace in the late 1820s, and his Romantic sketches do manage to incorporate some fact along with all the delicious – and deeply influential – whimsy:

> The amenity of its climate, where the ardent heats of a southern summer were tempered by breezes from snow-clad mountains, the voluptuous repose of its valleys and the bosky luxuriance of its groves and gardens all awakened sensations of delight, and disposed the mind to love and poetry. Hence the great number of amatory poets that flourished in Granada. ...

And so on, in a jasmine-scented haze of prose that can still cast a heady spell. For example, Irving's tale of the doomed passion of the poets Ahmed and Hafsah may owe more to Romantic convention than medieval chronicle, but Hafsa bint al-Hajj al-Rakuniyya (1135-1191) was a real enough person, and some of her amorous verses do survive.

Irving's vision of Granada as a citadel of sensual and intellectual glamour has proved remarkably resilient. In tourism, politics, even historical research, not that much of the myth has changed since he was:

> irresistibly transported in imagination to those times when Muslim Spain was a region of light amid Christian, yet benighted Europe – externally a warrior power fighting for existence, internally a realm devoted to literature, science, and the arts, where philosophy was cultivated with passion, though wrought up into subtleties and refinements, and where the luxuries of sense were transcended by those of thought and imagination.

But he wrote, of course, for Protestant and secular readers, to whom the grandeur of the Moors served as another stick to beat the barbarity of old Catholic Europe, with its prelates, torturers and inquisitors. Not that this 'black legend' entirely lacked a local foundation. In 1499, Archbishop Jimenez de Cisneros persuaded the Muslim judges of Granada – still formally protected, along with their community, by the guarantees given in the surrender treaty of 1492 – to bring out their precious Arabic books. He burned around 5,000 volumes, even refusing pleas from Christian scholars that they should survive.

For many local inheritors of al-Andalus, the picture of the past still looks decidedly different. If you pass, as I have done, from the consciously pluralist history on show in the Alhambra itself to the Catholic monuments of Granada, then the reconquest of 1492 swaps its costume: from catastrophe to triumph. In the Capilla Real, where the ruggedly modest tombs of Ferdinand and Isabella lie in the crypt, works of art still celebrate the capitulation of the Moors. Franco's ultra-Catholic Spain, 'One, Great and Free', had no time for diversity of any kind. Even today, the chapel's website defies critics of the Catholic kings over their persecution of Muslims, Jews and 'heretics' in Granada and elsewhere. It argues vigorously that the monarchs cannot be judged by modern standards and that 'every European country applauded the Spanish kings' initiatives, which represented safety for all of them'. In an outbreak of moral and historical relativism exceedingly rare in any institution attached to the church of Rome, the chapel's guardians maintain that 'Human beings' behaviour must be judged according to the conscience, laws and traditions under which they lived.'

Notoriously, Franco's godly forces liquidated the poet who had done most to reclaim his city's Moorish legacy: Federico Garcia Lorca, murdered in August 1936 at the start of the Civil War. Lorca, whose final volume of verses – *El Divan del Tamarit* – recovered and revitalised the *ghazal* and *qasida* forms of medieval al-Andalus, lives on in the Huerta de San Vicente, the pretty house where his family spent summers between 1926 and 1936. Now an evocative museum, it sits amid a rose garden in the high-rise suburbs of southern Granada. Though feted today, Lorca once accused his city of having 'the worst bourgeoisie in Spain', and the reactionary spirit that killed him is by no means dead and gone. Ancient culture-wars, moreover, have recently picked up a new momentum thanks to the politics of large-scale immigration: Spain now has a Muslim population of around 1.3 million.

This migration comes in a large part from Morocco, the destination of the many of the Spanish Moors ethnically cleansed from the Iberian peninsula between the fall of Granada and the formal expulsion of 'Moriscos' in 1609. And behind the new cult of al-Andalus and the praise heaped on the medieval '*convivencia*' lurks a gnawing fear. What if the Muslim Arabs of today were to lay claim to the lands of their ancestors? The paranoid politics that raises the spectre of an Islamic 'recovery' of al-Andalus hovers around the fringes of Spanish right-wing populism.

Its sole basis in fact lies, almost inevitably, in the rhetoric of Osama bin Laden, taken up by a few other al-Qaeda mouthpieces. From 1994, they did make the odd sweeping call for the reclamation of 'lost' Muslim territory. Needless to say, such delusions mean less than nothing to the actual migrants of today – who are rather less visible in Granada than in many working-class suburbs of Madrid, save for the Moroccan tea shops that cluster near the foot of the Alhambra hill or the craft emporia dotted around the old Muslim quarter of the Albaicin, across the river Darro.

However, on this happy hunting ground for illusion and fantasy, a few mavericks do yearn to turn back history's clock. Take, for instance, Sheikh Abdelqadir as-Sufi of the 'Grand Mosque' of Granada. Sited in a traditionally-styled building on Plaza San Nicolas in the Albaicin, the mosque was inaugurated in its current home by the ruler of Sharjah in 2003. I had passed the mosque, which commands magnificent views across the valley to the Alhambra, while wandering through the Albaicin, and had casually assumed it to be a mainstream institution born of the post-Franco reawakening of tolerance. But in Granada, refuge of dreamers, things can often be not quite as they seem.

Thanks to a comprehensive book on Iberia's modern Muslims by the Spanish-based journalist Marvine Howe, *Al-Andalus Rediscovered*, I now know more about the Sheikh and his mosque. In the 1980s, he founded the 'Murabitun World Movement' which calls for the non-violent restoration of the personal rule of the Caliphate and for currency reform through the circulation of an Islamic 'gold dinar'. For all his romance with the legacy of Granada, the Sheikh has more recently lived in Cape Town, where he founded a seminary.

As you might guess, Sheikh Abdalqadir is in fact a convert to Islam. It is his original identity that seems to fit so neatly with the record of modern Granada as a perennially appealing stage-set on which fantasists of every sort can play out their golden-age scenarios. For the Sheikh is in reality a Scot named Ian Dallas. Born in Ayr, Dallas trained at RADA, then acted and wrote plays and television scripts for the BBC. He even played a minor role in Fellini's self-reflexive classic of the director's life, '8 ½'. Dallas-Abdalqadir converted to Islam in Fes in 1967, and wrote prolifically before turning to Muslim Granada as the backdrop for the grandest production of his career.

On this historic stage where theatrical nostalgia can seize hold of religion, politics and scholarship, perhaps overt and undisguised fiction offers the most honest route back to lost world of the Alhambra. In Granada I also talked with Radwa Ashour, the Egyptian novelist and academic who is married to Mourid Barghouti and, for long years, shared his exile as another wandering star. Her 'Granada' trilogy dramatises the fall of the Nasrid kingdom and the slow extinction of its culture under Catholic rule, via the struggles of the learned bookbinder Abu Jafaar and his family. Not surprisingly, some critics have seen in her work a kind of allegory of the Palestinian *nakba* and its aftermath, as well as a resurrection of al-Andalus.

I asked Ashour how it felt to sit amid the settings of her fiction, with the legend made visible in – much-renovated – stone, brick and stucco all around. She was 'a bit troubled and confused' to be in Granada, she confided, 'because my characters are still living with me. I know they're somewhere here.' As Ashour put it, and no visitor would disagree, 'I feel that there are spectres hovering over the place, but they're very real ghosts.' Granada may still be Europe's prime location for conversation with those alluring ghosts. Nonetheless, any future golden age of harmony and tolerance will have to be built without any phantom assistance.

NINE POSTCARDS, NINE EXTRACTS

Alev Adil and Aamer Hussein

1st Postcard from Murad

Before breakfast, I walked back to last night's perfumed bush. It wasn't fragrant now: I must have smelt a night flower. We breakfasted beneath an orange tree. By the Alcazar gate, a chamber orchestra played the Habanera from Carmen. Only oranges and songs to take away.

We are leaving Sevilla. The bus station is crowded, proletarian. My companion wants water, a ham roll, the Ladies' loo. I fear we won't board on time.

A skirmish for seats, but they're numbered. We leave on schedule: midday on an August Tuesday.

1st extract from Refika's notebook

All those rainy London nights in Noura, Ozer, Melati and Taro when we'd plan our visit to Granada over leisurely dinners, how we might find the heart of who we were, this long-lost European Muslim civilisation, a place fragranced with orange blossom, whose existence challenged the clichés about two unbridgeable civilisations. Should we see the palace in the early morning or should we see it in moonlight, when there was less of a crowd? We already hated the other people we'd have to share the Alhambra with. It was our imaginary palace, far from our complicated lives with the clutter of difficult divorces, custody battles, demanding jobs, family feuds and disputes about inheritances.

All that talk came to nothing. The website that sold the tickets crashed. The hotel directed us to a travel agent down a long hot thoroughfare that stretched listlessly in the dusty heat, revealing the city's plain everyday face, a motorway, a dusty curb, rubbish. The travel agent was not only shut it had closed down, deserted like all the other shrouded shops.

We had Seville and the Alcazar instead. I was confused, which parts of the palace were Islamic, which Catholic aftermath? It didn't seem to matter. I couldn't imagine anyone actually living there. The gardens were loveliest. Reversed perspectives and geometries.

A weeping Madonna on the street. Inez Rosales *tortas de aceite* wrapped in greaseproof paper decorated with florid navy ink, flaking crumbs of anise and orange, tastes of North Africa on my lips. At breakfast I read *Tales of the Dervishes* by Idries Shah, its thirty-year-old cover once vibrant orange now a faded yellow. Murad writes a postcard.

'Whom are you writing to?' I ask him

'That's difficult to say,' he tells me.

2nd Postcard from Murad

On board, a confusing text on my companion's mobile. We try to calm each other: aren't we expected in Sanlucar? Is there some misunderstanding? Dun landscapes from the window.

The journey's shorter than expected. God, the vagaries of making electronic contact. My irritation makes my travelling companion laugh out loud.

I stole the term 'companion' from Pavese. In real life friends are all that matter, but 'friend' in a narration sounds coy.

Perhaps we laugh together.

2nd extract from Refika's notebook

I have passed through beautiful train stations like palaces, eaten oysters in Grand Central, seen the faded Ottoman majesty and stained glass windows of Sirkeci in Istanbul and watched gulls reeling outside the tiled splendour of Porto station, but bus stations have been tired ugly places in my experience. I've never encountered a charming one. Seville's is typical in its random concrete squalour and the pervasive smell of drains.

I spend a lot of time in bus stations in my nightmares. Bucharest, Ankara, Istanbul, Vienna, too often in the rain. Also at intersections on motorways, walking where there are no pedestrians, knowing I am once again in looks-like-Birmingham-but-is-really-Belgrade. I have never been to either city in my waking hours. My dreaming self is thirteen years old, if we suppose I sleep a third of my life. Her restless teenage soul prowls ugly peripheries and arteries, motorways and underpasses, refusing to return me to the real palace gardens I have seen.

3rd Postcard from Murad

My Spanish sister – I call her that, she calls me *hermanito* – is waiting at the little station. We have come to her for her birthday. She drives us to her new house: full of light as homes should be, with airy windows.

A year ago, she painted me, in oils. I'm dressed in blue and larger than life, sitting by a window of her London flat. Behind me there's a red brick wall. She complained of London's changing autumn light. Here she paints in her eyrie, in a tower. Her studio overlooks tall palms, jasmine bushes, bright flowers.

Later, with green figs, white peaches, local cheese, we drink summer wine. My sister calls it poor man's sangria.

3rd extract from Refika's notebook

We drove down the long avenue of cypresses hidden behind the tall dark green gates. For three consecutive Augusts we went to San Lucar to celebrate the Princess' birthday. Murad was her guest of honour, she called him her little brother. We drove down the long avenue to the new house in the old botanical gardens.

The first year we ate in the gardens at white damask-covered tables that shone silver under the full moon. The trees were ripe with butterfly lanterns.

The second year the women danced the Sevillana, their hands a forest of swooping circular gestures, a language I almost spoke, but not at all fluently, as I discovered when they insisted on drawing me into the dance.

The third year it rained incessantly and the party was held in the old eighteenth-century tower. Black umbrellas hung from the porch like malevolent bats. That was the year Death came with me, thought I could use the company.

4th Postcard from Murad

Satiated, seated by the blue pool now, hot as heaven. Anxieties disperse, join red petals scattered round on stone and grass. Birds dip their beaks in the pool's water. In the sun's blaze the leaves on their branches shine white. Now I think of the garden I once called home.

Shirtless, I lie on short grass. Its texture tickles my back. My companion, swimming, leaves me to my lonely thinking. (Once we shared summer ruminations. At times our silences run parallel. At others we're like strangers who don't meet.)

The cuckoo calls three times, as brazen as a rooster. Perhaps the sun estranges thoughts, reminds me of advancing age, grey hair, dull flesh. Still, in dreams, I fly before I fall.

4th extract from Refika's notebook

Murad is reading Pavese. The row of palms behind the tennis court is almost still. There is no breeze yet the pool wriggles with light. I dive into the blue and try to remember something about Pavese. Razed fields, miles and miles of burnt landscape, but I can't tell if these are related to something Pavese wrote, a memory of something else altogether or my nightmares.

'He came to me young, of his own accord', Death tells me.

I pull myself out of the water quickly as though I could escape my new companion easily, shaking him off with the tiny droplets of water as I walk across the lawn. Soon it will be lunch. There will be gazpacho. The gazpacho is delicious. The cook is famous for it.

5th Postcard from Murad

My sister, dressed in green, is dancing the Sevillana as we enter. Two friends are with her; one dances too, the other sounds the beat with flattened palms. They are sisters.

Sunlight dapples my sister's cheekbones, flickers on her fine drawn features. She dances with her face.

I'd love to paint her like this, in her green flamenco dress, dancing. If I could paint. But she could paint herself. *Tres morenas de Jaen, Axa, Fatma, y Maryen ... I.*

'What does *duende* really mean?' Someone asked my sister, at a London supper. '*Duende* means talent,' she responded. 'It's not a word we do not use much anymore.'

Tomorrow is her birthday. Her grandchildren are on holiday on another continent.

My sister, my companion remarks, looks twenty when she dances.

5th extract from Refika's notebook

Death is not good with dates. Time is a problem for him. All of it is happening at once. He tries not to remember everything, but it is impossible for him to forget. So busy all the time, for all of time. His to-do list gets longer and longer. There are seven billion of us now.

'I meet so few old souls these days,' he muses. 'And most of the tigers are mine already.' The wildness of beauty is on the other side now.

6th Postcard from Murad

Later, on the beach. Pavese called the sea a field. Tonight it is, a silver field. The sky reddens, darkens, scatters stars.

'We're at the mouth of the Guadalquivir,' my neighbour says. 'The Arabs called it something like *wad-el-kabir*.'

'Andalusian hospitality, too, is Arab,' someone says.

But this is not the sea. The yellow strand is not a beach. I'll stick to my terms. Sea or river, the line of water remains a silver field.

6th extract from Refika's notebook

The night air is warm as blood. Dark can be both wave and particle, gentle negation. Death lights my cigarette for me, whispers in my ear. He is in his element. I am barely aware of the dinner table conversation, hypnotised by the dance of reflections on the wine glasses, huge delicate balloons teetering on delicate stalks. Another covert Sevillana, the hands gesturing, lighting cigarettes, the raising and lowering of the glasses. I hear myself telling the table about the barrel signed by Faiz I had seen in the winery today. My voice sounds very far away to me. The Princess tells the story of Faiz's visit to San Lucar.

7th Postcard from Murad

We eat water-creatures: anchovies and anemones, cockles, langoustines and bream. My neighbour speaks to me of ragged love and separation. My mind and tongue unlock their Spanish. We are, at fifty, childless. My companion, eleven years younger, has a son.

'You should have a child, the two of you,' my neighbour says.

'Ah, I tell her, but we're not lovers.'

'We're best friends,' my companion adds.

'Do you still feel Pakistani?' The Venezuelan to my left asks me.

'I do, when I feel anything at all.'

The Venezuelan drones on.

'Muslims in Europe are a demographic problem. In Andalusia, I hear, they want to reclaim ancient sacred places. They should be loyal to their country of adoption. Wouldn't you say?'

'I guess I'm a Muslim in Europe too,' I say. 'And foreign everywhere I go.'

With one desultory gesture I dismiss an uncongenial conversation.

'I'm tired of romance,' I overhear my companion saying.

'But without love life's an uphill climb,' my sister muses.

Now, as I drink manzanilla, I see you in my glass. Perhaps I haven't thought of you as yet, left you behind with other things in London. Finger dipped in ink of manzanilla, I bring you into being from your place of absence, think of writing you into this narrative. (Like me, I remember, you can't swim.) Why do we see yesterday as shadow, tell me, call memory a haunting? Echoed crooked smiles, linked fingers, can thrill, become a sudden presence. Should I write: sometimes I think of you and wonder if you really happened, on occasion wish you were here to taste the green figs and the summer wine – B or remind you of an evening's words that spiralled from life's work into euphoria, an empty bottle's cork I kept at dawn, some other things you left behind?

7th extract from Refika's notebook

'You could just come with me and forget all this.' Death says. He would write my name in pomegranate seeds, 'I love you' in cocaine. Roses and razor blades are his idea of romance. Death knows how to seduce. They are talking about love now. I turn away from him, to the living.

'I am tired of romance.' I say.

8th Postcard from Murad

At midnight we sit on the patio. My sister smokes a cigarillo, I sip brandy poured on ice. A little lizard, startled, runs up the wall. The smell I remember from Sevilla fills the air, from a bush behind my left elbow.

'Jasmine,' my sister says.

(I must remember this, to tell you: there's no frangipani here, that makes it less like Karachi.)

Now it's nearly 2. My companion has retired to her room, her separate thoughts. (She wanted to visit the Alhambra. Short of time, we couldn't make it.)

Too often I treat friends like lovers, lovers as friends, give children the attention owed to adults. But friendship's all that matters. I have no time left for love. (One night B – November, and the moon was full – B you told me we had nowhere left to go. For a while I'd dreamed that we might travel on. It doesn't matter any more.)

My sister knows all this. I need to tell her nothing. We sit alone together. The sky hangs dark and low. We continue to talk, of small, of necessary things.

'The frangipani tree I planted will be in full flower the next time you're here ...' my sister breaks her sentence. Her eyes are very blue.

8th extract from Refika's notebook

The moon is full tonight. I watch her fanning herself with the palms from my bed. I lull myself to sleep by imagining I am walking barefoot through the red palace that is a pearl set in emeralds, the walls are made of a calligraphy of smoke, decorated with arabesques of remembered gestures, the fountains recite poems, the pools reflect the inky sky. But I know I'll dream again of motorways.

9th Postcard from Murad

Eyes shut, I breathe in, lost colours found again: jasmine white, fig green, hibiscus red and something new, unnamed: purple, perhaps.

The fan hums overhead. I recall one mad night's crossing, and a morning salutation: parted lips brush mine four times, and then – B an afterthought? – B a fifth. How should I name so accidental an exchange: inconsequence, or parting gift? What would you say?

Next door, my companion turns the tap on. What, I wonder, woke her? By my pillow, in a vase beside a jug of sparkling spring water, a twig of orange bougainvillea leans on jasmine. Like yesterday, it has no shadow and no smell.

9th extract from Refika's notebook

He takes me by the hand. We walk past the barking dogs, the white mare in the tall grass, down the avenue of cypresses, out of the gates, down the winding backstreets of the old town, to the edge of the land where the sea begins. And I take off my clothes and I take off my name and I swim off the page.

Death will come and will wear your eyes
– the death that is with us
from morning to evening, sleepless,
deaf, like an old regret
or an absurd vice. Your eyes
will be a futile word,
a cry kept silent, a silence.
Thus you see them every morning
when alone you stoop over yourself
in the mirror. O dear hope,
that day we too will know
that you are life and nothingness.

FOUR POEMS

Rowyda Amin

Of the Old Man of the Mountain

We were both bored, sitting on a wall when he
picked us up. His chauffeur drove for hours, too far
to change our minds and ask to be taken back,
up fenceless mountain roads to the gates
of a white villa hidden in low clouds and cedars.

The old man peeled oranges and poured retsina.
Leaning on cushions, he lit a glass pipe
and we watched the smoke curl into its stem.
He breathed the smoke from his mouth into ours
and stroked our hair as we fell asleep listening
to him tell of the garden where we would forever
be happy and fifteen.

We woke to the sounds of silver birds chiming
in the fruit trees over our heads, their filigreed
wings glimmering between the leaves. We shook
figs and pomegranates from the orchard. From over
a lake came the sound of laughter. Boys and girls
with long hair dragged us down with them to swim
and dry off naked in the warm grass.

The old man always sat a little apart. Each night
he wound the mechanical silver birds to wake us.
When we mentioned our mothers, he touched honeyed wine
to our lips and we forgot their names.

One night he brought the pipe, kissed our mouths again
with hot smoke and we opened our eyes at the foot
of the mountain, cheeks printed with gravel,
a dead dog buzzing with flies on one side of us,
on the other the buses and scooters from the village,
drivers laughing and leaning on their horns.

River Monkeys

They are the ones who slip
whilst grasping
for the moon's inconstant silver, who pitch
into ponds and streamlets
on nights when no one watches.

Simian-headed but webbed
at hands and feet,
they learn like frogs to breathe
through porous skins
growing cucumber green.

Slipping the meniscus, they return
while their parents sleep
to drop lunar currency on dressers,
leave behind small puddles,
a redolence of fish.

Claire

When we kissed on the cheek
on the Charing Cross Road
you smelled like yellow roses

and later when you unwound
your redbrown hair I thought
of horses and chestnuts, separately.

The taste of your name was pastel,
coral in milk and round
and small enough to roll

along the curl of my tongue
until it dissolved leaving almonds
and hot summer pollen.

The New Queen

The nurses chose me,
fed me rich jellies
to make me grow.

There were others, sisters
whose limbs thickened
and darkened with mine.

I sensed their movements,
turning head downwards.
Ready.

I forced an opening and called
into the dark passages. Found them
hiding in their cells.

I ransacked the nursery,
stinging the pale worms
until they were still.

The old queen was smothered
by her closest, expiring
in a nightmare of daughters.

I celebrated high in the sparkling air
with the drones,
mated them each to their death

and carried their gift home
to remind me
in my slow, swollen years

of our crazed flight,
their suicidal joy.

ARAB WINTER

John Liechty

Now that I've reached the land of dreams, let me tell you what it took to get there. Time, for one thing. I'm into my mid-fifties now, and it scares me. Bold posturing in the face of death is one thing when you're nineteen – I lost the taste for it decades ago. Here I am, far older than the mental images I keep of my parents, both dead before I was out of primary school. Khalsa and Anas ... I'm old enough to be their parent. Were they good people, good Muslims, salt of the earth? I frankly can't remember.

Unlike so many of my 'people', I am not steeped in family, culture, religion, a past. While everyone I knew growing up was wrapping themselves in what was expected of them, like naked souls dressing up against the cold, I was cutting myself free. I thought of myself as a man hacking his way through the jungle towards a clearing. I wanted to be naked, to feel the cold bracing my soul. Those others, swathed in layer upon layer of custom, duty, belief ... they struck me as mummies, doomed to suffocation by their own consent. I saw myself as relatively free, relatively fortunate, relatively courageous. I was too young to recognise that I was every bit as smug, conformist and blind as I held those living mummies to be, maybe more so. It hadn't yet occurred to me that a soul might die of exposure, or that I might merely be wrapping myself up in a different set of bandages.

I have no family ties, hardly even memories. To the rest, family was the ultimate safety net if not a religious obligation. It seemed to me just another obstacle or snare, something holding me back. I quarreled with my only surviving sibling, Fadwa, and made my exit a few weeks before one of the biggest days, I suppose, of her life – her marriage at age sixteen to a creature she'd barely met. We instantly lost touch. I did send her a postcard of Niagara Falls once I'd got a foothold in upstate New York – but it was more an occasion to gloat than an attempt to connect. I didn't even bother to indicate an address, apart from the name of the institute where I intended to do a two-year degree in electronics – a field in which I proved passably capable, but towards which I was largely indifferent. My energies at Remington Tech, for such was its name, were devoted to perfecting my English. When the degree eventually came round, I scarcely noticed it.

But what of Fadwa? Assuming she's alive and assuming she's still in the city, I have a fair idea what her life is like. She'll have three or four kids, one or two still at home, one or two married or contemplating marriage, all marginally employed. Her husband, Marwan, will be a grey nub of a man with bad teeth, as marginally employed as his offspring. The acme of his existence will be treating himself to yet another cup of syrupy tea, and moaning about Israel or America with his buddies, or maybe about the 'regime', as is the fashion this so-called Arab Spring. Fadwa will be consumed in the age-old struggle to keep the wheel of family turning, until, like some spent hamster, her heart gives out. The gas bottle, the quarter kilo of meat, the daily bread, the measure of rice, the weekly concessions to Marwan's still un-greyed libido, the endless concerns about children, and maybe grandchildren … the religious calisthenics (five-a-days), the hunt for change to finance a morning at the *hammam* …

Poor Fadwa. The centre of her life, apart from religion and the children, will be the veneered cabinet parked like a shrine in the gloom at the end of the living room, holding knickknacks from Taiwan (via Mecca), some musty books, an ornate copy of the Qur'an on a broken wooden Qur'an holder, a just-functioning television set, a just-functioning video player, a collection of battered videos (Adil Imam, Chuck Norris, and half a dozen weddings), a weird blonde shepherdess someone's brought from Dubai, ghostly tinted portraits of Marwan's parents, one of our Uncle Safwan (who took us in when Khalsa, and two months later, Anas died) and who knows … a thirty-five-year-old postcard of Niagara Falls?

All I wanted was to get away from the world Fadwa was getting into. I'd figured that out from day one. I spent the pocket money wheedled out of Uncle Safwan on black-market Levis, tee-shirts, and now and then, a bottle of obscenely overpriced bourbon called Gold Kentucky. The rest of what I could scrape together went for English classes at the American Language Centre on Nasser Avenue. I was a groupie at that place, eventually commandeering one of the handful of free tuitions they gave out (grandly referred to as 'scholarships'). The director was a fish-faced guy named Reggie Shields from Seattle. He had no personality to speak of, but I kissed his ass like he was Stevie Wonder. I used to practically camp in the vestibule to his office, where a frizzy-haired woman named Barbara served as secretary. A one-time acolyte of The Grateful Dead, she'd fried whatever brain cells she'd been initially granted, and ended up in my country. My country ... Where America's airheads could get a decent job and eat meat by the kilo and take two months a year for travel while the natives scrambled for the right to breathe. But I didn't resent the foreigners their privileges. Fascination overrode my envy.

My ultimate goal was a visa to the United States, and those weren't easy to come by. Meanwhile, the Americans didn't even need a visa to my country. They just paid a few dollars for a stamp at the airport, and I never heard of anyone being refused. We'd have let Charles Manson in. But to get a visa to the States? Short of having big money or big connections, the only surefire way I was aware of was fucking the vice-consul. The vice-consul was a pig of a man (unbeddable even by my standards of the period) named Sidney Halstead III. The first time I applied for a visa, I glimpsed the man-pig through the bullet-proof glass barrier separating Us from Them. Us being a waiting room full of nowhere boys. Us ... The Ay-Rabs. Him ... Captain America.

I remember the notices on the bulletin board in the waiting area. I'd had plenty of time to look them over. Lots of stuff that didn't concern Us, for example, LOST! Kimmy, my irreplaceable Persian Cat, if you see her call Jennifer ASAP at blah blah blah. American Embassoid chatter ... Barbecue at Geoff's Sunday after Softball, BYOB ... The AWA (American Women's Association) invites you to a Coffee Morning with special guest Khadija Nabhani, PhD. This Month's Topic: Risk of Lead Poisoning from Ceramics in the Souq ... Salsa with Felicia, Reasonable Rates ...

And then there was the notice that did concern Us, the one in my face as I was walking away from the plate-glass window, where I'd just been informed by Halstead III that I wouldn't be getting a visa this time around, and that the rejection would diminish my chances of getting one next time around. I gathered up my impotent dossier, which the turd (a Turkish girl at the language centre once made me smile by pronouncing his name 'Sidney Halstead the Turd') hadn't even glanced at, and headed out the chute with a hot lump in my throat. Despite my distraction, the poster grabbed my eye. We'll Give You a Million Good Reasons to Fight Terrorism ... There was some stylised rendition of Us, some embittered *shab* in a balaclava thrusting the barrel of a gun in civilisation's face, and below that a pledge from the US government that a useful informer might come out a million dollars ahead.

I pressed the red button of the thick steel door, with its little square of frosted glass crisscrossed by strands of reinforcing wire, heard the click, and pushed. I walked to another glass window, behind which sat one of Us in name and genotype, in reality just another of Them, an old local in uniform, a man sufficiently innocuous to have been given a job staffing the exit. He didn't bother to look at me or address me, just took my name tag, returned my ID and pen knife, and hit a button. There was a click, and the massive door swung slowly outwards. It was like leaving an airlock from Their world back to Ours, or what was left of it.

I had to walk half a mile before I could catch the number 8 downtown. I walked along the corniche awhile, letting the afternoon sun shift the chill of the embassy from my bones. I entered a café, ordered a cup of tea instead of my usual can of Coke, half-watched the asinine quiz show on the TV screen like everyone else. I thought about getting a balaclava and a rocket launcher and blasting Halstead the Turd to Kingdom Come. I drank my tea. I reopened my dossier. I seemed further away than ever from America. The thought of reapplying for a visa filled me with dread. It occurred to me that if I wasn't welcome through the front door, I might slip in through the back.

I finished my tea and headed for Nasser Avenue. The American Language Centre was quiet, not like in the evenings when it buzzed with students. I went up to the vestibule. Barbara was typing. She wasn't beautiful but she wasn't ugly. She had a pleasant smile, slightly vacant, but you sensed that whatever might have been there to begin with had been essentially good.

'Hi Sam', she said.

'Hi Barbara. I brought you something.'

'Hey, that's sweet.' She took the little newsprint-wrapped 200 gram cornet of dried apricots, set it on her desk, and smiled up at me. Plan B was underway. Operation Backdoor.

I said I have very few memories of family. There is in fact one memory that has stuck with me through the years. I can see and hear my uncle, smell the smoking bread and the cardamom they put in the coffee … Uncle Safwan had taken me along for breakfast to a place he liked in the heart of the old city. The memory is fresh as a new-minted coin – the bland block walls, the fierce cold (it was December, and very early in the morning), the *bisht* the bear of a Bedu a couple of tables away was wearing. I sat there sullenly watching my own breath, doing my best to indicate that I wished I was still in bed.

The waiter ignored me, and my uncle didn't ask what I wanted, not that I expected him to. He ordered *khubz* and *ful* and *chai*. I clutched the tea with frozen fingers and sipped while Safwan dropped pinches of salt and cumin on the beans, cut up the half an onion the waiter had brought, and bit at one of the hot peppers.

'Listen,' he eventually said in his thick voice. 'Listen to me. I can see what you're doing. I'm not blind. The other day I smelled alcohol, not for the first time. There's no respect. You wear western clothes. Look at you. You stopped your prayers a long time ago. You speak English as much as Arabic. I don't like it. That's where I stand. I took you and your sister in, your father's dying words to me, *wullah*: "Take care of them Safwan, take care of my kids." And tired as I was already, I swore I'd do my best. *Wullah*.'

More bread came steaming. Safwan tore open a loaf and dabbed at bean and onion. I picked at the food. 'Eat!' he roared. '*Kul*! *Kul*!' I nibbled a little bread but the beans didn't appeal to me, or the onion and peppers. Let's face it, I wasn't the man my uncle was. He ate like the place was on fire, and scoured the bottom of the bowl with the last bits of bread.

'What can I tell you,' he said at last. 'God knows best. But a donkey still thinks he knows better.' He sighed and eyed me with scorn. 'My mother used to say: Eat what you like, but dress as others do.' I sat shivering in my ridiculously expensive genuine Levis jeans and ridiculously inadequate ersatz Levis jacket, and underneath, my ridiculously ridiculous Jefferson Starship tee shirt. All I could do was look at my hands and say nothing.

Nevertheless, I had something to say. Something downright monumental. It was about six months after the visa rejection. I'd been working on Plan B awhile, and it was more or less coming to fruition.

'Uncle,' I said. 'I've got something to tell you.'

'Inshallah,' he murmured thickly. He always sounded like he had a cold. He lit a cigarette and two streams of smoke rolled from his nostrils. 'Well?'

'I'm getting married. To an American girl. Who I met at the language centre.'

Uncle Safwan let out a string of *Istaghfarallahs*.

'And I'm thinking about entering a college in New York. It's called Remington Tech.'

'A green card wedding?'

I blushed in spite of myself, and shrugged. 'We get on together.'

'Sure,' Safwan said. 'She's a life support system for a visa.'

I smiled, and for a strange couple of seconds my uncle and I felt like cronies.

He'd hit the nail on the head. It was as green card a wedding as they came. Barbara was under no illusions. She knew what was in it for me – a ticket out, no more, no less. Or if she didn't know, she didn't care. It was all the same. And what was in it for her? Access to the best hashish in the country, risk-free at nominal cost. Lots of the foreigners smoked, but they paid foreigner prices and they were always subject to intrigues and a string of middlemen. With me on the scene, Barbara had an inside track to the most important substance in her life.

And I wasn't bad to look at. I may have been a little squirrely, kind of a slight James Dean figure, a little dishevelled and edgy. But she liked me that way. I had some fashionable connections, I got her into parties she'd not otherwise have attended, and apparently I wasn't too inadequate a lover once I'd completed Barbara's seminar on how best to proceed.

Six months later Barbara and I were in Middleton, New York, renting a place not far from her mother's. It wasn't until nearly a year after that that I started at Remington Tech. Barbara had persuaded her mother, Anita, to put up the tuition, not very substantial in those days. My English by this time was remarkably fluent. I made few grammar mistakes (fewer, it occurred to me, than Barbara), and hardly had an accent. I used to sit up late by the radio or TV working on that. Americans took it for granted that you would speak their language and understand their culture, such as it was. Not so in my country. Reggie Shields had been there fourteen years running his lucrative language institute, and he was still struggling with 'Salaam Aleikum'. You could count on one hand the foreigners who spoke even rudimentary Arabic.

Ah, the American culture. A moment ago I unleashed a dismissive 'such as it was', but of course it was there and there were certain boundaries you didn't want to cross, certain rules you had to adhere to. It was trickier than the language. I watched sitcoms, I talked to Barbara's mother and her sometimes boyfriend Pete, I read. I read a lot more than most of the people I bumped into. And I thought I knew a thing or two, to the point that I lowered my guard and made mistakes. Not many. In general I knew how to keep my mouth shut. If there's one thing Americans love, it's for you to keep your mouth shut and listen while they're opening theirs.

One time in particular I stepped over the line. I was at Anita's place watching TV with her and Pete. We were all three on the sofa, drinking margaritas. At our knees was a bowl of corn chips on a glass-topped coffee table, with a dish of guacamole and another of bean dip. Barbara had stayed home to nurse Najma, our cat. By this time she preferred the cat's company to mine, and she wasn't getting along with her mother. So it was just the three of us there on the sofa and we'd all had a few. Things got a little chummier than they should have, I guess.

We were watching some CBS special about the Statue of Liberty. They'd just given it a makeover, reinforcing the torch and polishing the surface, at some ungodly cost in dollars. Ronald and Nancy Reagan, George and Barbara Bush, and a bunch of celebrities were out there waving their arms back and forth as if the whole world was their friend. I can't remember what year it was exactly, but Reagan had bombed Tripoli a time or two and the US Navy was doing 'exercises' off the Libyan coast. Much as I thought Qaddafi was an asshole, it stank of provocation. And unlike many Americans, who seemed to think Reagan was some kind of savant, I thought he was a senile old fart. Watching those children in adult bodies waving their arms with Lady Liberty at their backs, it occurred to me how gratifying it would be to see the smug smiles wiped off their faces. Pete didn't seem too fond of Reagan himself. Maybe that's why I said what I said, maybe it was the margaritas, maybe it was the moon.

'If I was Libyan,' I said, 'right now wouldn't be a bad time to blow that statue sky high.' Look at the sentence. Do you appreciate how idiomatic the English is? Wouldn't it have brought a smile to your face? I'd submitted for a second to the illusion that I was an insider. I thought my comment was funny. I was visualising some wildass Libyan pilot screeching into the festivities just long enough to at least strip Freedom of her torch. I waited for them to laugh

I waited, but they weren't laughing. They were sitting there looking like parents who've just found out their kid is gay, or communist, or a Jew, or an atheist, or a Republican, or whatever it is that strikes them as the ultimate disappointment. A moment ago we'd been munching corn chips on the sofa of democracy. Suddenly there was a line between us. They sat uncomfortably on one side. The recently exposed Ay-rab sat alone on the other. I knew better than to wait around for things to return to normal. They never would. We'd go to our graves with that line between us. It might diminish in time, or even disappear from sight, but it would be there forever.

I soon rose and made my excuses, something about needing to see how the cat was doing, and left them to their world. Left them with the chucklehead in charge of their country, his televised arm still wagging like a limb on one of those bobble dolls people attach to their dashboards ... His perfect teeth, his glossy cowlick. They seemed relieved. 'Come back anytime,' Anita said. I hardly ever went back, and when I did the line was still drawn.

I'd broken the golden and largely unspoken rule that everyone should observe when dealing with Americans. Like the customer, an American is always right. No matter what sort of nonsense they happen to endorse, you have to appear to be taking it seriously. Not it, in fact, but them. They don't actually care if you can't condone their drivel but you've got to hear out their perspective (just don't expect them to hear out yours). They want to be taken seriously on a personal level. They want to be liked, to be respected. After all, they've had to be the Greatest People in the World for as long as they can remember (their memories aren't much longer than their attention spans), and I suppose it's a challenging row to hoe.

I need to accelerate the next thirty years if we're ever going to get to the bottom of this. Barbara decided to go back to her old job at the language centre. She missed the hash, she missed the parties, she missed the job. She'd forgotten that Americans typically work like dogs, then have to beg for their annual week off. She'd forgotten how nice it had been to do a little typing in exchange for health insurance, a cheap apartment, and two months' vacation a year. At the same time, she was finding out that living with me was a lot less fun in her country than it had been in mine. She wrangled with her mother. She didn't care for Pete. She wrote to Reggie Shields. A couple months later he wrote back to say he had something, and the next thing I knew Barbara and Najma were on a plane.

In spite of the fact that Barbara and I were now openly separated (we only got around to an official divorce years later when Reggie Shields' mid-life crisis induced him to propose marriage and Barbara, fifteen years his junior, accepted), Anita continued to pay my way at Remington. She was amazingly impartial in this respect. She'd promised to put up the money for two years, and she did, notwithstanding my remark about blowing up the Statue of Liberty. I wasn't a total mooch. I worked nights at a convenience store, and paid my rent.

I kept up my reading. I read a lot of junk. But I also read Hemingway and Fitzgerald and Steinbeck and Kurt Vonnegut. I read Truman Capote and Updike. I went back a century, and struggled with Melville and Thoreau. I worked on Mark Twain until I could figure out when to laugh, and sometimes why. I tried Faulkner, but never figured it out. I read foreigners. I read J.M. Coetzee and Dostoevsky and Kafka and Camus. I read Hardy and Hesse and, yes, Naguib Mahfouz. Was he a foreigner? And Ghassan Kanafani? Sometimes I wrote things down in a notebook. I was fond of Somerset Maugham, who referred to Americans as 'that tumultuous conglomeration of humanity, distracted by so many conflicting interests, so lost in the world's confusion, so wishful of good, so cocksure on the outside, so diffident within, so kind, so hard, so trustful and so cagey, so mean and so generous ...'

I don't want to give the impression that I was some kind of contemplative, or some kind of scholar. It's true that I lived to myself, and was never really attracted back to the distractions of sex, or companionship, or status, or whatever trappings of normality I might have been expected to subscribe to in the Barbara Era. And of course I didn't read and absorb all that stuff all at once. It took years of my life. Books were my main companions. I was something of a loner, without feeling particularly lonely – or not lonely enough to go out fishing for friends.

Getting a job in America was easy, at least at first. Even a diploma from the un-prestigious Remington Tech meant something. You just had to be minimally competent and willing to work, and plenty of Americans were neither, frankly. I was distinctly employable. I drifted around for a decade, living in Tampa (armpit of Florida) for a time. I lived in Gainesville (the other armpit); Dubuque, Iowa; Norman, Oklahoma. At the age of late thirty-something, I finally settled in Denver, where I worked for a company called Front Range Compu-Solutions. It was a good job, in the generally accepted sense – that is, I had two weeks a year paid vacation, I had health coverage after a fashion, I made a living wage.

As I became increasingly familiar with the United States, I began to realise how silly some of my initial assumptions had been. The place wasn't heaven. I was now an American citizen and had a valid US passport in my desk drawer – to have known at nineteen that such miracles would come to pass would have brought tears to my eyes. But the passport felt less like an accomplishment than just something that had happened. It wasn't taking me anywhere. Most Americans didn't have passports. Even if they had them, they rarely travelled. And even if they travelled, they rarely seemed to see anything.

I turned forty. Over the next decade, I settled in to a life of work and worry, which I guess is what good citizens do. Still, I kept reading. In my thirties I had toyed with the idea of going to university and getting a degree, maybe a PhD, in literature. I always seemed to be stopped by the notion that it was too late, that I was too old. The years ran on, and it wasn't long before I really was too old. I had some dental work done. I developed hypertension. I got promoted. I started making payments on a small apartment. It no longer felt like I had plenty of money. It no longer felt like the world was my oyster. I got sick, and had to take a month off. The people in charge at work didn't seem to mind too much. But I knew them well enough to understand I'd become a question mark.

It was during that period that I met Nabil. I met him in a Middle Eastern grocery out on Parker Road. As a rule, I didn't spend a lot of time in the company of Arabs. I didn't spend a lot of time in the company of anyone. My defences were down due to my illness, which didn't even have a name. I'd been losing weight and wasn't sleeping well. My blood pressure was up. The doctor changed my prescription from the diuretic I'd been taking to stronger stuff, a blood thinner. He suggested that stress was behind the changes in my health. He recommended a specialist and gave me a card. It wasn't until I was out in the clinic parking lot that I realised he wanted me to see a shrink. I considered throwing the card away. I ended up putting it in my shirt pocket.

But back to the grocery. It was a big place, and crowded. I was standing at the meat counter, regarding the lamb. I must have blanked out for a few seconds. When I came back, the butcher was looking at me. 'You okay?' he said. I was holding tight to the bar on my shopping cart, suddenly conscious of the little crowd that had converged.

I think I blushed, despite feeling cold and pale. 'Yes, it's nothing.' I tried a little laugh. 'Nothing to worry about.' I nodded reassuringly to the woman beside me, and she moved on. 'I'll take that piece,' I said, pointing. 'The neck.'

'Sure.' He leaned into the counter, took the meat, and put it on the scales.

'Say brother, you don't look so good.' The speaker was one of the several people who'd seen what happened. The others had resumed their shopping.

'I'll be all right.'

'*Inshallah*. But I'd be happy to drive you home.'

'Thank you, that's a very generous offer. I'm sure I'll be all right.'

'Let's just see how you feel. It's not a problem for me. My name, by the way is Nabil.'

We shook hands. 'I'm Sam,' I said. 'Sami.'

On the way to the cashier, I added a bottle of olive oil and a packet of figs to the cart. I had intended to buy quite a few other things, but felt like getting to the car. Nabil helped me open the hatch, and he put the groceries inside. I could feel sweat beaded on my forehead, and a shiver took hold of me.

'C'mon,' Nabil said. 'I'll drive you home. I'm at your disposal. You live in Aurora?'

I nodded.

'I can take you to the hospital if you think you should go.'

I shook my head. 'Home,' I said. 'Sorry for this.'

'It's not a bother, brother. You're talking like an American.'

And that's how Nabil came to be handing me a cup of tea in my own flat. I drank it, and lay back on the sofa, and must have napped a little. When I woke I recognised the sound of the pressure cooker coming from the kitchen. Something smelled good. I felt better, and realised I was hungry, and wanted to eat.

'What's gives in here?' I asked at the entry to the kitchen.

'I went ahead and made some soup. How are you feeling?'

'A lot better.'

'You look better.'

For the first time I found myself feeling well enough to take a good look at my nurse. He had a wispy beard, and was younger than I'd imagined him, perhaps in his mid thirties. He was slightly built. His eyes were sharp, he had a fine hawkish nose, his lips were not overly friendly, his skin was smooth and gingery. He actually reminded me (apart from the beard) a little of those aliens who are forever abducting the good citizens of Roswell, New Mexico. He had been born in Najran and had a Saudi passport, but as he explained, that was merely a quirk of bureaucracy – he considered himself Yemeni.

The soup was better than I could have managed, and I'm not a bad cook. He'd used some of the lamb, along with garlic, dried leeks, a bay leaf, chili, carrots, potatoes, a turnip.

'This is delicious,' I said, sitting at my table, sipping the salty broth from a spoon. 'You should try some of your handiwork.'

'I had a few tastes in the kitchen. It's time I was going.'

'Give me just a minute and I'll give you a ride back to your car. I feel much better.'

'No need, I called a friend at the mosque. He's on his way. He'll drop me off.'

'Thank you, Nabil. You've been a godsend.'

Nabil's expression could have been a frown or a smile. 'I wonder,' he said. 'I don't mean to intrude, but would you care to join me this Friday over at the mosque?'

I'd been afraid this was coming. Always a catch. Normally I would have said no without hesitation. 'I … I'm not particularly religious.'

'I figured that. I've seen your books,' Nabil said, glancing into the living room at the shelves. 'Lots of books, but nowhere the Book. Don't you miss the Qur'an?'

'No,' I said. 'I was never too attached to it.'

'So which are you, Sam or Sami?'
'I've been Sam so long I guess I'm Sam.'
'Which are you in your own head? And your heart?'
I didn't answer either question. Nabil took a card from his wallet and handed it to me. 'In case you change your mind, here's my number. And even if you don't change your mind. Okay?'
'Okay.' I put the card in my pocket. There were two of them there now. I still hadn't called the shrink.
He looked at his mobile phone. 'All right, brother, *Salaam Aleikum*. My ride is here. You look after yourself. I'll let myself out.' I tried to get up to at least walk him to the elevator, but he was too quick for me. The elevator had already kicked in by the time I opened my door. I went back to the table and finished the soup.

Friday came and went. On Monday I had to get a prescription filled, and ended up at Wal-Mart. It seemed like every entry to the parking area had someone in a flannel shirt or old army jacket holding a piece of cardboard with their plight written on it. The sign at the entry I took read: 'Help – Disabled'. The guy didn't look disabled. He was able enough to spell 'Disabled' at any rate, and stand holding his piece of cardboard half a day. You really couldn't blame these people too much. There weren't many jobs available. The country was broke and fighting two expensive (and silly) wars. There'd been talk among the colleagues that Front Range CompuServe (where I was due back in two weeks) was considering a move to China. I might have to start looking for my own piece of cardboard before long. I wondered what to write on it. 'Homeless' had potential.

Inside the store, I headed straight for the pharmacy and took my place at the end of a short queue at the prescription window. Ahead of me was a woman in one of those self-propelled wheelchairs. Judging from the back of her neck and what I could see of her arms, she was obese, and I assumed she was simply another of the many leviathans one saw tooling about Wal-Mart in motorised chairs because they were too fat to walk. Then I saw that she was missing a leg. Here was someone who really was disabled, and a minute later I understood why as she pivoted her chair from the prescription window.

An image of the American flag billowed across the woman's breasts, each like a pan of jelly. The tee shirt read: 'I Fought for Freedom in Iraq'. She couldn't have been twenty-five. The stump of her leg winked at me as she whirred to the end of the aisle and rolled out of sight. I thought of words from the quote in my notebook: '… so lost in the world's confusion, so wishful of good …' You might dislike these children, but it was difficult to actually hate them.

I collected my prescription, aware I wasn't feeling very well. I went to the men's room and stood at a urinal, producing the limp trickles and spurts that mark the tail end of middle age. I washed my hands and daubed my forehead with a paper towel. As I left the store, I read for maybe the fifteenth time that morning Wal-Mart's thought for the day: 'Save Money. Live Better.'

'Hey guy, spare some change?' It was a long-haired bony man wearing a cowboy hat, a pearl-snap checkered shirt, tight jeans, and pointy-toed boots. He let up scratching at his arm. I shook my head and gulped a few mouthfuls of air. To the west the snowcapped mountains glistened. There was sweat on my forehead. 'Even a couple bucks would help out.' I looked at him and shook my head again. He muttered something and headed for fresh prey, scratching.

I made it across the parking lot to my car, and sat shivering behind the wheel. I thought I might black out again, like I had at the grocery. I started the engine, and waited for the heater to drive off the cold.

But I couldn't wait that long. I felt stripped to the bone. The cold was moving in. I drew out both cards that I'd cached in my wallet, selected one of them, and punched the number into my phone. A voice answered.

'*W'aleikum Salaam*,' I said. 'It's Sami.'

ET CETERA

CITATIONS

Introduction: Return to al-Andalus by Ziauddin Sardar

The quotations from al-Ghazzali are from his *The Book of Knowledge*, translated by Nabih Amin Faris (Ashraf, Lahore, 1962), p1-2; and *The Incoherence of the Philosophers*, translated by Sabih Ahmad Kamali (Pakistan Philosophical Congress, Lahore, 1963), pp.1-3; 88; 163-167; 176 and 181. Others books mentioned by al-Ghazzali are widely available in translations of various qualities. There are several translations of ibn Rushd's *The Incoherence of the Incoherence* but the best is by Simon van Den Bergh (Luzac, London, 1954, combined two volumes). Similarly there are a number of translations of *On the Harmony of Religion and Philosophy* but George F Hourani (E J W Gibb Memorial Trust, Cambridge, 1961) cannot be surpassed. My quote from the historian Marrakushi is taken from him, p.8; the quote from Hourani himself is from p.11. Volume 1 of *The Distinguished Jurist's Primer*, translated by Imran Ahsan Khan Nyazee is published by Garnet (Reading, 1994). Simon Ockley's 1708 translation of *Hayy ibnYaqzan* can be downloaded from here:
http://www.muslimphilosophy.com/books/hayy.pdf
Ibn Hazm's quotes on the prophethood of women are from his *al-Fisal fi al-Milal wa-al-Ahwa'i wa-al-Nihal*, which can be downloaded from: http://globalwebpost.com/farooqm/study_res/islam/gender/women_prophethood.html
A J Arberry's translation of ibn Hazm's *The Ring of Dove* can be downloaded from:
http://www.muslimphilosophy.com/hazm/dove/ringdove.html

See also A G Chejne, *Ibn Hazm* (Kazi Publications, Chicago, 1982); Majid Fakhry Averroes, *Ibn Rushd: His Life, Work and Influence* (OneWorld, Oxford, 2001); W Montgomery Watt, *Muslim Intellectual: A*

Study of Al-Ghazzali (Edinburgh University Press, 1963); Iysa A Bello, *The Medieval Islamic Controversy Between Philosophy and Orthodoxy* (Brill, Leiden, 1989); Salman H Bashier, *The Story of Islamic Philosophy: Ibn Tufayl, ibn al-Arabi and Others on the Limits Between Naturalism and Traditionalism* (State University of New York Press, 2011); and Peter Adamson, *In the Age of Averroes: Arabic Philosophy in the Sixth/Twelfth Century* (The Warburg Institute, London, 2011), which contains an illuminating essay on *Hayy*.

The quotes from Ebrahim Moosa's *Ghazali and the Poetics of Imagination* (University of North Carolina Press, Chapel Hill, 2005) are from p.38 and p.39; Sadakat Kadri, *Heaven on Earth: A Journey Through Sharia Law* (The Bodley Head, London, 2012) p.87; and C. Snouck Hurgronje, *Mekka in the Latter Part of the 19th Century* (Brill, Leiden, 2007) p.210 and p.217. Jeremy Cox's *The Burial Chamber* (Stroud Green Book, London, 2012, £8.99) can be downloaded as kindle version for 77p!

The Jasmin Breeze by Robin Yassin-Kassab

The quotations from Titus Burckhardt's *Moorish Culture in Spain* (Allen and Unwin, London, 1972) are from page 90 and 10; and Robert Irwin's *The Alhambra* (Profile Books, London, 2005) from pages 69, 64 and 88. Giles Tremlett's *Ghosts of Spain* (Faber and Faber, London, 2006) offers useful commentary on contemporary Spanish attitudes to the civil war and Franco periods, on Gypsies and Spanish subnationalities. There are several editions of Washington Irving's *Tales from the Alhambra*, which was originally published in 1832. Salman Rushdie's *The Moor's Last Sigh* is available as a Vintage paperback (1996). On the ideas of ikhwan as-safa' see *The ikhwan as-safa and their Rasail: An Introduction* edited by Nader al-Bizri (OUP, 2008).

A recitation of Iqbal's 'The Cordoba Mosque' (1933) can be heard at: http://www.youtube.com/watch?v=CAKH2ZHmE-A
And Jorges Luis Borges' poem 'Alhambra' can be downloaded from: http://www.poetryintranslation.com/PITBR/Spanish/Borges.htm#_Toc192667914

Jose Maria Aznar's September 2004 lecture at lecture at Georgetown University, 'Seven theses on today's terrorism' can be found at: http://es.groups.yahoo.com/group/clubliberaldecastillayleon/message/256

The Andalusian Secular by Nazry Bahrawi

For the work of the Andalusian philosophers discussed in this article see ibn Tufayl, 'The Story of Hayy ibn Yaqzān' (1169-79) in *Two Andalusian Philosophers*, translated by Jim Colville (Kegan Paul International, London, 1999); ibn Rushd (Averroes), *Tahafut al-tahafut* (The Incoherence of the Incoherence), translated by S. van Der Bergh (E.J.W. Gibb Memorial Trust, London, 1978); and ibn 'Arabi, *The Bezels of Wisdom*, translated by R.W.J. Austin (Paulist Press International, New Jersey,1980). See also al-Ghazali, *The Incoherence of the Philosophers* translated by Michael E. Marmura (Brigham Young University Publications, Utah, 2003); and Majid Fakhry, *Averroes (Ibn Rushd): His Life, Works and Influence* (Oneworld, Oxford, 2008).

For novels based on *Hayy*, see Daniel Defoe, *Robinson Crusoe* (Oneworld, Oxford, 2007; original 1719); Jean-Jacques Rousseau, *Emile, or On Education*, translated by Allan Bloom (Basic Books, New York, 1979; original 1762); and Rudyard Kipling, *The Jungle Book*. 1894. (Penguin, London, 1989; original 1894).

The quotations are from Syed Muhammad Naquib Al-Attas, *Islam and Secularism*, (International Institute of Islamic Thought and Civilisation, Kuala Lumpur, 1993, original 1978), p. 48; Nader Hashemi, *Islam, Secularism, and Liberal Democracy: Toward a Democratic Theory for Muslim Societies* (OUP, 2009), p. 145; xi; 144; Charles Taylor, *A Secular Age* (The Belknapp Press, Cambridge, Mass., 2007), p. 4; John Locke, *Some Thoughts Concerning Education* (A. and J. Churchill, London,1693), p.2; Jean-Jacques Rousseau, *The Social Contract and The First and Second Discourses*, edited by Susan Dunn (Yale UP, London, 2002; original 1762), p. 165; Ziad Elmarsafy, *The Enlightenment Qu'ran: The Politics of Translation and the Construction of Islam* (Oneworld, Oxford, 2009), p.

119; Immanuel Kant, *Critique of Practical Reason*, translated by Werner S. Pluhar (Hackett, 2002, original 1788), p.185; Friedrich Nietzsche, *The Gay Science*, translated by Josefine Nauckhoff (Cambridge UP, 2001, original 1882) p.109.

Other works mentioned include Ian Almond, *Sufism and Deconstruction: A Comparative Study of Derrida and Ibn 'Arabi* (Routledge, London, 2004); Talal Asad, *Formations of the Secular: Christianity, Islam, Modernity* (Stanford UP, 2003); and Yusuf Qaradawi, *'Al-Hulul al Mustawradah wa Kayfa Jaat 'alaa Ummatina'* [How the Imported Solutions Disastrously Affected our Ummah] (Maktabat Wahbah, Cairo, 1977).

A Thousand and One Histories by Gema Martín-Muñoz

The quotation from Mª Antonia Martínez Núñez is from, '¿Por qué llegaron los árabes a la Península Ibérica?' *Revista AWRAQ*, 3, nueva época, 2011, pp. 28-29; Menéndez Pelayo's quote is cited and analysed by María Rosa de Madariaga, 'The Image of Morocco and an Interpretation of History in the Spanish Educational System' in Gema Martín Muñoz, editor, *Learning to Know Oneself: Social and Cultural Perceptions Between Spain and Morocco* (Fundación Repsol, Madrid, 2001) p.133; the quotations from Eduardo Manzano are from *Epocas Medievales*. Volume 2 of the *Historia de España* edited by Josep Fontana and Ramón Villare (Crítica/Marcial Pons, Madrid, 2010), p.127 and p.128, respectively.

On al-Andalus advertising posters, see *Brisas de Oriente: The Spanish Advertising Poster 1870–1970* (Colección Carlos Velasco. Casa Árabe, Madrid, 2011). See also, Américo Castro, *Spain in History: Christians, Moors and Jews* (Grijalbo Mondadori, Barcelona, 1983), and Claudio Sánchez-Albornoz, *The Kingdom of Asturias: Origins of the Spanish Nation* (Biblioteca Histórica Asturiana. Gijón, 1988).

The Original Enlightenment by Emilio Gonzalez-Ferrin

The six volumes of Edward Gibbon's *History of the Decline and Fall of the Roman Empire* was published in 1788-1989 and Thomas Carlyle's *On Heroes and Hero-Worship* and the *Heroic in History* appeared in 1842 – both are widely available.

The reinterpretation of Renaissance is best illustrated by Jerry Brotons, *The Renaissance Bazaar: from the Silk Road to Michelangelo* (OUP, 2003) and Juan Vernet, *What Europe owes to Islam in Spain* (Acantilado, Madrid, 2006). On Akhbar Majmu'a, see David James, *A History of Early Al-Andalus: The Akhbar Majmu'a* (Routledge, London, 2011). Other works mentioned include Charles Homer Haskins, *The Renaissance of the Twelfth Century* (Harvard University Press, Cambridge, Mass., 1927); Dimitri Gutas, *Greek Thought, Arabic Culture: The Graeco-Arabic Translation Movement in Baghdad and Early 'Abbasid Society* (Routledge, London, 1998); and Americo Castro, *The Structure of Spanish History* (Princeton University Press, 1954). See also, Emilio Gonzalez-Ferrin, *Al-Andalus: Europe between East and West* (Almuzara, Cordoba, 2010, in Spanish and French).

The Memorandum of Fernando Nuñez Muley by Matthew Carr

For the complete text of the memorandum see Francisco Nuñez Muley, *A Memorandum for the President of the Royal Audiencia and Chancery Court of the City and Kingdom of Granada*, edited and translated by Vincent Barletta (The University of Chicago Press, 2007). For more on Moriscos see Henry C. Lea, *The Moriscos of Spain: Their Conversion and Expulsion* (Lea Brothers, Philadelphia , 1901); L.P. Harvey, *Muslims in Spain, 1500 to 1614* (University of Chicago Press, 2005) and Matthew Carr, *Blood and Faith: the Purging of Muslim Spain 1492–1614,* (Hurst, London, 2009).

Sephardic Judaism and the Levantine Option by David Shasha

The quotations from Moses Angel are from *The Law of Sinai and its Appointed Times* (London: William Tegg and Co., 1858, p. 288 and p.289 respectively), which can accessed online at http://archive.org/details/lawofsinaiitsapp00ange
Ibn Paquda's *The Book of Direction to the Duties of the Heart* has been translated by Menahem Mansoor (London: Littman Library of Jewish Civilization, Routledge and Kegan Paul, 1973), and his quotation is from p 317. Other works cited include: Haym Soloveitchik, 'Religious Law and Change: The Medieval Ashkenazic Example,' *AJS Review* 12:2, (Autumn 1987), p. 207; Ross Brann, 'Hebrew Literary Culture in Spain (al-Andalus) in the Age of the Geniza', *The Solomon Goldman Lectures*, (Chicago: The Spertus College of Jewish Studies Press), 2003, pp. 14-15; Bernard Lewis, *What Went Wrong? Western Impact and Middle Eastern Response* (London: Oxford University Press, 2002, p. 155); and Peter Cole, editor and translator, *The Dream of the Poem: Hebrew Poetry in Muslim and Christian Spain 950-1492* (Princeton University Press, 2007). See also pages 77 and 471 of the 1950 Penguin edition of *Don Quixote* translated by J.M. Cohen for references to the fictional Arab historian; and Maria Rosa Menocal, *The Arts of Intimacy: Christians, Jews and Muslims in the Making of Castilian Culture* (London: Little, Brown 2002), where she expertly shows that the early years of Christian victory of Muslims was a good period for Jews.

Books on Sephardim worth exploring include: S.D. Goitein, *A Mediterranean Society: The Jewish Communities of the Arab World as Portrayed in the Documents of the Cairo Geniza* (University of California Press, Five Volumes and Index, 1967-1993); Haim Beinart, editor, *The Sephardi Legacy*, (The Magnes Press of Hebrew University, Two Volumes, 1992); Jerrilyn Dodds, Maria Rosa Menocal, and Abigail Krasner Balbale, *The Arts of Intimacy: Christians, Jews, and Muslims in the Making of Castilian Culture* (Yale University Press, 2008); Ammiel Alcalay, *After Jews and Arabs: Remaking Levantine Culture* (University of Minnesota Press,

1993); Joel Kraemer, *Maimonides: The Life and World of One of Civilization's Greatest Minds* (New York: Doubleday Books, 2008); Ilan Stavans, editor, *The Schocken Book of Modern Sephardic Literature* (New York: Schocken Books, 2005); Jose Faur, *In the Shadow of History: Jews and Conversos at the Dawn of Modernity* (State University of New York Press, 1992); Colette Sirat, *A History of Jewish Philosophy in the Middle Ages* (Cambridge University Press, 1985); and Elijah Benamozegh, *Israel and Humanity*, Translated from the French by Maxwell Luria (New Jersey: Paulist Press, 1995).

A Musical Passage by Cherif Abderrahman Jah

The quotes from Owen Wright are from 'Music in Muslim Spain' in Salma Khadra Jayyusi, editor, *The Legacy of Muslim Spain* (Brill, Leiden, n.d., two volumes) p.564. See also Owen Wright, editor, *On Music: An Arabic critical edition and English translation of Epistle 5 (Epistles of the Brethren of Purity)* (OUP, 2011); Fadlou Shehadi, *Philosophies of Music in Medieval Islam* (Brill, Leiden, 1995); Earle H. Waugh, *Memory, Music, and Religion: Morocco's Mystical Chanters* (University of South Carolina Press, 2005); and Jean Jenkins and Paul Rovsing Olsen, *Music and Musical Instruments in the World of Islam* (Horniman Museum, London, 1976).

Empowering Women by Brad Bullock

My statistical analysis derives primarily from the Pew Research Center report on The Future of the Global Muslim Population, (as of 27 January 2011) and the UN's Human Development Report, 2011 which, appropriately enough, shows on its cover a young woman wearing hijab and reading a text in Arabic. The works referenced for Andalusian women are: Asma Afsaruddin, 'Poetry and Love: The Feminine Contribution in Muslim Spain' *Islamic Studies* 30 (157-169), 1991; and Maria Viguera, 'On the Social Status of Andalusi Women', in Salma Khadra Jayyusi (ed.), *The Legacy of Muslim Spain* (Brill, Leiden, 1992, two volumes) Volume 2 pp.709-724.

Parvin Paidar's essay 'Encounters between Feminism, Democracy, and Reformism in Contemporary Iran' is in Maxine Molyneax and Shahra Razavi (editors), *Gender Justice, Development, and Rights* (OUP, 2002); Fadia Faqir's 'Female and Fighting' appeared in *Critical Muslim 1: The Arabs are Alive* (Hurst, London, 2011) pp.105–111; as did Merryl Wyn Davies's 'On Saudi Women Drivers', pp.254-258. See also Samia Rahman, 'The Race of Women', *Critical Muslim 2: The Idea of Islam* (Hurst, London, 2012), pp.57–74. Thomas Lippman's article on Saudi lingerie shops appeared in the *New York Times* (January 2012) and may be found here: http://www.nytimes.com/2012/01/22/opinion/sunday/saudi-women-break-a-barrier-the-right-to-sell-lingerie.html?_r=0

Iberia's New Muslims by Marvine Howe

For a more detailed reportage of Muslim communities in Spain and Portugal see Marvine Howe, *Al-Andalus Rediscovered: Iberia's New Muslims* (London, Hurst, 2012). For statistical information on Spanish Muslims, see Gema Martin Munoz, *Muslims in Spain: A Reference Guide* (Madrid: Casa Arabe-IEAM, 2009). The essay by Abdennur Prado, 'New Islamic Thought in Al-Andalus Today' appeared in *Islam in the Kingdom of Spain* (Bubai, Al Mesbar Studies and Research Center, 2011, in Arabic).

The conclusion of Islamic feminist conferences, as well as Laure Rodriguez Quiroga's report of Carboba TV, can be found at webislam.com. The website for the Islamic Community of Lisbon can be found at: www.comunidadeislamica.pt. Islamic Junta's education website, which offers course on Islam, culture, halal production, and gender relations, is at: www.educaislam.com. Clara Teixeira's profile of Zeinal Abedin Mohamed Bava appears in *Visao*, Lisbon, 27 March 2008.

Reconquista 2.0 by Jordi Serra del Pino

The Balaguer programme can be downloaded from: http://www.tv3.cat/videos/3991571/Balaguer-una-ciutat-musulmana-per-descobrir

On Catalonia's independence aspiration, see Matthew Tree, 'A country can exist quite happily without a state of its own' in *the Guardian*: http://www.guardian.co.uk/travel/2012/nov/23/barcelona-catal-onia-spain-culture-independence

Gandhi and Palestine by Vinay Lal

This essay first saw light as the S. K. Bose Memorial Lecture, delivered at St Stephen's College, Delhi, 19 February 2011. I am grateful to Alok Bhalla, K. P. Shankaran, and many members of the audience for their thoughtful questions, and would especially like to thank Daniel Neuman for his probing questions and comments.

The Collected Works of Mahatma Gandhi (New Delhi: Government of India, Ministry of Information & Broadcasting, Publications Division), published over three decades, is the standard source for Gandhi's writings. The entire set of 100 volumes [often cited as CWMG] is available online in pdf at www.gandhiserve.org. Gandhi's statement on 'The Jews', published in the *Harijan* on 26 November 1938, is in Vol. 74, pp. 239-242; for his two letters to Hitler, see CWMG 76:156-57 and CWMG 79:453-54. The most detailed biography remains D. G. Tendulkar, *Mahatma: Life of Mohandas Karamchand Gandhi*, 8 vols. (new ed., New Delhi: Ministry of Information & Broadcasting, Publications Division, 1962), though it is barely analytical. Gandhi's response to the Reuters correspondent in 1947 is to be found in Vol. 7, p. 390; information on Sonia Schlesin is in Vol. 1, pp. 60, 71, and 139, though Tendulkar underestimated the significance of Gandhi's Jewish connections. Those of Gandhi's pronouncements which have the largest bearing on the subject matter of this essay have been put together by E. S. Reddy, 'Gandhi, the Jews, and Palestine', at http://www.gandhiserve.org/information/writings_online/articles/gandhi_jews_palestine.html

The Khilafat issue is one among several on which Gandhi is commonly thought to exhibit vulnerability. His autobiography, available in a few dozens editions, ought to be the first source for his views: see especially Part V, Ch. 36. For an assessment of one national pastime in India, see Vinay Lal, 'The Gandhi Everyone Loves to Hate', *Economic and Political Weekly* (4 October 2008), pp.55-64.

There is a growing literature on Gandhi's views on Palestine, Arabs, and the Jews. The most useful works include Gideon Shimoni, *Gandhi, Satyagraha and the Jews: A Formative Factor in India's Policy Towards Israel* (Jerusalem: The Hebrew University, 1977), and Simone Panter-Brick, *Gandhi and the Middle East: Jews, Arabs and Imperial Interests* (London: I. B. Tauris, 2008). There are shorter articles of much interest, such as Yunan Labib Rizk, 'Gandhi in Egypt', *Al Ahram Weekly*, 716 (19-25 December 2002).

Martin Buber's letter to Gandhi of 1939 is widely available. It has been published in Martin Buber, *Pointing the Way: Collected Essays*, ed. and trans. Maurice Friedman (New York: Harper & Row, 1957), pp.139-47; as well as *The Letters of Martin Buber: A Life of Dialogue*, eds. Nahum N. Glatzer and Paul Mendes-Flohr, trans. Richard & Clara Winston and Harry Zohn (New York: Schocken Books, 1991), pp. 476-86. The former volume also contains Buber's essay from 1930, 'Gandhi, Politics and Us'. The Jewish Virtual Library [www.jewishvirtuallibrary.org] carries the entire text of Buber's letter, as well as the essays of his other Jewish interlocutors, Hayim Greenberg and Judah L. Magnes; the same texts are available at www.gandhiserve.org. Maurice Friedman, *Martin Buber's Life and Work*, one-volume edition (Detroit: Wayne State University Press, 1988), may be consulted profitably. Arthur Hertzberg, ed., *The Zionist Idea: A Historical Analysis and Reader* (New York: Atheneum, 1976), is still quite useful.

Nathan Katz, *Who are the Jews of India?* (Berkeley: University of California Press, 2000), is among the leading scholars of Jewish Indian history; his views echo those of Joan G. Roland. Hanna Krall, *Shielding the Flame: An Intimate Conversation with Dr Marek Edelman, the Last Surviving Leader of the Warsaw Ghetto Uprising*, trans. Joanna Stasinska and Lawrence Weschler (New York: Henry Holt & Co., 1986), is enthralling. A brief estimate of Edelman is to be found in Paul Foot, 'Palestine's Partisans', *Guardian* (21 August 2002), and the text of his letter to Palestinian commanders is at: http://1humanity.blogspot.com/2009/10/marek-edelmans-legacy-israels-most.html (accessed 30 August 2011).

Muslim Dogs by Barnaby Rogerson

For more on Muslim dogs see *The Superiority of Dogs over many of Those who wear Clothes* by Ibn al-Marzuban, translated and edited by G.R.Smith and M.A.S. Abdel Haleem (Aris & Phillips, London, 1978); and Javad Nurbakhsh, *Dogs From a Sufi Point of View* (Khaniqahi-Minatullahi pubications, 1978).

The Writing on the Wall by Boyd Tonkin

Books mentioned in this essay include Elias Khoury, *Gate of the Sun* (Vintage, 2006); Marvine Howe, *Al-Andalus Rediscovered* (Hurst, London, 2012); and Radwa Ashour, *Granada* (Syracuse University Press, 2003). There are several editions of Washington Irving's *Tales of the Alhambra* and *El Divan del Tamarit* by Federico Garcia Lorca; for an English version see *The Tamarit Poems: A Version of Divan Del Tamarit*, translated by Michael Smith (Dedalus, Dublin, 2002)

Abu al-Baqa al-Rundi's 'Lament for the Fall of Seville' can be found here: http://www.muslimphilosophy.com/ip/abubaqa.htm
Other Andalusian poets, including ibn Zamrak and ibn Jakh of Badajoz, can be found in Cola Franzen, *Poems of Arab Andalusia* (City Lights Book, San Francisco, 1989). For more on Sheikh Abdelqadir as-Sufi, particularly his early life in London and Norwich, see Ziauddin Sardar, *Desperately Seeking Paradise* (Granta, London, 2004).

Nine Postcards, Nine Extracts by Alev Adil and Aamer Hussein

The poem at the end is by Cesare Pavase [22 March 1950]; translated by Marco Sonzogni it appeared in David Wheatley, *Modern Poetry in Translation*, Oxford, No18, 2001.

Reimaging the Cordoba Mosque by Zara Amjad and Gulzar Haider

The quotation from Nuha Khoury is from 'The Meaning of the Great Mosque in 10th Century' *Muqarnas* Vol.13 (Brill, 1996), p.80; the quotation from Charles V is from Natascha Kubisch, 'The Great Mosque of Cordoba's original construction under Abd al-Rahman I' Architecture', in *Islam: Art and Architecture*, edited by Markus Hattstein and Peter Delius (Konemann, Cologne, 2000), p.222. See also D F Ruggles and H Silverman, *The Stratigraphy of Forgetting: The Great Mosque of Cordoba and Its Contested Legacy* (Springer, New York, 2010); and N Khoury an G Necipoglu, *The Meaning of the Great Mosque of Cordoba in the Tenth Century* (Muqarnas, Issue 13; 1996, 80-98 (Brill, Leiden, 1996).

THE ANDALUSI DOZEN

Three monotheistic faiths lived and thrived side by side for eight centuries, from 711 when Muslims first entered the Iberian Peninsula to their expulsion in 1492. Al-Andalus was an astoundingly liberal and open multicultural society where Muslims, Jews and Christians collaborated to produce a period of unsurpassed intellectual development and artistic and cultural ferment. The science, philosophy, poetry, music and architecture, as well as the fashion and culinary delights, of al-Andalus are wonders to behold. Islam has not seen or experienced anything better than the brilliance of al-Andalus. The fountains of al-Andalus fertilised the dry intellectual life of Europe, transformed the uncouth barbarians beyond the Pyrenees, and changed the course of western civilisation. Yet our knowledge of this incredible period of human history, ignored by Islam and suppressed by the West, is rather limited.

Al-Andalus is not a culture and a period that exists simply in a remote past. Its achievements can be experienced when we visit a restaurant, admit ourselves to hospital, travel around the world, yearn for spiritual enlightenment, argue about religion and science, and struggle for a multicultural society.

Here then is a reminder of some of the different ways al-Andalus intervenes in the present: a list, in chronological order, of our favourite Andalusian personalities.

1. Ziryab (789-857)

His real name was Abu l-Hasan ʻAli ibn Nafi, but he was better known by his nickname, Ziryab, meaning blackbird; and he could sing like one too! Ziryab was a brilliant musician, poet, cosmetician, gourmet cook, and fashion icon. He left Baghdad to settle in Cordoba, where he established one of the first schools of music. He is credited with adding an extra string to the Oud, establishing beauty parlours for women, and introducing the idea of a three-course meal that should be eaten properly, sitting down, on a well laid-out table, accompanied by fine beverages that should only be drunk in crystal glasses. He disapproved of people who did not take a daily bath or use deodorants (of which he concocted many types), shampoos or hair preparations (he developed a special one from rose water and herbal salts). Men who did not shave received a reprimand. Clearly the 'civilising mission' was travelling in the wrong direction.

2. Abbas ibn Firnás (810-887)

This Andalusian Leonardo was always forging instruments and bubbling with ideas. When he wasn't building a planetarium, designing a water clock, cutting rock crystals or setting up astronomical tables, he was writing poetry. In 875, he built himself a glider and flew from a tower: the flight was successful but the landing, on the main street of Cordoba, was less so. His critics suggested he hadn't paid enough attention to how birds pull up into a stall; like the birds, his glider should have been equipped with a tail. He died twelve years later, probably from the injuries he sustained. Fittingly, after the departure of Saddam Hussain, the Iraqis named an airport after him.

3. al-Zahrawi (936-1013)

Considered 'the father of modern surgery', al-Zahrawi was a brilliant physician and surgeon. His thirty-volume encyclopaedia of medical practice, *Kitab al Tasrif*, was a standard text in Europe for five centuries. He was the first to describe the life-threatening condition of ectopic pregnancy and the use of forceps in childbirth, he introduced new and effective methods to treat a dislocated shoulder, recognised that haemophilia was passed down through families, and used catgut for internal stitching. He invented a number of surgical instruments which continue to be used in operating theatres today.

4. Recemundus (d. 961)

Or Rabi ibn Zaid, was Bishop of Elvira and Secretary to Abder Rahman III (812-961), Emir of Cordoba. A man of immense wisdom, he was renowned for his tremendous diplomatic skills. In 953, Recemundus stepped in to sort out a rather undiplomatic exchange of letters between the Emir and Otto I (912-973), the founder of the Holy Roman Empire. After patching up the relationship between Islam and Christianity, he became ambassador to Christendom and took the message of peace to Constantinople and Jerusalem. In between his diplomatic missions, he developed an Arabic calendar of Christian holidays, which included days commemorating the martyrs of Cordoba.

5. Ben Nagrella (993-1055)

Prime minister of Granada and prolific Jewish poet, was also an expert calligrapher. His *Diwan* includes over 1700 poems, mostly of a secular nature. In Hebrew, he is known as HaNaguid, prince of the Andalusian Jewry.

6. Solomon ibn Gabirol (1021-1058)

The renowned Jewish poet and philosopher tried to reconcile Jewish theology with Neo-Platonism, although his theory of emanation is held by some to be irreconcilable with the Jewish doctrine of creation. His philosophy is summed up in *Fountain of Life* (Fons Vitæ), regarded by many as a seminal text. He is also credited with creating a *golem*, the animated anthropomorphic being of Jewish folklore, now a standard feature of cartoons and Hollywood blockbusters. We blame him for crafting the genre of self-help literature – how to improve yourself while going through menopause, how to attain enlightenment by wearing a *dhoti* and beating drums in a shopping mall – the kind of books which now emanate from the US and litter bookshops all over the world, promoting the idea that good citizens can best look after themselves by denying social relations. If only ibn Gabirol knew where his intellectual efforts would end!

7. Azarquiel (1029-1087)

Old 'blue eyes', as he was called, was a brilliant astronomer, instrument maker, and all round genius. He perfected an astrolabe known as 'the tablet of al-Zarqali', built a water clock capable of indicating lunar months, invented compasses as well as a great gadget known as Azafea that served to locate a traveller in motion – a sort of Google Map for the eleventh century. He was the first to demonstrate the motion of the solar apogee relative to the fixed stars, to estimate the correct length of the Mediterranean, and to show that the orbit of Mercury is elliptical. His famous Almanac enabled its users to find the days on which Coptic, Roman, lunar, and Persian months begin. No wonder they named the moon's Arzachel crater after him. But Muslims today still find it difficult to spot the new moon of Ramadan, and pass their time arguing about the correct length of beards and which trousers to wear for prayers.

8. Ibn Quzmán (1078-1170)

The most famous and original poet of al-Andalus, known for his use of colloquial language, and not infrequent use of bawdy jokes. His *Diwan* contains 149 songs which were sung in the streets of Cordoba, where he was born, and in the alleyways of Seville, where he spent most of his life. His work is a fusion of Arabic oral strophic poetry known as *zajal* and the medieval romance tradition of western Europe. Some of his poems celebrate music and dance, while others describe his numerous relationships with young men: 'To the Souk went a boy/You know his name/ but I dare not name him'. Et cetera.

9. Ibn Tufayl (1110-1185)

Polymath, physician, vizier, and an all-round genius, ibn Tufayl was the author of the first ever philosophical novel, *Hayy ibn Yaqzan*, and the father of the pedagogical novel (or *Bildungsroman*) in Europe. His novel had a profound impact on both Islamic and modern Western philosophy, and became the foundational text of scientific revolution and the European Enlightenment, influencing Thomas Hobbes, John Locke, Jean-Jacques Rousseau, Isaac Newton, Immanuel Kant, and a string of imitators, such as Daniel Defoe. There would be no Europe as we know it without *Hayy*.

10. Ibn Rushd (1126-1198)

Another all-round genius and polymath, ibn Rushd was a mathematician, geographer, psychologist, musical theorist and expert on Islamic jurisprudence. He has left an indelible impact on human history as a commentator on Aristotle, defender of reason, harmoniser of philosophy and religion, establisher of scholasticism in medieval Europe, catalyser of the Renaissance, and inspirer of a 'dangerous school' of free-thinkers in Europe, called Averroism. Quite simply the greatest Muslim philosopher who ever lived.

11. Maimonides (1135-1204)

One of the most influential figures in Jewish history, Maimonides was a physician and a philosopher. He is an indispensable religious authority in times of trouble, and an invaluable guide for the bewildered. His *Mishneh Torah*, exceptional for its logic and learning, codified Jewish law and ethics, and produced the thirteen principles of faith. Maimonides is embraced by traditionalists but also claimed by modernists and postmodernists. Driven out of al-Andalus by fanatics, he became the chief physician to Salahuddin Ayyubi (Saladin). His *The Guide for the Perplexed*, originally written in Arabic, is essential reading for all self-respecting intellectuals.

12. Ibn 'Arabi (1165-1240)

Thinker, traveller, poet and visionary, ibn 'Arabi is the greatest mystic of all time. He spent a long while living in Mecca, where he fell in love with both a woman and the *Kaaba*, and wrote his famous work, *The Meccan Revelations.* In Cordoba, he had a mystical vision in which he met all the Prophets in their spiritual forms. His *Diwan*, or anthology of poetry, runs to five volumes; its mystical outpourings, exploring the essence of the soul and its mystical annihilation, and covering the essentials of the mystical path and purpose, are both bewildering and immense. If you are fortunate enough to fathom any of his numerous books, do let us know what he is on about.

Great achievements only emerge within a society and polity that provides appropriate support. Al-Andalus was brimming with rulers who appreciated thought and learning, science and innovation, and cultural refinement. Rulers like Muhammad al-Mu'tamid (r.1069–1091), the King of Seville, who loved poetry and liberalism in equal measure; Caliph Abu Yaqub Yusuf (r.1163–94), also of Seville, whose love of philosophy and learning knew no bounds, and who befriended ibn Tufayl and ibn Rushd; and Caliph al-Hakim II (915–976) of Granada, the patron of al-Zahrawi, who was himself an accomplished scientist in possession of a library of 600,000 books. And let us not forget Alfonso the Wise (1221–1284), king of Castilla, sometimes considered the last king of Western al-Andalus because of his respect for and determination to preserve and translate the legacy of Muslim Spain. He was the kind of multiculturalist that Europe direly needs today.

ON 'GRANADA'

Merryl Wyn Davies

Granada, I'm falling under your spell,
And if you could speak, what a fascinating tale you would tell.

Granada! I hear it as musical climax, which somehow reminds me of the fanfare that greets the *torreros* as they enter the bullring. Then the tune takes off again in that distinctive rhythm of all things Spanish to the accompaniment of castanets. The tenor concludes his song, in the original Spanish, with the phrase '*sangre y sol*' (blood and sun). In my head I hear the refrain of the English version where 'Granada will live again the glories of yesterday.' And I wonder once again whose glories; when and what will be revived?

Augustin Lara's song *Granada* is an operatic standard, one of those classy *divertissements* regularly included in recitals. It featured in the very first, the unmatchable, meeting of the Three Tenors: Pavarotti, Domingo and Carreras. They gathered at the Roman ruins of Carracalla, lit to perfection under a clear Italian night sky, to mark the FIFA World Cup football final of 1990! It sounds incongruous but it worked so well it became a global phenomenon. It was celebration, joyous entertainment full of *joie de vivre* and *esprit de corps* – yet with the unmistakable undertone of gladiatorial combat: each tenor vying to state their case for being the head honcho in larynx to larynx duels. In the midst of it the 'other one', as the Spanish tenor Jose

Carreras became known, belted out *Granada* as he tried so earnestly to match the supreme glories of Domingo and the big fella, Pavarotti.

The pairing of opera and football is typically Italian, for both are passions of the masses. And not just in Italy, as the tenors proved. In Britain the triumphal conclusion – *vincera* – of Luciano Pavarotti's signature aria *Nessun Dorma* became a massive hit thanks to its inclusion in the title sequence of the BBC's wall to wall coverage of said World Cup finals. Wonderful and extraordinary as Pavarotti is and was, perhaps the ultimate Italian opera singer, picking heroes of such ilk is a matter of personal choice. For me, it is the mellow richness, the lyricism and supreme musicality of the voice of Placido (ah Placid!) Domingo that is supreme above all others. So when it comes to singing *Granada* my choice is Domingo. It seems even more appropriate when one remembers that, although born in Spain, Domingo is actually Mexican like Lara, the song's composer.

The Three Tenors is more than a clue to the popularity in song of *Granada*. The phenomenon is an example of what it takes to construct heroes and mythology. An eccentric occasion, that night in Rome had perfect timing, context and marketing to deliver popular acceptance and endorsement of something that is taken to possess inherent merit. This classic combination enables people, places and events to live long and fondly in memory. It does not help, however, to explain the enduring enigma I find in the Granada that is imagined in song, the one that will live again.

Why would a Mexican composer dream of Granada? I keep coming back to the question since all I know of Mexico's modern history, artistic and social, is about peeling away the era of colonialism, the conquest that came out of Granada. Think of the art of Diego Rivera and Frida Kahlo with their vivid efforts to recover the Indio soul of Mexican existence. Their work excavates the overlooked, the relegated unpopular living history that underpins Mexican identity. And they used their art to make political common cause with the revolutionary spirit by which generation after generation of Mexicans have sought to overturn the political and social order founded on the Spanish conquest. The arrival of Spain created a totalitarian hierarchy, an all-embracing stratification of everything that afflicts all Latin American societies, and which had been experienced by all colonised societies. Modernity arrived on ships from the east, the ships of the Admiral of the Ocean Sea, Christopher Columbus, of Cortes who burnt his ships to stiffen the resolve of his project of dominion over what became New Spain (Mexico) and eventually made his lieutenant Francisco Pizzaro, a pig herder from Extramadura, master of the downfall of the empire of the Incas. Modernity is a moment in time that divides us from the past, and such a moment happened in Granada. Is that the triumph – *vincera* – that lives again and again? Is the Granada of the song really revitalising the time and the place where all that is pre-modern and non-western loses any claim to popular acceptance, endorsement of their inherent merit and their right to live long and fondly in memory?

The fall of Granada, the last Moorish kingdom on the Iberian peninsula, in 1492 is a clear and precise historic moment. I remember this Granada as the time the life blood of plurality was drained from European consciousness. It was the day plurality died (think of it to the tune of *American Pie*!) to be replaced by *limpieza de sangre* – yes blood as in the final words of the song. The blood synonymous with Spain after 1492 would be judged by a single quality: *limpieza*, its cleanness or purity. Flushed with their victory – a rising crescendo of *vincera, vincera, VINCERA* – the Spanish monarchs Ferdinand and Isabella started the march and spirit of modernity. Their closing of the Spanish frontier at home emboldened them to license the speculative venture of Columbus to open a new frontier by sailing west to find the east. The new frontier he stumbled upon, the Americas, would be structured by the ethos honed and fashioned on the old frontier: singularity of lineage and heritage. This ideal was embraced, expanded and expounded across Europe to become the line of demarcation between 'us' and 'them', the basis of a hierarchical view of humanity, history and ideas.

Spain not only vanquished the last remnant of Muslim rule at home, its *conquistadores* sought to continue the old purpose: the overthrow, subversion and circumvention of the economic, political and intellectual power of Muslim civilisation. The day Columbus set sail his were not the only ships leaving Spanish shores. Other vessels carried the Jews summarily expelled from Spanish land. It was the unhappy birth of modern nationalism as singular, exclusive, exclusionary and eventually murderous, genocidal ethnicity. This exodus would be followed in time by that of the Moriscos, the remnants of the Muslim population. New institutions would be established to seek out the questionable *conversos*, those new Spaniards produced by forced conversion, and inquire whether in fact they remained closet Jews and Muslims. Those deemed dubious would have their flesh sacrificed, the better to save their souls.

It was the fall of Granada which gave meaning to the heroes and myths that define the project of empire, the creation of the dominant hegemony of modernity. Is this the Granada a Mexican eulogises? What heroes and myths were vanquished in that Granada and destined never to live again? I choose that other Granada, the one dimly referenced by the song's mention of 'Moorish eyes'. It is the Granada of the *convivencia*, the living together and mutual interaction of Muslim, Jew and Christian that endured, for better and worse, for seven centuries. The heroes I dream of are ibn Rushd and Maimonides, and my favourite of all, ibn Hazm, author of the argument for the prophethood of women on the grounds of the equal opportunity application of the criteria established by classical Muslim scholarship. I choose the Granada of libraries and scientific institutions, of learning and debate, poetry and music that fed the imagination of Europe. I choose what went before modernity, the more flexible and diverse forms and ideas that continued to exist relegated to the margins of modernity. I choose the potential transmodernity these margins signify, the transcending of the flaws and limitations of the west-centric, mono-cultural instrumental modernity. Transmodernity as the spirit and substance to be gleaned from engagement with and inclusion of the Other that we desperately need to construct (reconstruct?) in the twenty-first century to reform and redeem humane futures for everyone.

The past is not an unquestionable self-evident progress leading in only one direction. History is a choice from among the accumulated rubble of past time, the myriad variety of human actions and thought. What stories get told and who chooses, has much in common with the phenomenon of the Three Tenors. History loves romance and a good story populated by heroes and myth. History is that plastic arena in which we invest past time with our own imagination, collect and select from among the available evidence to support how we see the past. In that process context and timing as well as marketing are all important. It is hard work to overthrow the collective might of heroes and myths that have gathered popularity and lived fondly in memory generation after generation. It often sounds churlish to attempt to displace the hold of one model of the past with an alternate theory. Deconstruction inevitably leads to backlash, else why would Niall Ferguson sell so many books?

Alternative history itself is no simple matter. The glories of Granada before its fall are everywhere eulogised by Muslims, many, perhaps even a majority of whom are, in this present day dedicated to a vision of civilisation and interpretation of Islam that is thoroughly monolithic, totalitarian, authoritarian and entirely antithetical to tolerance, openness and most of all debate and intellectualism. Try debating ibn Hazm's theory with your average maulvi in Pakistan or Britain, a sheikh in Saudi Arabia or Egypt, and see how far you get before being declared a heretic.

The trouble is that history is not just imaginative recollection backed by evidence. History is also politics, the assertion of power over the present for control of the future. Heroes and myths are wielded with instrumental rationality to determine events, actions and policy to secure power. The song *Granada* is just such a case in point. Its composer Augustin Lara was an approximate contemporary of Diego Rivera. Rivera declared himself the offspring of a *converso*, a Jew forced to convert to Catholicism, and therein he found his point of access to alternate history and dedicated himself to the cause of deconstruction. Lara, on the other hand, chose Spain and became a favourite of Generalissimo Francisco Franco, the fascist leader of the victorious Nationalist forces in the brutal Spanish Civil War who held all Spain in his authoritarian thrall until his death in 1975.

As is usually the case with opera, it is a good thing *Granada* has a great tune and is sung in a foreign language. Being somewhat linguistically challenged in everything except English – which Niall Ferguson assures me is a positive triumph of the British Empire, the enforced closure of all Other worlds of thought not withstanding – it has taken me some time to find exactly what Lara imagined about Granada. It turns out the lyrics resolve themselves into a ragbag of references to flowers, bullrings, songs, gypsies, girls with 'Moorish eyes' and of course blood and sun, images conventional and familiar enough yet without any apparent logic that I can discern. In fact translations of *Granada* remind me of nothing so much as that Europe-wide pop hit of the 1970s *Y Viva España*. It was a manufactured pop song that became the anthem of the era of mass cheap package holiday tourism. This annual migration has turned out to be a double-edged sword, it has corrupted and cheapened travel as a means of broadening the mind as much as it has corrupted and now ruined the economy of Spain.

Just like Lara's *Granada*, *YViva España* is another ragbag of images that sum up just how this new Granada came to live fondly in the memory of the hordes of North European working classes: sun, sand, sangria (lots of cheap booze in fact) and the flirtatious assignations of holiday romance among bullfights and binges. Talk about context, timing and marketing, even now *YViva España* is the pernicious kind of catchy tune one simply cannot get out of one's head once recalled. Matters were much worse one particularly painful holiday I spent in Spain in the 1970s. The song was blaring from every shop, bar and hotel all hours of the day and night. It became so infernal a racket, such a recurrent curse of physical torment, that my friends felt an incessant need to liberate Cuba to anaesthetise the pain. A fitting riposte, a liquid (the fusion of rum and cola) rejection of the dominant hegemony raised in honour of one of the various revolutions that dethroned Spanish imperialism, and in modern times has ousted, confounded and denied American imperialism.

In the final analysis however, it is the Engish lyrics added to *Granada* by the American Dorothy Dodd that really bother me. That insistent line: 'Granada shall live again the glories of yesterday' as I have tried to show is not so much a pleasant invitation as a challenge and a potential threat. If historical imagination and its manipulation of heroes and myth is an exercise not merely of personal choice but political power, then we all have cause to pause and reflect.

The British government has declared it is preparing for 'celebrations' to mark the hundredth anniversary of what is now called World War I, otherwise the Great War of 1914-18. That is the war that turned out not to be the war to end all wars, but, as is the norm, the breeding ground of further wars. What war will we be invited to memorialise? Which war will live again the glories of yesterday? Will it be the idealistic English poet Rupert Brooke war of 'God be thanked/ Who has matched us with this hour' and then bloated into years and so liberally made extensive corners of foreign fields 'forever England' as the resting place of the dead. Or will it be the war in which Welsh poet Wilfred Owen encountered the reality concealed by the rhetoric of how sweet and proper it is *pro patria mori*, to die for one's nation, walking behind a wagon bearing the body of a soldier gassed as he stumbled back from the front all writhing eyes and hanging face 'like a devil's sick of sin'. Will it be the war in which Wilfred Gibson, British Georgian poet, wrote of soldiers who eat breakfast 'lying on our backs/ Because the shells were screeching overhead.' When simply raising one's head to accept a humble bet about football was an instant death sentence. Or the war of English poet and soldier Siegfried Sassoon's *cri de coeur* 'O Jesus, make it stop!'

These are neither easy nor comfortable questions at a time when ordinary squaddies are being manufactured as unquestionable, incontrovertible heroes in all their actions and fidelity to duty. Are these heroes, are our present day soldiers, so very different from the forefathers we are about to remember? The technology of war may have changed but is war in all its death, dearth and devastation ever anything different? And is the construction of these soldier heroes today any different than what went before, or will the reconstruction of fond memory, the history that will live again, be anything other than the fate that befell those innocents slaughtered by millions from 1914-18?

Heroes and myths are not mere personal choice, they are political. Today's heroes are convenient creations because they subvert, circumvent and divert debate from what should be its real target: the politicians who make the illegal, misguided and ineffectual policy, despatch the troops, and tolerate the collateral destruction caused by war. How is it possible to memorialise the sacrifice of soldiers and not in some way romanticise the craven politics and horror of war? If the only face of war we recognise becomes the squaddies coping with impossible tasks as best they can on the frontline, must we inevitably not also lose sight of the malign inhumanity that causes real death and destruction collaterally on innocent bystanders based 'on the best intelligence' by remote-controlled-unmanned drones directed from half a world away?

Be careful with Granada lest the one you would not choose is conjured to live again.

CONTRIBUTORS

Alev Adil is the Head of the Department of Communication and Creative Arts at University of Greenwich, London • **Rowyda Amin** is a poet of Saudi Arabian and Irish origins • **Zara Amjad** is Visiting Faculty at Beaconhouse National University, Lahore • **Nazry Bahrawi** is a research associate at the Middle East Institute, National University of Singapore • **Brad Bullock**, Professor of Sociology at Randolph College, Lynchburg, Virginia, specialises in social and development issues • **Matthew Carr** is an author and journalist; his latest book is *Fortress Europe: Dispatches from a Gated Continent* • **Merryl Wyn Davies** is the Director of the Muslim Institute, London • **Emilio Gonzalez-Ferrin**, writer and historian, is the author of *Al-Andalus: Europe between East and West* and *Bikes are not for Cairo*, a novel about the Arab Spring • **Gulzar Haider** is Dean, School of Architecture, Beaconhouse National University, Lahore • **Marvine Howe**, a journalist, is the author of *Al-Andalus Rediscovered: Iberia's New Muslims* • **Aamer Hussein** is senior editor of *Critical Muslim* • **Cherif Abderrahman Jah** is President, Islamic Culture Foundation, Madrid • **Vinay Lal**, cultural critic and prodigious author, is Professor of History at UCLA • **John Liechty** is a writer and translator based in Colorado • **Gema Martín-Muñoz**, Professor of Sociology of the Arab and Islamic World, Autonomous University of Madrid, has published extensively on Arab and Muslim issues • **Jordi Serra del Pino**, a futurist and consultant, is agitating for Catalonia's independence • **Barnaby Rogerson**, writer and publisher, is the author of the acclaimed *The Prophet Muhammad: A Biography* • **David Shasha** is the director of the Center for Sephardic Heritage in Brooklyn, New York, and editor of weekly e-mail newsletter *Sephardic Heritage Update*: http://groups.google.com/group/Davidshasha • **Boyd Tonkin** is the Literary Editor of *The Independent*